MW01616216

How I Learned to Love the World

My Epic Journey from Solving Equations to Healing Hearts
Through Writing, Therapy, and Memoirs

Copyright ©2024 by Jerry Waxler

ISBN: 978-0-9771895-8-8
Book Cover by Lexi Schnabel

"The ultimate aim of the quest must be neither release nor ecstasy for oneself, but the wisdom and the power to serve others." Joseph Campbell, author of *The Hero with a Thousand Faces*

"The greatest act of rebellion in a sick society is to heal yourself, then softly help others heal too." - Unknown.

Recovering from the sixties 1977

On a Saturday afternoon, I stood outside the large house in the woods, anticipating the arrival of the rest of the pack. About ten or twelve of us gathered every week, for a long, hard bicycle ride on quiet country roads. Having grown up in a city, the natural beauty of forests and farmland in this semirural corner of Bucks County, Pennsylvania soothed my soul. While I was waiting, I leaned my bike against the house.

This house. Thank God for this house. I'd been so alone before I moved in here. Now I had friends whenever I wanted, and privacy whenever I wanted. The perfect combination for a loner who was trying to climb out of himself.

While I was waiting for others to show up, I strolled toward the sound of bubbling water that whispered in the background. The stream was only a few steps away, down a short path, obscured by the bushes and trees that crowded in from all sides.

I crept into the glade without making a sound, hoping to get a glimpse of our resident blue heron. And there he was—standing still and tall, and yet ready to fly on a moment's notice. When he saw me, he lifted off, as if there was only room in this special place for one of us. I gasped with delight.

Three years earlier, when I visited the house for the first time, I discovered this spot by the stream. The joy it evoked confirmed my intuition that I'd come to the right place.

The peace of this place was disturbed only by the splashes of water, gliding over rocks, sliding under the surface, then bursting into view again. Like me, the rivulets were always on the move, striving to figure out where they belonged. Until I'd moved into this house, though, I'd had to do my seeking alone.

Ever since I could remember, I'd been on the outside looking in. As a teenager in the early sixties, I got a part-time job at Temple University Medical School. My boss there encouraged me to borrow books from their library, which I took home and studied as if they held the key to my future. I assumed they did, since being a doctor ran in my family. My brother was already in medical school, and I intended to follow him.

Occasionally I'd get up from my desk to watch kids in the back alley playing stick ball or jump-rope. How did they have time to play when there was so much studying to do?

When I left Philadelphia to attend the University of Wisconsin in Madison, I'd go to classes, and then afterward stop at the Student Union. Standing off to the side, I looked out over hundreds of students in the cavernous coffee shop. Instead of joining them, I was still asking myself the same question. How were they able to enjoy each other's company? This time though, the question was more urgent.

Trudging back to my apartment, I'd sag onto the sofa. Instead of studying, I'd get stoned, listening in the dark to my collection of jazz, rock and roll, blues, and classical symphonies, watching the sounds dance through my mind as the hours and years slipped away. Numbed by my loneliness, my killer instinct for grades haunted me, like a ghost from another life.

Through the rest of the sixties, loneliness, marijuana, and discouragement about the Vietnam War spun an alternate reality, in which down was up and despair was the only thing that made sense.

After college, I moved even farther away from home, to Berkeley, California, to follow the counterculture. I lived in a shed behind a house and sometimes went for weeks without speaking to anyone. As my college money, generously provided by my father, ran out, my loneliness turned almost to madness.

The madness ended when a fellow loner handed me a book. He said it had brought him peace. I'd never had any interest in Eastern mysticism before, but this book by a Westerner named Kathryn, about her experience traveling to India, spelled out the laws of the soul as clearly as Sir Isaac Newton had described the laws of physics.

I felt as though I'd been trying to figure out a painting hung upside down, and this spiritual teaching came along and turned it right side up. Once I saw life through this lens, I looked around at my mattress on the floor and all my belongings in cardboard boxes and I realized how far I'd fallen.

My parents were the only two people in the world who might help me get back up, so I retraced my steps, returning to the East Coast. When I arrived at their doorstep, though, their frightened stares reminded me they were looking at a young man who bore little resemblance to the one who had left six years earlier. I didn't blame them for not knowing who I was. I didn't even know myself.

Realizing my problems were too strange and unsettling to fit back into this old groove, I fled into the wilds of Philadelphia to try to work out this new version of myself on my own.

During the next couple of years, I lived alone, went to work, and meditated. To ease the pressure of my isolation, I attended local meetings of the spiritual teaching I'd been following. The small gatherings, with only a dozen members and an occasional visitor, became the extent of my social life—better than the solitude I'd imposed on myself in Berkeley, but not by much.

When I arrived for one meeting, my host announced that we'd be joined by special guests. Then a couple walked in, about my age, both of them tall and lean. The woman was blonde and attractive and the man, handsome, full of smiles and warmth. The minute I met them, their genuine interest in me made me feel safe. As if to confirm the mysteries of the universe, the woman I'd just encountered was Kathryn, the author of the book that had lifted me out of my downward slide.

I spent more and more time at Kathy and David's house in the woods, where other followers of the spiritual path gathered. Soon, they asked me to move in and join their growing community of wanderers and seekers. When every room in their house was filled, a dozen more of my new friends rented apartments nearby and regularly stopped by to participate in birthday parties, meetings, and outings.

Our joy fit perfectly with the most basic rule in the spiritual teachings: to love people. I felt an increasing desire to do exactly that.

Here in this glade by the stream, the never-ending dance of water and sunlight reminded me to enjoy the moment, even while stirring me to wonder where I was heading next. I still hadn't figured out a romantic relationship. I didn't have any idea how I was going to earn a living. And above all, I had a lot of work ahead of me if I was ever going to learn how to love the rest of the world.

Other than the warm and nurturing connection with my friends, I had not yet broken my old habit of seeing everyone else as though they were on the other side of a canyon.

"Jerry. Where are you?" While I'd been down by the stream, I'd lost track of time. My friends were ready and I didn't want to hold them up. I retraced my steps and came around the house to the driveway.

As I approached, David broke into a big grin. "There you are."

Almost a dozen riders, vibrant in their colorful jerseys, were busily clipping water bottles to their bikes and topping off tires while discussing their route. Surrounded by my people, I grabbed my bicycle, ready to go.

Love God and do your duty

When I'd graduated college, I had a Bachelor's degree in physics, but had no thought of ever getting a job. I had been caught up in the hippie philosophy that jobs were evil. To get by, I became a beggar, a thief, and a con artist. And, in order to maintain the delusion that joblessness was noble, I had to carefully avoid thinking too clearly about my choices. So being a hippie was not only making me poor; it was also turning me blind and stupid, as well.

When I first discovered Eastern mysticism, I assumed it would support my "do nothing" approach. However, once I read the fine print, I realized that the rule, "Don't be a burden on others" translated to "Get a job." It took me a few seconds to grasp that my grand ideas about poverty were not shared by my newfound value system. Once I looked at the impact my behavior had on others, I recognized the absurdity of my former position. Unfortunately, I had disengaged so completely from the working world, I had no idea where to start.

My first job was as a shipper in a gift store in downtown Philadelphia, packing expensive, fragile gift items all day. After a few months, I thought I could do better. On my day off, I walked around town until I saw a sign for an engineering company. I told them about my degree in physics and they hired me to analyze schematic drawings of nuclear power plants to ensure the pipes wouldn't break during an earthquake.

The daily routine wasn't so bad. I liked my coworkers and I was intrigued by the insider view of such an important industry. Being a working man wasn't as miserable as I'd feared. By the time I moved into the house, I already had taken a first step toward a real career as an engineer.

I eagerly anticipated the end of every workday, when I could join my friends for dinner. Mealtimes were informal, with each of us throwing together simple fare, with as little preparation time as possible. The real attraction was the conversation around the table.

All I had to do to get ready was to take off my button-down shirt and tie. For the others, the end of the day meant showering off the sawdust, machine oil, or food stains from their factory or food service jobs. At dinner, we compared notes about our workdays. At least they did. I just listened. Their stories were always more entertaining than mine.

When the environmental risk of nuclear power became apparent, the entire industry collapsed, along with my budding career. At that time, David was the manager at a small foundry, and he offered me a job as his assistant. Factory work? Me? The notion at first seemed absurd. But back in my hippie days, I'd glorified the earthiness of producing something you could hold in your hands. Working in a foundry would let me experience that idealistic concept for myself.

Even if I felt out of place, I hoped the black sand, acrid smoke, and loud blast furnaces would drown out the noise in my mind. After all, my main job on the spiritual path was to get closer to God–what I did while on this earth was just superficial stuff. The real inner growth was taking place on other levels. So I tried to calm down, accept my fate, and do my duty.

At first, watching the process of turning brass and aluminum ingots into a variety of metal parts intrigued me, but my fascination quickly wore off. Walking around the plant, I looked for things to do, such as keeping maintenance schedules for the equipment and repairing small machines. But in the absence of intellectual challenges, my mind began crashing in on me. Before long, I spent most of my time worrying about what I was doing there.

When I became too caught up in my inner pressures and confusions, I talked with Kathy about my frustrating inability to relate to my own mind. Instead of soft-pedaling the problem or telling me to meditate more, she stayed with me, listened—and suggested that I start keeping a journal.

"Write whatever you think and feel. The act of writing, in itself, can help you."

I embraced that advice, viewing my daily writing as a lifeline. Alone in my room, at a diner nursing a cup of coffee, or sitting on a rock by the stream, I filled page after page with outpourings of misery, hope, doubt, and longing. As the flowing ink revealed my words, I felt empowered, as if I was coming to know myself.

Kathy always had so many projects and places to go that it wasn't always easy to find a time to meet, but I could write anytime I wanted. My journal became my trusted companion.

And when I was feeling better, and wasn't obsessing on my broader purpose, my life wasn't so bad. Being around those smelly furnaces, the brawny men, and the noise so loud you had to shout directly into each other's ears, gave me, for the first time, some interesting stories to share with my hard-working housemates.

A partner!

I'd always found myself in an impossible bind when trying to talk to a member of the opposite sex. The more I was attracted, the worse I felt. The only way I could control the confusion raging in my heart was to avoid girls altogether.

This strategy worked well when attending an all-boys high school. And I never saw girls at my dad's drugstore on the weekend. But when I went to college, there was no way to avoid them. They were everywhere. Despite my growing wish to get to know at least one, I was as lonely as ever, thanks to my awkward, self-conscious way of speaking and my nervous habit of withdrawing at the first sign of interaction.

Those obstacles magically disappeared in 1969 within weeks of arriving in Berkeley, California. At a party, I danced with a six-foot tall, sunny, athletic, blonde girl. My infatuation was so extraordinary, it temporarily overrode my fear. She responded accordingly. I fell hard for her, losing myself in the other-worldly bliss of her smile, her eyes, her laugh. I couldn't believe this was happening.

But then, in only a few months, an emotional upheaval rose up from some deep wellspring of pain within me to drown those heavenly sensations. To save myself, I tore away. What should have been one of the happiest, most exciting times in my life turned into one of its great disasters. The experience left me with the impression that too much love was more dangerous than none at all.

In 1975, when I moved into Kathy and David's house, I had to face the new challenge of girls living under the same roof. This was the first time in my life I'd had the chance to chat with females amiably and even laugh with them. It was a heady experience, given my life-long drought in that regard. But the possibility of ever falling in love awakened self-doubt and confusion. So I joined in on everything, and kept so busy that I was able to skate along without disrupting the joy that the group brought me.

The spiritual path encouraged committed relationships, so it wasn't as if the house was a hotbed of random sex. On the contrary, we were all sizing one another up as romantic partners, and ultimately, spouses. This search for a long-term relationship helped me impose a bit of order on what sometimes felt like an avalanche of unsettling emotions.

Even in this more contained environment, though, there was still a learning curve, and in the first year of the group, I managed to slip across the line. One too many smiles led to a kiss, which for me, felt like pulling the pin on a hand grenade. Some incompatibility of temperament made it unworkable. It was only a matter of time before it exploded, threatening to destroy this precious sanctuary of interlocking friendships.

Thankfully, the generosity of spirit that kept the group together was big enough to contain the emotional pitfall of stumbling into a relationship that didn't work. Instead of turning into a disaster, my indiscretion was somehow put back in the bottle and we moved on, returning from failed lovers to good friends.

One year, Kathy and David arranged a vacation for the whole group on Nantucket Island. A bunch of us piled into our cars and drove up in a caravan. We stayed in a string of cabins on a small campground, taking bike rides together, walking around town, and just hanging out with each other.

One girl, Ruth, had been a good friend. Like me, she was Jewish, which created an invisible, shared cultural bond. And since she already had a boyfriend when she moved into the house, I didn't have to waste energy worrying about whether or not we could be a couple; I was able to open up to her.

Just before our trip to Nantucket, her prior relationship fell apart, and in the relaxed atmosphere of the vacation, our friendship turned to touching and hugging, and lo and behold we became a couple. We liked each other. We were both lonely. It was like magic. I had a girlfriend. I couldn't believe it. After all this time. I didn't mind that we never actually fell in love. In fact, I considered it a plus. Because of my track record of falling all over myself when I fell in love, simply liking her felt much safer.

Computers opened doors

While David and I were working at the foundry, Kathy saw an article about a newfangled gadget called a personal computer. She bought a plain-looking box from Radio Shack called a TRS-80. When she discovered that Apple computers could display color, she shifted her allegiance to the Apple brand. Kathy started going to computer expos, taking several of us along with her, to investigate the big splash these little devices were making.

I knew computers were powerful, having encountered mainframes in college and at my engineering job. But I didn't understand why these little ones were causing such a big fuss. Surely, they were just toys. To prove my point, one of the guys in the group, Gene, figured out how to write programs that automatically drew art on the screen.

What I'd written off as a fad rapidly gained momentum. By the following year, Ruth had been awarded a grant to run a computer graphics exhibit at Bucks County Community College and Gene had landed a real job as a programmer.

Coming home dead-tired after each day at the foundry, I was unable to imagine how I was ever going to get involved. Fortunately, Ruth's boss at one of her jobs had a boyfriend who was hiring programmers and lined up an interview for me. I was skeptical. No one would hire me based on one measly computer math course I took in college and a couple of programs I'd coded when I was an engineer. But at the job interview, it turned out I had a secret weapon. Because of my extensive experience writing in my journal, I mentioned that I love to write. He hired me to write their computer manual.

When I broke the news to David that I was going to quit, I felt like I was abandoning him. But he was generous and kind and understood working in a foundry wasn't my dream job. He wished me well.

As a technical writer, I enjoyed the challenge to clearly explain the computer systems at my new job. In order to write about them, I had to learn every nuance of the technology. It was a perfect stepping stone for me to gain insight into the technology. So a year later, when I spotted a higher paying position in the coding department, I applied and got the job.

I quickly adapted to the new position-and just as quickly felt I needed bigger challenges. So when I wasn't working on a problem at my own desk, I walked among the cubicles asking people what they were doing. One of them, a PhD mathematician from Egypt, was exceptionally friendly, and when I asked him questions, he stopped what he was doing and offered detailed explanations of the algorithms he was coding that would enable a computer to interpret images.

To learn more, I bought a book, teaching myself image processing on weekends, but my learning was slowed by the fact that it required math beyond what I'd needed for my physics degree. Living in a suburb of Philadelphia, I had a half a dozen colleges to choose from. It wasn't long before I was taking classes at night, learning the kind of math that would lay the foundation for the increasingly esoteric topics I encountered at work.

The rest of the house joined the wave

While I was enjoying the thrill of learning all I could about computers, the conversations at dinner became increasingly varied. Janet, who had been waitressing, got a job as a bookkeeper, and soon her boss said, "Let's try personal computers." Then Bill, who had been a machinist, sent away for a mail order course and taught himself to program computers.

David was also taking notice. He had been a student at the University of Pennsylvania's Wharton business school, and the increasing involvement of his housemates in the new industry provided him with some ideas about how to earn a living that was both cleaner and possibly more lucrative than casting and grinding metal.

Before long, the stories at the dinner table became more conspiratorial as David and a few others brainstormed how to start a computer business. Then David quit his foundry job, and through a complicated series of job changes and realignments, this crew formed a software company.

Other than David, none of them had ever started a business, but that didn't slow them down. On the contrary, the newness of everything created an atmosphere of joy as they shifted from the grit of manual labor to the tribulations of learning computer skills and business development. Every evening, the dinner table would be almost like a comedy show, the way they all carried on about their adventures.

Janet would speak of her fledgling attempts in sales. With Bill, the new programmer, she drove to local industrial parks, walked into each factory and tried to sell software, only to return to the car a few minutes later with another rejection. Considering my own tendency to avoid strangers, she seemed as courageous as a warrior in battle. But when I tried to compliment her, she turned it upside down, claiming that Bill's job was harder than hers, "He's the one who has to listen to me cry."

They broke up the monotony of office life with pranks, which they'd recount at dinner. For example, David, the new boss, kept a suit and tie in his office in case he needed to look sharp in front of customers. In one often repeated story, the pranksters stuffed this suit with packing peanuts and laid it on the floor. The punch line was David's cry of mock-horror when he walked into his office and saw himself like a clothing-store dummy taking a nap. Such stories at the dinner table always resulted in peals of laughter.

I enjoyed these evening storytelling fests, soaking up the energetic camaraderie, picturing their adventures as if I'd participated myself. But with my mind clogged with algorithms and my days spent in a cubicle staring at a screen, I couldn't think of a single thing worth telling. So while they entertained me with stories about their work, I kept my thoughts to myself, grateful for all the vicarious fun.

The scientific fruits of my Philadelphia roots

I wasn't moving up the ladder fast enough at my computer programming job, so I impatiently studied the classified ads and regularly sent out resumes. One position caught my eye: a research programmer in the medical imaging department at the Hospital of the University of Pennsylvania.

I'd been dreaming of that institution ever since my high school history teacher sent us to the campus to research a paper. When I emerged from the underground trolley and walked a couple of blocks to the campus, I fell in love with the tree-lined walkways bustling with smart students. The musty smell of old books in the cavernous stacks of their library made me feel right at home.

So the following year, when my high school math teacher announced a city-wide search for smart math kids to participate in a summer program at the university, I felt it was essential that I participate. During the long weeks waiting for the results of my application, I learned that Penn was the home of the first electronic computing machine in the world. It was another reason to admire this institution and to feel proud of being born in such a great city.

My application was rejected, and I was devastated.

To ease my pain, my math teacher arranged for me to go down to the campus anyway to take a free course in computer programming. Naturally when I applied for college, the University of Pennsylvania was my first choice. They rejected me again.

Twenty years later, the possibility of getting this job in medical imaging gave me one more chance. Of course, they'd want to know how smart I was, so I included my fabulous college admission scores on the job application. It worked.

My boss, Gabor Herman, a Hungarian Jew with a deep voice and thick accent, mentioned that he'd developed some of the mathematical equations that had made CT scans possible. His research department continued to push the envelope, attempting to contribute additional advancements to the field of medical imaging. I thought I'd arrived in science heaven.

My tiny office was carved into the basement of the old part of the hospital with pipes running along the ceiling. On my lunch break, I'd burst out into daylight. The crowds of smart, competitive students fascinated me, but even more compelling were the heroes this campus evoked in my imagination.

On my lunch time walks, I was drawn to old parts of the campus, which reminded me of my childhood history lessons. While others hustled past me, I lingered at the historical plaques, reading them slowly, as if I could send my gratitude back through time. In my heart, I thanked the old Philadelphians whose principles of religious freedom had made it possible for my Jewish ancestors to find safe haven in this country.

One of my duties at my medical imaging job was to attend the weekly meetings of the medical imaging department. I sat in the background while professors and PhD candidates spoke about the latest developments in magnetic resonance imaging as well as CT and PET scans. Medical doctors and computer scientists debated whether a computer would ever be as good as a human at spotting abnormalities in lung x-rays.

I understood most of what they were saying about the physics and medicine, but their math equations contained symbols and logic I'd never seen before. To push my math training up a notch, I wondered if it might be possible to take courses at Penn. I knew it was a gutsy idea, but it paid off. The admission policies for part-timers were more liberal than for their full-time programs.

I jumped in, enrolling in unbelievably difficult courses. Learning math in those University of Pennsylvania classrooms scratched some itch deep in my soul. The fact that I had to spend all weekend on homework was a small price to pay.

Despite this grueling schedule, the social interaction at home kept me warm and safe. The only person I missed was Kathy, who had practically disappeared. I was accustomed to her immersion in huge projects, usually for some artistic goal like setting up a photography darkroom or a music recording studio. During these times of deep concentration, we all knew to let her alone to do her thing.

When I heard that her latest project involved taking math courses, I wanted to know more. At the first opportunity, I slipped into her office to say hello. Instead of the usual bright smile to which I had been accustomed, she seemed preoccupied. Glancing at the pile of difficult textbooks spread on her desk, I immediately recognized what was going on. Math is a harsh taskmaster and does not permit much attention to slip out to other people.

She obviously wanted to focus on her work, but I couldn't move. Finally, I asked, "Why are you doing all of this?"

"I'm preparing for a doctoral program."

"Really? What will you study?"

"I want to learn more about the brain, from a scientific point of view. I'm going to study neurobiology."

I left her to her work, trying to make sense of such a radical shift in her trajectory. We had very little interaction that year, as her need to maintain a hyperfocused state of mind overrode the involvement she usually had with us housemates.

The following year, she signed up for a biochemistry course at the University of Pennsylvania. *Biochemistry.* Just the word felt like a Siren call from my past. During the last couple of years in high school, when I'd pictured myself as a future doctor, every scientific inquiry into the human body drove me wild with curiosity.

Since she'd be taking the class only a few blocks away from where I worked, I asked her if she minded if I sat in on it with her. Even though I knew she'd be busy doing her own schoolwork, I thought the whole experience might ignite some of my dormant interest in medicine. She thought it was a great idea.

I ordered the textbook, but when I flipped through it, the illustrations of chemical structures and reactions reminded me that memorizing formulas had never been my forte.

I walked across campus to join Kathy at her first class, figuring that no matter how difficult it was, I would be able to learn something. When I arrived, she gave me a warm smile, but when the class started, she switched into student mode. Within the first few minutes of the class, I was lost. Kathy, on the other hand, sailed right through it, shredding any stereotype I might have been harboring about my superior intellect.

I put the book on my shelf, astonished at myself for attempting to take an advanced chemistry course for which I had no preparation. It was similar to the gutsy decision I'd made years earlier, when I enrolled in an organic chemistry course in Berkeley. When I'd failed back then, I'd accepted it as the last gasp of my dream of being a doctor. Why was I still trying? I couldn't answer my own question. I once again felt restless, looking for the next step.

The never-ending climb to nowhere

During my four years at the University of Pennsylvania, I'd formed an easygoing relationship with my boss, who didn't mind me drifting away from my desk to walk around the beautiful urban campus or take classes with Penn students. Even though I couldn't always understand the high tech talk at departmental meetings, I was learning and growing, and beginning to feel my identity as a scientific researcher in a scientific tribe. Then one day, I heard my position had lost its funding. I'd been kicked out of paradise. I had to scramble to find a new home.

After extensive searching, I found an opening at the Sarnoff research labs in Princeton, New Jersey, the place where the color television was invented. This division had recently been purchased by Intel, the chip manufacturer, so I'd be working for a company whose name was recognized by just about every technical person in the world.

There were some things about the job that made it less attractive. My commute would be four hours every day. I shouldn't have even considered it.

But they liked my image processing experience, and the pay was good. And there was one more reason why I couldn't let it go. I felt that being in the vicinity of Princeton University would make me a better person—after all, Albert Einstein had taught there. So I overrode practical concerns about having to spend half my life in the car. I took the job.

Once I settled into my cubicle and absorbed the scope of my responsibilities, I felt like it was a good fit. Based on my experience and skills, I was learning and contributing in equal measure. But rather than being content with my new position, I immediately began to scheme for yet another run up the mountain.

Attending Princeton seemed like such an outlandish idea when I first considered it. But when I asked my boss at Intel if he'd be okay with me taking off during the day to attend class, he broke into a smile. He'd earned his PhD from Princeton, and proudly shared that their math department was the best in the world. It was a good omen when he offered to write me a letter of recommendation.

After decades of practice applying to schools, I went through the motions, assuming there was no way that I could ever get in. The admissions officer seemed to agree. "Don't think you can just walk in and take a course with our full-time students," she said in a posh British accent. "This is a rare privilege."

If she meant to defend Princeton from intruders like me, why had she bothered calling me in for an interview? Perhaps her unwelcoming tone was meant to intimidate the faint of heart. But she hadn't said no.

When I received my letter of acceptance, I should have been elated. In a way I could look at this as a form of redemption for the misery I felt when I was seventeen and received a rejection to every single college I applied to. But instead of joy, I felt a new round of fear. Was I really ready for this challenge?

On the day of the first class, I sat at my workstation, staring at the timeAll my blood felt like it was pooling in my stomach, which was a concern because I really needed it in my brain. Was I really taking a math course at Princeton University? I must have been crazy to even try. At the appointed time, I sprinted to my car for the short drive across town.

When I entered, I furtively glanced at the other students, each one selected to be here because of their placement at the top of their entire high school class. I was accustomed to being around smart people, but this was insane. Slumping into my chair, in the front row, so I wouldn't have to look at them, I focused all my attention on the still-empty blackboard. Apparently, my dyed chestnut hair hadn't fooled anyone, because when the professor walked in, I saw a glimmer of surprise on his face. He might as well have spoken the thought I imagined in every one of these nineteen-year-old students' minds: *What's he doing here?*

I held my breath and pretended I belonged.

The professor began scribbling on the board. Cycles... groups... permutations... I loved this stuff. Ever since I was fourteen, I'd appreciated the way math exercised my brain to its fullest capacity. It was a glorious feeling, both terrifying and blissful. Each time I tackled a difficult math equation, it was like jumping out of an airplane. If I didn't solve the problem in time, I'd fall to my death. Finding the solution was like the yank of the parachute. I did it that time.

If it just wasn't for my obsession with being smart, this class would not be a big deal. The concepts were the same as what I'd learned at the University of Pennsylvania a couple of years earlier. I'd received an A in that course, so I knew I could handle the material. But Princeton was more competitive than Penn. What if that meant that on the exams, I'd be expected to solve harder problems, faster? And what if the unthinkable occurred—I received a B? I couldn't imagine it. Like some sort of existential annihilation, if I wasn't the best I might cease to exist.

I was losing myself, again

In 1989, Ruth and I married with the whole group in attendance. Much full-throttle dancing marked the event. My sister, who was witnessing the group for the first time, asked how we could let go with such abandon in the absence of alcohol. I smiled and shrugged. Dancing was our drug of choice. To us, to dance was to celebrate the joy of life.

After the wedding, Ruth and I continued to live in the house as before. Neither of us cared that this wasn't the type of living arrangement most people might expect. For us, it was perfect. When we weren't withdrawing into our separate rooms, we were good friends. She was always kind and respectful to me, and I to her. And she was smart and creative. When we tied the knot, I felt I had fulfilled an essential prerequisite of my life's journey.

The year we were married, Ruth was free-lancing for a small marketing firm, and I asked around at Intel to see if anyone might be interested in hiring her. Much to my surprise, she landed a small contract. I was impressed by all the hard work and clever salesmanship it must have taken to get the job, and was pleased to have played a role.

The day she came in for her first meeting, I was so absorbed in my computer screen that I'd forgotten she was bustling around somewhere in that enormous room, filled with quiet workers hiding in a warren of cubicles. Her sudden appearance at my side startled me. All I could muster was a whispered "hello."

She stood there as I continued to work. Realizing she actually expected more from me, I was at a loss as to what to do. This was not a chatty environment. Several times a day, on my way to the water fountain, the rest room, or the printer, I'd offered a cheery hello to someone, and they'd walk past me without even meeting my gaze. To Ruth, I whispered, "I'm sorry. I just can't talk right now." She looked disappointed and stomped off.

That night at the house, she burst out, "You didn't even look at me. You looked so withdrawn, like you were barely there. What are you doing to yourself?"

I was surprised by her intensity. "That's the way I am at work."

"I hate it," she said. "You're better than that."

Even though her criticism felt unfair, I detected the kind, respectful intention beneath it. She saw my behavior as being a form of self-harm; that I was smothering an important aspect of my authentic self.

Until then, I had seen my emotionally barren work environment as the harmless side effect of a topnotch job. Her reaction made me wonder if allowing myself to be swept along by this behavior was awakening some of the isolating tendencies I'd been struggling with my whole life.

I had good reasons for taking the job: great pay and a prestigious company that would look awesome on my resume. Until Ruth pointed out the emotional starvation she perceived, the only negative had been the four-hour-a-day commute.

How ironic that the engineering specialty practiced at this company was called "communications theory." We were certainly knowledgeable about the way computers talked to each other, but apparently not so good at relating to people.

Even though my home life was congenial, this office environment suggested my anti-social habits had a deeper hold over me than I'd realized.

That Christmas, when I received an invitation to the office party, I thought of all the reasons I ought to skip it. I would be miserable. I had no use for the free booze; I hadn't had a drink in almost twenty years. I was a vegetarian; there'd be nothing for me to eat. There was no way Ruth would go. She hated office parties as much as I did. And it's not like my coworkers had exhibited one iota of warmth toward me.

On the other hand, I had sensed some esprit de corps during departmental meetings, when reviewing our technical successes and failures. Perhaps in the informal setting of a party, I'd be able to increase my sense that we were all on the same team. In the end, I decided to attend alone.

During the dinner, one of the senior fellows walked to the front of the room. Brian had a PhD from Cambridge or Oxford; regardless of which one, I was impressed. In a voice slurred from too much alcohol, he said, "When I received a lifetime appointment as a senior research scientist at Sarnoff Labs, I thought I was set for life. Now, look at this place. All I'm doing is helping a manufacturer sell more chips." The bitter sarcasm in Brian's voice cut the air as his colleagues coaxed him to relinquish the mic.

Driving home from the party that night, tired and discouraged, I felt that my rosy view of being the smartest in the room was beginning to fade. I'd been trying to join these engineering gods at the top of their technical Mount Olympus. But Brian's dark diatribe called attention to the futility of my plan. I was already as high up this mountain as I could hope to go and here was one of the most successful intellectuals I'd ever met, complaining that even his achievement wasn't so great after all.

My lifelong goal of proving myself to be smart was just a pipe dream. Instead of leading me to the top of some mountain, the path I'd chosen was leading me in circles.

Could I ever change?

I bulldogged my way through the Princeton math course, so by the end of the semester I would qualify for an A. But I still had to pass the last hurdle. Entering the hall for the final exam, I could barely feel my body, while my mind raced in two directions at once: Part of me knew I would crush it, and part of me felt like a small child whimpering, unsure why he was even there.

The situation reminded me of the recurring dream I'd had for years: being on some generic college campus, feeling completely out of place, and walking endlessly without knowing where I was going. But this compulsion to take yet another college course felt like the dream had come to life, and I couldn't wake up.

A few days later, I saw the email in my inbox. Its contents could signal one of the great academic achievements of my life, or one of the most humiliating defeats. Since I was taking this course a second time, receiving a B would be absolute proof that I'd reached the uppermost limits of my intellectual capacity.

When I saw the A, I felt a whoosh of relief. I should have been elated. And yet it was only valuable in some altered reality where people cared how much math I knew. My wife and housemates were happy that I felt good about my math work, but they regularly let me know that their love had never depended on my grades. As for the brilliant, competitive guys at work, getting a good grade in one course barely rated a mention.

Perhaps this experience at Princeton meant I could scratch an item off my bucket list. But I couldn't think of anything else I'd gained.

My obsession with proving myself to no one in particular demanded oceans of mental effort and returned only occasional bursts of satisfaction. It wasn't worth it. I decided not to sign up for a second course. This race was over.

The decision to stop taking math courses gave me more time to go to movies with my friends, and to ride my bike on rural roads while pushing my forty-something year old body to stay fit.

Ruth had recently bought a horse, and I often visited her at the barn, soaking up the earthy presence of those gentle four-legged giants, and participating as a so-called horse-husband in the mostly-female camaraderie of barn culture. But no matter how much I enjoyed weekends, each Monday morning, I was up before dawn, stumbling into my car for the two-hour trek to dullsville.

Now that I'd abandoned my quest to become some sort of middle-aged math genius, I saw more clearly than ever that my fellow engineers had little interest in offering emotional support. The only important currency in this place was brilliance. If I wanted to find love, I would need to look elsewhere. However, quitting my job was a lot more complicated than quitting my math courses. I couldn't just stop altogether. I had to figure out what to do instead.

I continued to send out resumes, but my options were limited. While hundreds of ads called for business programmers, few wanted mathematical or scientific ones. I felt trapped in a prison constructed of my own intellectual hang-ups.

One Saturday morning, I sat in the living room as I often did,, drinking a cup of coffee with David, in front of windows that extended to the peak of the A-frame. Gazing at the small stream visible through the lush forest behind the house usually brought me peace. But on this occasion, I felt increasingly frustrated.

"I keep taking jobs that make me miserable. If I follow the same pattern, I'm going to end up in the same place. Do you think I'll ever change?" My stomach hurt when I said this, because in that moment, I feared I never could.

"Hang on a minute. I have something that might help." David went into his room and returned with a large brown-paper shopping bag full of audio tapes. I picked one off the pile. *The Greatest Salesman in the World* by Og Mandino.

"I can't imagine how anyone could be a sales person," I sighed. "That's not me."

"Just keep an open mind," he said. "These tapes are about all kinds of things. Perhaps you'll get a few ideas."

I placed the bag on the passenger seat of my car and forgot about it. Monday morning, about an hour into my predawn ride, I felt awake enough to pop a tape into the player.

The narrator presented an enchanting allegory about a salesperson who felt desperate to earn a living, and yet was discouraged by the difficulty of asking people to purchase his products. In his darkest hour, he met a wise stranger who proposed that the solution to all his problems could be found by opening his heart to others.

I was shocked by the way this author had linked earning a living with the fundamental principle of loving other people. That was exactly the quality missing from my work life. But the aspect that surprised me the most was the narrator's implication that opening one's heart is a learnable skill.

This suggestion gave me a glimmer of hope that I might be able to lower my guard and embrace the love that connects all people. I knew I had a long way to go, considering I could barely stammer a hello when introduced to a stranger. But I was accustomed to tackling difficult problems. If I kept chipping away at it, step by step, perhaps someday I could learn to be more open.

Good cheer, hard work, an easier road? 1991

My attempt to find another super-high-tech scientific programming job closer to home had been a bust. Month after month, my attempts to leave Intel went nowhere. This tension was growing unbearable. No matter how hard I tried, I couldn't pry myself loose.

Then one day, all my hopes and dreams about earning a living bounced in a new direction. David told me his software company was growing and asked if I wanted to join. Because of our friendship they were not worried that my experience did not exactly match the needs of the job. They just trusted I would learn.

My friends' software company had intrigued me from the beginning. And because of our nightly debriefs around the dinner table, I felt like I was already involved.

However, actually accepting this offer raised complex issues about my identity and what I wanted in life. For one thing, it would mean admitting the failure of my ten-year urgent climb toward the pinnacle of specialized image computing. In my new position, I'd have no globally recognized company name. No bosses with doctoral degrees from Ivy League schools. No more frantic search for the newest technology. I'd just be a business programmer. I told him I had to think about it.

To ponder my decision, I returned to the little stream behind the house. Like me, the babbling water was still searching for the right spot, and yet, in every moment, it was always exactly where it was supposed to be. How could I learn to strive endlessly, and to also be content? The ultimate paradox. And yet I had to keep trying.

Pulling myself away from these abstract thoughts, I weighed my situation more practically. Working so much closer to home would mean less time in the car. And working with friends would enable me to be around people who believed that human warmth is more important than a rigid fixation on complex ideas.

I wanted to know what it felt like to be happy at work. I wanted to be near my friends. And there was always that ultimate hope that I could learn to love people someday. This move felt like a small but significant step in that direction.

I looked at my tenuous toe and finger hold, clinging to this rocky cliff of high-tech ambition, reaching toward the rocky peak. It appeared that the engineers who attained those lofty heights were just as lonely as I was. Then I looked back at David's extended hand, offering warmth and people and possibilities. It was time to try a new direction. My heart took over. I made the leap.

Needed a new way to be smart

Within weeks of starting to work with my friends, I fell into the rhythm. I loved the shorter commute, the easy conversations, and the smiles in the hallway. It wasn't perfect, though.

For one thing, switching from scientific programming to business programming required that I learn to use an entirely new set of tools. Without the glamor and pressure of famous scientists seeking international recognition, the technical challenges felt like drudgery. I'd grown weary of coding in symbols that could only be understood by computers.

So when my friends at the software company needed someone to write their user documentation, I saw it as an opportunity to return to a type of work that I loved. Earlier in my career, at my very first job in the computer industry in 1979, I wrote a computer manual. But I was younger then, and eager to race up the hill. The real hotshots were programmers. I wanted to be one of them.

After years of chasing that attractive illusion, I discovered that other than the good paycheck, the work itself was often tedious, and reinforced my bad habits of remaining disconnected from people.

So I offered my services as a technical writer, and since no one else wanted it, the job was mine. Now, even though I was sitting in a cubicle staring at a screen, my mental focus all day would be on attempting to communicate with people.

The pay was less, but I didn't have an expensive lifestyle. And as a technical writer, I'd no longer need to stay up-to-date on the latest marketable computer languages. *Good riddance.* I was finished with all of that.

But after a few months in my new job, I noticed a new problem arising in my overly active brain. Without sickeningly difficult problems in an advanced math course at Princeton, or painfully obscure technical explanations at a departmental meeting at the University of Pennsylvania, I felt something was missing.

"What next?" I asked myself. The question repeated over and over like a mantra. What next? What task, or mission, or purpose would allow me to settle into adulthood and finally feel I was fulfilling my duty as a human being?

A different type of getaway

Just as my mad pursuit of intellectual achievement had reached a conclusion at the end of the eighties, so had Kathy's. After she finished her PhD, she put away her textbooks. I had no doubt she would soon find another intense project to focus on. She always had in the past. And soon, I learned that the new project was going to be an adventure for us all.

Traveling together had been one of our regular activities from the beginning of the group. That first year, we drove in a caravan of cars up to Marblehead, Massachusetts, and slept on the floor of the gymnasium of the church where Kathy's father was the pastor. The next morning, we attended a worship service that doubled as a ceremony to honor Kathy's mother, who had been the church pianist. That afternoon, we drove to the beach and performed a magnificent dance, swaying rhythmically on boulders overlooking the Atlantic Ocean. Since then, we'd ridden bikes on Nantucket Island; we'd swum with dolphins in Florida, took a boat tour among the alligators in the swampy outback of the Everglades; and snorkeled with colorful fish off the Cayman Islands.

One of the most unusual of our group's adventures had been in a gritty hotel in New York City when we all went to see the grand opening of Stephen Spielberg's *Close Encounters of the Third Kind*. The movie portrayed aliens as being loving and curious, which seemed to imbue the universe with a sense of wonder. Kathy liked it so much we went back over and over – I only saw it twelve times but others bragged about having seen it more than twenty. For years, we used quotes from the movie as punch lines to house jokes.

At the dawn of the nineties, she announced a very different type of group vacation: a week-long retreat at a campground Kathy and David had rented. While there, we'd meditate and observe a vow of silence.

The summer of 1991, Ruth and I packed enough food and clothes to last a week and drove up to the property in the Poconos for our first summer retreat

As we approached, I felt a growing sense of dread. Since talking had always been such an important feature of my life in the group, I couldn't imagine surviving without it. Ruth must have felt it too, because just as we pulled into the driveway, we both spontaneously screamed, in one final vocal outburst. That was it. No more speaking for an entire week.

The campground spread before us, with rustic cabins around a lovely lake, but we could utter no appreciation of the view. Finding our rooms and unpacking our things in total silence, we muddled through the first few hours, thanks to the ubiquitous supply of small writing pads Kathy had provided.

On the second day, our notes to one another became less pressured, and by the third day we had adapted to this quiet mode, communicating mostly by smiling and waving. We walked around the small lake and enjoyed the sunshine, or sat and read. Every day, Kathy gave us a spiritual pep talk to keep us engaged. Devoting so much time specifically to meditation and rest felt decadent, a bold willingness to stop all the bustle and haste in order to insert a period of reflection.

Kathy encouraged us to write, and to this end, she gave each of us a blank journal. Waking up in that pristine place, with pen in hand, I filled page after page with reflections on all that had taken place the year before. All my accomplishments. All my challenges. It was like my very own, annual life review. Then, after getting it all on paper, my mind slipped into the present. I let go of my worries about my life and was ready to absorb my peaceful surroundings.

At the end of the week, we returned home, armed with a wellspring of energy, feeling far more rejuvenated than I ever had from an ordinary vacation. As had happened so many times in the past, one of Kathy's projects had turned into a benefit for the group. I was always grateful at the way her desire for adventure and self-improvement kept helping me grow.

That fall I heard that Kathy and David were cruising around rural Pennsylvania looking for a property to buy. At first, I didn't think much of it. Kathy was always trying new things. But as their cruising developed into a full-scale search, I sensed hints of a major shift.

By December they had selected a wooded parcel in the Pocono Mountains. One Sunday, we all drove up to check it out. Arriving at the remote spot, surrounded by thousands of acres of wildlife preserves, with snow on the ground and the crisp mountain air some ten degrees colder than it had been at home, it felt like we'd traveled to a different country. That appeared to be the point. She said that this was our new retreat center, and a retreat was meant to remove us from our humdrum routines.

Kathy spent an increasing amount of time up north, planning the buildings that would serve us on future retreats. Unlike previous projects, which she had managed on her own, this time David joined her. Before long, it became clear they both intended to move there. The retreat center would become their new home.

What about the house?

My entire adult life had been formed in the house by the stream, surrounded by my friends. Over the years, some of them had outgrown group living—some having kids, others simply choosing to find their own places—but the house had continued to serve as the hub. It was where Kathy held meetings, where we did our creative projects, where David's bike rides started, where we still celebrated birthdays, and where we decompressed after work. If any of us was looking for conversation, we could stop into the kitchen and likely find someone to talk to.

I thought back to the first year the group formed, in 1975. What a motley crew we were, refugees from the sixties, climbing into the house like survivors of a capsized boat into a life raft. That was a remarkable turnaround from my freshman year in college, when I pretended my dorm roommate didn't exist.

When I arrived on their doorstep, Kathy and David's loving friendship and expert community guidance gave me a chance I never would have taken myself. Somehow, over time, Kathy's instinct for activities and entertainment brought me out of my shell.

That first year I moved into the house, Kathy asked members of the group to act out the parts of the various characters she'd been creating in her novel about Jesus.

I felt like she'd asked me to walk barefoot on hot coals. I'd grown up Jewish, so in my childhood, Christianity had been an endless source of persecution. To add to my discomfort, the idea of playing a part terrified me. As a socially awkward person, I barely knew how to play myself.

But I overcame my reluctance and did my best to read the part she assigned me. Muddling through what must have been one of the stiffest dramatic readings in history, I learned three things.

First, Kathy's book showed Jesus' disciples as caring people, thirsty for deeper wisdom about their place in the universe. This was easy for me to relate to, and helped bust me out of a lifetime of my own prejudices. Second, she showed me that pretending to be someone else wouldn't kill me. I could imagine that with a little practice, play-acting could be fun. Third, and perhaps most important, she showed me that being vulnerable around my housemates brought us closer together.

That small reading project in the very first year of the group's existence gave way to a far more ambitious project in the second and third years. Kathy was interested in Tarot cards, citing her belief that this system had been invented in ancient times to help steer spiritual seekers toward the search for higher consciousness.

During the first few years of the group, she'd engaged us more and more in this mysterious set of images, inviting the artistic among us (Frank, Nancy, Ruth) into her craft room for endless hours of drawing the cards. But that was only the beginning.

She conceived of a project that dominated our spare time for the following year. We were going to reenact and photograph a version of the Tarot deck. She turned the living room into a photography studio and the laundry room into a dark room. At the end of our workdays, we transformed into a troupe of actors and stagehands. Ruth was the costume designer. Frank and Mel were the artists responsible for sets and backdrops. Just about everyone in the group took turns dressing in homemade costumes and wielding household items cleverly disguised as props in front of hand-painted backdrops, to play the roles on each card.

Nancy operated the camera and even learned how to develop the film and make the prints. Nancy and Kathy then had long discussions about the color saturation, which prompted a new series of prints. This production work often kept them both up all night.

When it was my turn to pose, I sat on a makeshift throne, wearing a gold-painted, cardboard crown and a lush-looking robe while the whole group shouted at me to smile less and open my eyes more. They were all laughing, while I was trying to look serious.

Apparently, I'd made good progress in my willingness to open up. Unlike the awkwardness I felt when I first read a part from Kathy's novel, all this attention broke through my defenses—I had never felt more accepted or loved in my life.

At the end of the Tarot project, Kathy briefly attempted to have the cards published, but after a few attempts, she set aside her cards, pulled down the backdrops, and moved on to a different project, unrelated to the Tarot but totally related to bringing us together as a group. Two of the guys in the house tried to start an acting class, but with Kathy's guidance the regular evening meetings morphed into music-and-dance workshops in which we all participated.

During my loneliest times in college, wild dancing had given me a few rare glimpses of total freedom. Back then, the light shining through the darkness lasted for only a few moments until whatever girl I was dancing with decided she needed to be somewhere else. Here in the house, that glorious force of music lifting me out of myself became one of the strands of the social fabric we were weaving together. Kathy orchestrated these ensemble activities with such a natural grace and ease, it made me wonder if helping us grow together had been her goal all along.

Now, fifteen years after we came together, she was moving out, and the chances of me ever again finding a group of people with whom to live seemed impossible. I wondered if we had learned enough and cared about one another enough to survive as a group without her. I tried to be brave, and as soon as I could line up a private talk with her, I told her I worried my life would never be the same.

Much to my relief, Kathy assured me they wouldn't dismantle the house. We could all continue to live there. And I felt relieved to learn that David would come down to the house, most weeks, to run the business. We still had each other. But I feared that wouldn't be enough.

"You know the path is always meant to be an inner journey," she said.

"I know," I replied, "but I also worry about my ability to navigate in the world. Your presence here has always been such a crucial part of that."

"Don't worry, Jerry, it's not over. Having our own place for retreats is going to be good for everyone."

Another curious person

Occasionally, Ruth or I wondered out loud if we should find a place of our own. Such musings didn't last long. Without the ready companionship of our other housemates, I was terrified I might return to the deep loneliness that haunted me. Ruth, too, appreciated the social support of the group.

She occasionally fell into depression, needing to be alone, sometimes for days at a time. I completely understood. My own life had been filled with the struggle to rise above dark moods. Somehow this committed partnership helped me fill the empty space in my heart.

In fact, we agreed this living situation provided the perfect environment for our marriage. When Ruth's mood swings struck, or I was gripped by self-doubt, Kathy was available to provide moral support or suggest a more positive way to look at our lives. Her kind and thoughtful perspective helped us rise above whatever was bothering us. How we would cope after Kathy moved out remained to be seen.

One day, Ruth said to me, "I've been seeing a therapist."

This stopped me for a moment.

"What could a therapist tell you that we couldn't learn from Kathy or the spiritual path?"

"Kathy's the one who suggested I talk to someone. She told me it was important for me to realize not everything was my fault."

"What does she mean by that?"

Ruth shrugged. "I guess that's what I'm going to find out."

"But how do you talk about our spiritual beliefs? Doesn't your therapist think it's weird?"

"That doesn't come up. Mainly we talk about my crazy family."

"Like what?"

"Like the way my father paid so much attention to my sister that it made me invisible. Sometimes I felt I was alone in my own house."

I'd heard many stories about the miseries of her childhood, but it had never occurred to me that talking about it to a therapist would have much benefit.

"Is the therapist helping?"

"I've only been seeing him for a little while, but I think so."

Wasn't it enough that we could speak with Kathy about our issues? Apparently Kathy didn't think so, since she was the one who suggested Ruth see a therapist. A thousand more questions sprung to mind. I'd always assumed that psychology was only interested in generalities. Perhaps I'd been wrong about that. What if a trained therapist could help me relieve my inner pressures?

I asked Ruth if I could come along with her the next time she went.

"I have to check with my therapist, but if he says it's okay, sure."

At her next appointment, I sat in the waiting room with Ruth, not sure what to expect. When Curt opened his door to usher her in, his warm, welcoming smile set me at ease. When halfway through the session he invited me to join them, I was relaxed and looking forward to the encounter.

I sat with Ruth on a comfortable sofa, and after a few pleasantries, Curt turned to me. "I understand you wanted to meet me. I'm glad you came. I wanted to meet you too."

Rather than wasting time with small talk, I jumped right into the question that was bothering me. "I was wondering how you deal with the fact that Ruth has a spiritual teacher."

"I'm not sure how I deal with it. I've never been in this situation before. If you guys are following a guru, that might make it difficult for me to conduct therapy."

I grimaced. There it was. The guru problem. I didn't blame anyone for having a cynical view of gurus. The whole world, including me, had been sickened by Charles Manson, who used his charismatic control over impressionable followers to turn them into murderers. And the Jim Jones mass murder-suicide was another example of sincere seekers being led into the abyss.

Because of the dark shadow of these highly publicized catastrophes, I'd become accustomed to avoiding any mention that I followed a spiritual teacher. But the whole point of therapy seemed to rely on complete honesty. To honor that, I needed to get the guru problem out in the open.

Finally, I said, "It's true Kathy is our spiritual director, but she's also our friend and mentor. Why would that be a problem?"

Curt looked thoughtful, as though he were trying to process this whole, novel situation. "The thing is," he said, "I don't know what Kathy might tell Ruth that would contradict what I say."

I glanced at Ruth, hoping she didn't mind me hogging a few minutes of her session. She seemed to be curious to know his answers as well, so I pressed on. "How is this situation different from what you would tell a young person who is also juggling advice from their father or mother?"

"That's a good question. You tell me. Is that the way it is?"

"I never thought about it this way before," I said, scrambling to try and explain our relationship with Kathy to someone who didn't know her. "We do look to Kathy for spiritual guidance," I said, thinking out loud, "but this is different from those scary stories in the news. In those situations, individuals had handed over their entire moral direction to a leader, even when that leader stepped outside the bounds of normal behavior. Our spiritual teaching is actually founded on mutual respect and love for people. When we look for guidance it's to help us figure out how to live more responsibly."

He was quiet for a moment, but still exuding that kindness I had felt when I first saw him. "Ruth's therapy has been working out fine, so I don't see any issue."

His answer excited me. The spiritual path provided advice for my relationship to God, and some practical advice for getting along in the world. But after years of applying myself to the teachings, I still had no idea how to relate to people. Seeing a therapist could potentially provide me with advice from an entirely new source.

Kathy had just opened a door for Ruth, and I wanted to slip through that door right behind her. I hoped that on the other side, I'd find more tools to improve my relationship with my sometimes-tortured mind. The next day, I called Curt. Would he be willing to take me on as a client?

He said that while some therapists would not be willing to do individual therapy with two partners, he didn't see a problem in our case. I set up an appointment.

Would talking help?

At my first session with Curt, I complained to him about my worst problem: how my thoughts got tangled up and made me unhappy. He seemed open and eager to engage with me on every nuance of my concerns. His comments and questions led me from one thing to another so easily that when it was time to go, I couldn't believe an hour had passed.

During the following week, I filled pages in my journal with thoughts raised during our session. By my next session, I had a whole list of questions to ask and memories to share. Over the following months, journaling and therapy worked in tandem to help me sort out the questions and quandaries that seemed to eternally bounce around in my mind.

During one session, I was describing an interaction with a coworker that ended badly. The guy walked away, shaking his head. Curt asked me what I'd said. After I repeated our conversation, Curt said, "Not everyone is interested in irony." Through his eyes, I was able to see that I was only amusing myself by being so clever. It never occurred to me that others might not be amused.

I decided to pay attention the next time I experienced a similar glitch. The following week, when I was speaking with the same guy, I spotted a confused look. I replayed the conversation in my mind and realized that once again I'd added a layer of irony. Apparently, it left my listener bewildered. I'd never paid attention to these signals before, so I'd never known when I'd succeeded or failed to connect.

Gradually, I noticed that in addition to helping me understand myself, Curt's tips were helping me get along with others.

My efforts at self-improvement were adding up. Through the study of spirituality, self-help, and now therapy, I was improving my confidence and social skills, allowing me to navigate my loneliness, unnamable despairs, and infinite longings. I still had all those feelings, but now instead of drowning in them, I was finding ways to swim through them.

Somehow, meeting with Curt each week seemed to organize my progress and make it more integrated and accessible. These talk sessions didn't seem to follow any particular theory or method, at least none that I could see. So, what was it that was so valuable about simply talking? I tried to pick apart the process of therapy, listing the various ways it helped, but in the end, I kept coming back to one fundamental aspect of our interaction. He listened, just like Kathy.

I'd always assumed that her ability to deeply hear and understand me was related to her ability to see the God within each person. But my therapist had no particular spiritual training, or even leaning, and yet he too patiently listened to my complicated thoughts with complete attention.

For only the second time in my life, I felt I was being truly heard.

Looking for a better wall

Even though David's residence was up north at the retreat center, he stayed at the house during the week in order to be closer to work. During early morning hours, I often found him in the living room, studying a book. One day I asked him for a recommendation. He disappeared into his office and returned with a heavily underlined copy of Stephen Covey's *The 7 Habits of Highly Effective People*.

A business book? *Hmmph*. Then I caught myself. My old prejudice against the shallowness of business people no longer seemed relevant. After watching my housemates evolve within their growing company, I had to admit that many of the skills that make a good business person could be useful for living a good life.

"I have an extra copy if you want to read it," he said.

At my desk the next morning, I was immediately impressed by the book's introduction. After years researching the history of self-help all the way back to antiquity, Covey had identified seven basic concepts. Within each one, he had piled layer upon layer of meaning.

If I'd been listening to a tape while driving, the finer points might have blown past me. But at a desk, I could reread a section, ponder it, and even take notes.

Reading at home also gave me access to a perfect study partner. David had embraced Covey's ideas so thoroughly, he could expound on all seven principles, reciting entire paragraphs from memory. Our discussions added a depth to my studying that I wouldn't have been able to achieve on my own.

One of Covey's fundamental ideas opened a door into entire new dimensions of my attitude about life. He said that to find more lasting fulfillment, I had to expand my vision and pursue satisfaction beyond my job.

Of course, Covey had nothing against succeeding at work. On the contrary, he advocated advancing in every realm, including the one that earns a paycheck. He just wanted to call attention to the importance of other roles, such as family, community, physical and mental health, hobby, and so on. Anyone who wanted to be more fulfilled needed to focus constructive energy on these other aspects of life, too.

This was a radical shift from my assumption that my career was the only project I needed to plan for, and that the other parts of my life would take care of themselves.

Covey wanted me to get off of autopilot. He was saying, "Don't coast. Pay attention." It reminded me of the familiar spiritual concept of "be here now," which I'd always interpreted to mean "stop and smell the roses." Covey extended it to include working toward goals. Do your best at whatever you are doing.

When I thought about it more, I realized I'd had plenty of experience focusing on a project when I'd been immersed in math courses. But now that they'd stopped, I needed to find another project.

While Covey couldn't tell me exactly what to focus on, he urged me to select something that served my long-term purposes. He used a prison-break metaphor. If you're going to the trouble of climbing a ladder, be sure it's leaning against the right wall.

I wasn't sure which wall to lean against, but I was convinced that Covey himself was providing a good ladder. His sophisticated overview of the field of self-help seemed to offer limitless possibilities for personal development.

One of Covey's points was important enough to be embedded into the title of the book. Because it was so central to his teaching, Covey had compressed his appreciation for habits into a slogan so catchy, I followed David's lead and memorized it. "Sow a thought and you reap an act; sow an act and you reap a habit; sow a habit, reap a character; sow a character, reap a destiny."

A number of habits had already proven to be crucial for my ongoing effort to feel good about myself: meditation, journaling, exercise. And now I could add the habit of studying self-help.

Let there be light

All of us at the house were morning people, since, according to the ancient wisdom of our Eastern teachings, the best time to meditate was early in the morning.

There was a second reason why the house was a haven for morning people. Kathy's very modern scientific research into the sleep-wake cycles of medical students and residents had demonstrated that their irregular schedules disrupted their stress hormone cycles, making them prone to mistakes and mood disorders.

In the eighties, when she shared this information, a few of the others in the house began to sit in front of bright lights each morning, creating an even greater sense of quiet contemplation in the early morning hours. Back then, I was already in my car by five a.m., so I let the initial suggestion of morning lights pass me by. Now that I had a shorter commute, I wanted to revisit this advice. The next time I visited the retreat center, I asked Kathy if she thought it would be a good thing for me to do. It was a topic she was happy to talk about.

She said that the human brain works best when it's on a regular daily cycle. But maintaining this cycle required more than simply getting to bed on time each night.

"Our body clocks slip out of sync with the rhythm of the day. The result is a problem called Seasonal Affective Disorder. It feels exactly like depression, and it affects a lot more people than you might think."

I'd experienced deep despair back in college, during the cold, dark Wisconsin winter. Back then, I'd assumed my misery erupted like black clouds from the volcano of anger I felt against the Vietnam War. Kathy's insights suggested those steel-gray skies may have contributed a biological component to my foul mood.

Jerry Waxler

"I can see how the harsh winters up north would be depressing," I said, trying to digest this information. "But why here in Pennsylvania?"

"The problem," she said, "is that indoor lighting is not bright enough to reset your biological clock. Bright, full-spectrum lights mimic the sun's influence on your brain, and get your biorhythms back in line."

Light. … The suggestion seemed so elegant.

I went to the electrical supply store in town and bought two banks of lights, with full-spectrum bulbs that mimicked the type of light emitted by the sun. Although the fixtures had been designed to hang from the ceiling, I propped them against the wall at the back of my desk, so I could comfortably look at them.

The next morning, I forced myself awake extra early and sat with open eyes facing the lights. They were a little too bright, but that seemed like a small price to pay, considering that I felt sharp and alive every morning.

More science of mind

Covey's book had provided a roadmap through the field of self-help, showing me how to think differently about my priorities, and even how to cultivate a more loving attitude. Armed with my new habit of sitting in front of bright lights every morning, I now had a perfect time to pursue the study of self-improvement.

The self-help shelves at the bookstore were crowded with names I'd already encountered while listening to tapes. I felt a sense of gratitude to them, as though like old friends they had banded together to show me how I could grow.

As I searched for new material, I paused at the section labeled "Psychology." I had always ignored that section as a result of a bad experience I'd had many years earlier. In 1965, just after high school, I had taken Psychology 101 at a local university to see if it would teach me anything about the way my mind worked. But instead of providing insight into my own consciousness, it focused on things like training pigeons to peck for food and rhesus monkey babies hugging wire-frame mothers. I never took another psychology course.

My meetings with Curt, combined with Kathy's interest in the brain, convinced me to take a closer look. Of the titles in the Psychology section, one stood out because of its large size and audacious claims. *The Feeling Good Handbook* by David Burns stated that in order to feel better, I had to improve the quality of my thoughts. What a radical idea—a book that tackled problems of the mind by teaching me how to adjust the way I think.

Balancing my thoughts had always been one of the goals of meditation. Closing my eyes and pulling away from thoughts about the world created an oasis of peace at a designated time each day. But when actively engaged in life any other time of the day, I still felt confused by my emotions and my ongoing issues of feeling distant from people.

The Feeling Good Handbook proposed that faulty thinking leads to misery and by improving my thoughts I'd improve my feelings. This approach appealed to me, but I remained cautious. Thinking about thinking sounded like an invitation to teeter on the edge of a cliff. What if this scientific approach pulled me right back into the tornado of overthinking that had almost destroyed me?

After Kathy moved out of the house, most of her attention was consumed either by running the retreat center or by retreating herself. When at last I was able to get together with her, I jumped right into the quandary of whether it was okay to think about thinking. As usual, she took the time to be fully present to my concern.

"It's true our ultimate goal is to rise above thinking," she said. "But until you've transcended your mind, you still rely on thinking. If, in your daily activities, you feel depressed or anxious, it's certainly okay to take advantage of these psychological tools. That's common sense. Clear thinking doesn't hurt your meditation at all. In fact, having loving thoughts during the day helps you concentrate when you sit for meditation."

Reassured by her words, I returned to my study of Burns' book. By practicing the do-it-yourself exercises he recommended, I found that in times of mental distress, adjusting my thoughts really did make me feel better.

After soaking up the wisdom of improved thinking, I grew increasingly curious about other books in the psychology section. They used more technical language than the self-help titles and referred more often to evidence-based science. I vowed to become familiar with these authors as well, hoping that someday they too would feel like old friends.

Unsplitting a divided world

Just as I feared, after Kathy and David moved out, living together as a group wasn't nearly as much fun. Fortunately, a fresh supply of their friendship was within easy reach. We just had to drive north a couple of hours to the retreat center. Sometimes we went up for a Sunday, sometimes all weekend. But the main event was the annual retreat.

The first summer they were away, we packed for a week-long silent retreat, this time on our own property, where the trees, meadows, and wildlife had drained the complexity from my mind and replaced it with beauty.

Emerging from my tiny cabin each morning, I moved super-slowly so as not to startle the deer grazing on the dewy meadow. Mesmerized by their gentle presence, I tuned in to the breeze that made music through the leaves. Not being able to speak forced my gratitude inward and upward. I felt thankful for the gifts of nature, the years of companionship, and the sense of spiritual purpose that made life seem so worthwhile.

Midmorning, about ten of us gathered to hear Kathy offer insights into the basic teaching that God is present in every impulse of kindness, and that all living creatures are connected through our shared longing for love. The message was perfect for someone like me who had always felt isolated and alone.

During these daily meetings we broke our silence with a mix of banter, laughter, and an occasional comment or question. It felt good to touch one another with our voices. Afterward, we withdrew to our cabins to meditate. Meditation at midday felt like taking an extra helping of peace.

During unscheduled parts of the day, we ambled, explored, hiked, read, meditated, or did anything else we liked, sometimes coming together in silence, other times, going off on our own.

When the mood struck, we stepped into the shared kitchen in the lodge to prepare our own meals. It could get hectic if half a dozen of us happened to be hungry at the same time, but over the years, we'd learned to navigate around one another in what we called our "kitchen dance." During the retreat, we were able to harmoniously bob and weave in complete silence.

One afternoon we reconvened to watch a video, in which Joan Rivers interviewed Raymond Moody, a leader of the near-death experience (NDE) movement. His investigation into people returning to life after having been declared dead proposed that visions of glorious wisdom and higher consciousness await us on the other side.

I'd already read a few books about these accounts. But seeing the video while I was on retreat added nuances I had not previously considered.

First was Kathy's comment that by bringing people back from death, modern science had offered Westerners a new source of insight into the journey of the soul. The other thing that caught my attention were the numerous survivors who felt they needed to enter a life of service. If these accounts could be believed, getting closer to God really does lead to a sense of closeness with other people.

After returning to my routine at home, when the crush of real-life circumstances made it difficult to remember that more peaceful state of mind. I'd pull myself out of the slump through friendship, meditation, and occasional weekend visits to the retreat center.

The next summer, we again lingered for a whole week in the warm embrace of extra meditation and silent appreciation for nature. On several afternoons, we were again treated to videos. The first one was about Mother Teresa transforming her faith in God into a bottomless well of compassion on the streets of Calcutta. Another day, we met Huston Smith, who had spent his life studying the spiritual essence hidden amid the diverse practices of world religions.

After the retreat, I noticed my mind returning to the simplicity and power of Mother Teresa or Huston Smith, as if their inner drive to spread spiritual truths had permeated my soul.

The third year, we watched a series of videos about Jon Kabat-Zinn who showed Western doctors how a type of meditation he called "mindfulness" could benefit patients in chronic pain.

That winter, I read Kabat-Zinn's book *Wherever You Go, There You Are*. I loved the underlying principles of mysticism, but I always feared the word *meditation* would evoke unwelcome images of turban-wearing, robed men sitting cross legged on the floor. By introducing meditation into a prestigious teaching hospital in Boston, Kabat-Zinn broke through that stereotype and placed Eastern teachings into the inner sanctum of Western medicine.

By this time, I was beginning to appreciate how much the video tapes in the afternoon were gradually, year after year, increasing my insights into the way other people offered their spiritual beliefs to the world. In this slow and steady way, Kathy was helping me heal a wound that had been tearing me apart my whole life.

In high school, I was certain that the equations of math and physics were sufficient to explain everything. I had no idea back then that focusing so much attention on my analytical side was smothering my emotions.

When my self-destructive tendency reached its inevitable conclusion, I had no choice. I had to reject science and embrace mysticism. I dove into my new belief system with all the desperation of a lost soul. After it helped me heal, I had a new challenge. I quickly realized that I couldn't simply throw away Western science. Somehow, I had to make peace between the two systems. And the entire time I'd been seeking to understand the connection between East and West, I'd benefitted from Kathy's lifetime passion to achieve the same goal.

In fact, it was Kathy's book about traveling to the East that had brought me to the path in the first place. And when I met her in person in the seventies, she was writing a novel about a group of disciples in ancient Israel who were learning the secrets of consciousness from an itinerant preacher named Jesus. His esoteric teachings, at the very foundation of Western civilization, sounded remarkably similar to ours.

The Tarot photography could be included among her East-West projects since, according to her, that mysterious deck of cards had its origins in ancient Egypt. And of course, Kathy's pursuit of a scientific education represented a multi-year investigation into the rigors of Western thinking. Now, through these explorations of world spirituality, we accompanied her on another chapter in her search for a globally recognized understanding that God is within all of us, at all times, in all places.

She'd been right when she told me that we could carry on in her absence. By seeing her occasionally, and following the path of healing and meditation, year after year, I felt the two halves of my world gradually fusing into one.

The universal code hidden in plain sight

One year at retreat, Kathy shared a series of interviews between the journalist Bill Moyers and a man named Joseph Campbell, who had spent his life studying myths. For every question Moyers asked, Campbell responded with stories, such as Native American warriors who traveled beyond the edge of the world and Egyptian gods who created the universe. He liberally sprinkled in dragons, secret powers, magic swords, and potions. Campbell's stiff, intense demeanor, combined with the magical impact of these mysterious tales, completely captured my attention.

Walking back to my cabin, I considered how I'd dismissed myths long ago. The Greek gods in Homer's ancient epics had behaved like spoiled teenagers. The Norse god Thor seemed to be a primitive attempt to explain the phenomenon of thunder. I didn't know what to make of Hindu myths about blue gods and flying chariots. What could modern humanity possibly learn from such nonsense?

In the subsequent afternoons, though, Campbell took these strands and wove them into an elegant tapestry. Stories in which a hero went forth, overcame hardship, gained wisdom, and then returned home in order to share the experience with the community were evident in every culture since the beginning of time.

How could one storyline have existed from the jungles and savannahs of Africa to the outback of Australia, from Alaska to the Amazon? To evaluate this astonishing idea, I considered the Old Testament account of the Jews. They went forth from their home in Israel, faced hardships in the land of Egypt, and then returned home, having acquired wisdom. This journey fit nicely into Campbell's model.

What broke through any remaining skepticism was the way Campbell's system matched the story at the heart of my spiritual beliefs. In our teaching, at the core of every person was a soul attempting to find peace. If at the end of one incarnation the soul had not completed the journey, it returned in another birth to try again. The ultimate payoff at the end of all this effort was the soul's return to its true home.

My mind raced with excitement. If Campbell's proposal was right, and humans had been attempting to follow the same storyline since the beginning of time, perhaps I could use his system to help me understand the drives and needs of being human. My enthusiasm was dampened by one huge problem: Campbell's stories were mired in ancient symbolism. How would someone in the modern world apply the principle of the hero's journey to their own lives?

I was delighted when the interviewer in the video asked that very question. Without hesitation, Campbell answered, "To travel the hero's journey, follow your bliss." His cryptic choice of words made no sense. Follow my bliss?

In my immigrant family, becoming a doctor was practically like becoming a god, so perhaps fulfilling that dream might have been blissful. But I'd never know. Once my plan fell apart, the memory of it became a source of misery. How was I supposed to pick up and move toward my bliss again? I turned the question over and over, until I realized I might be wiser to meditate. Perhaps I could solve the puzzle some other time.

On the last day of the retreat, we broke our silence. At first it felt awkward to speak, but soon we were chatting away, happy to be sharing words. As I moved back into the real world, though, the hero's journey resonated like a call to some future that lay just out of sight.

Searching for my bliss, 1997

Thanks to my shorter commute, I relished my added time to meditate, write in my journal and study self-help books each day. But after my morning session, I'd go off to work and stare at my computer. I appreciated that my job was now devoted to writing sentences in English, rather than in the cryptic algorithms demanded by computer code. Yet, when I thought about how I was spending my life, discouragement continued to creep into my mind. Perhaps I ought to leave instructions to etch "loving son, husband, and computer guy" on my tombstone.

One day, in 1997, I took a break from my technical writing and walked into a coworker's office to chat. Todd typically kept his space neatly organized, so the book on his floor looked out of place. Absent-mindedly, I picked it up. It was filled with listings for hundreds of graduate schools throughout the United States that offered degrees in counseling, psychology, and social work.

"What do you have this for?" I asked.

"I was thinking someday maybe I could find a way to help people."

"Me too. Could I borrow it?" I asked.

Back at my cubicle, I flipped through the pages, fascinated that this book even existed, and even more surprised that it had appeared as if from nowhere. It didn't make sense. But I'd spent so many hours of my life scanning college catalogs that looking through it felt perfectly natural.

As I lingered over the pages, I discovered that many of the programs accepted applicants whose undergraduate degrees were in fields other than psychology. My heart quickened as I considered this new possibility.

My previous attempts at adult education had done little more than prove I could still pass tests. By contrast, a master's degree in counseling psychology could have a real impact on the direction of my life. In addition to qualifying me for a new career, the process might further my dream of making sense of human nature.

To take a tentative step on this path, I made appointments at nearby institutions. After visiting a couple of them, my intention to pursue this degree grew more certain. I set my sights on Villanova University. The school had a good reputation, wasn't too far away, and the beautiful campus with old stone buildings and large courtyards. Several years earlier, I had even taken a night class in computer science there.

I dove into the application process, requesting transcripts from all the colleges I had attended. Since the official acceptance would not arrive in time for the approaching semester, I requested permission to take a first course while I waited. They agreed, and I enrolled immediately. Just eight weeks after I had seen the book on Todd's floor, I was on my way to my first class.

Back to school to develop a different part of me

On my drive to Villanova on Philadelphia's Main Line, I was dizzy with anticipation. Even though I'd taken many challenging courses, this was my first one about understanding people. But when I opened the door to my classroom, I went from excitement to panic.

I'd long ago become accustomed to being the oldest student in the class, so that wasn't the problem. What threw me was the furniture. The chairs were arranged in a circle.

In almost every class I had attended since I was six years old, students faced the front of the room, making it easy to focus only on the teacher. In this class, we would be facing one another. I felt naked.

My teacher, Stephen Weinrach, was a gruff old guy, bald, and a bit overweight. When he explained how the class was going to work, I quipped that it sounded like an encounter group. To my surprise, Steve didn't laugh. Without expressing any emotion at all, he said it really was an encounter group.

I was stunned. My only knowledge about such groups came from my reading about the intense self-help movement of the seventies, often cited as proof that Californians were crazy. I didn't even know encounter groups still existed, and suddenly, I was about to experience one for myself

The unnerving thing about the professor's answer wasn't its content, but his stony demeanor. Having always taken school so seriously, I'd developed the knack of tossing out a few comments in order to ingratiate myself to the teacher. After he answered my question, Steve looked away dismissively, signaling that he recognized this trick and it wouldn't help me in this class.

He continued his overview. "We have one rule," he said. "Only speak about things that you know about each other or that you are feeling." Then he stopped talking.

We sat in silence. My mind spun. I wanted to make a good impression but didn't know what to say. Since we didn't know anything about one another, there was no way to follow that rule. And I really didn't know what I was feeling, so there was nothing to say about that either. By the end of the first evening, only a few sentences had been spoken. I was worried.

At home, I read the first few chapters of the thick textbook, *The Theory and Practice of Group Therapy* by Irvin Yalom. In it, I learned that in the sixties and seventies, encounter groups were considered a miracle cure that would allow people to get in touch with themselves and one another. But this historical background would not help me. Our grades would be based on the degree to which we were able to connect with each other. I was screwed.

The second class again started in awkward silence. I fretted, trying to imagine saying something. Anything. But nothing sensible came to mind and I sat there terrified by my own awkwardness. No one spoke until a student walked in and said, "Sorry I'm late. There was a traffic accident." Steve reminded him, "Nothing about the outside world, please." Turning to the group, he said, "How do you feel about Alan being late?" We all looked at each other, bewildered. Steve continued. "It's important we all get here on time."

The room remained silent for the bulk of the second session. Steve's authority over the room felt spooky. While we sat squirming, he could start up a conversation anytime he wanted. What was he up to?

At the third session, someone said, "I feel really awkward." Steve perked up. This was a "here and now" topic worthy of discussion. His curiosity, and more important, his failure to criticize her, gave us permission to make similar comments. Another person responded, "I feel awkward too." It gave us just enough of a toehold to be able to speak.

In the following weeks, conversation gained momentum and Steve remained in the background, interrupting only if someone talked about things outside the room. Week after week, we shared how we felt about ourselves or about one another.

In that circle, I felt terrified they would judge me for my miserable communication. I had learned from years of disappointment that when I was nervous around people, which was most of the time, I came across as obscure and furtive. My sentences were intellectually overwrought, broken with pauses while I searched for just the right word, and by the time I found that word, the conversation had moved on. I worried that the same thing was going to happen here.

In one session, after I commented on something, one of the students said to me, "I have a hard time understanding you." Beads of sweat pooled on my forehead and upper lip, a familiar occurrence when anyone focused on me. I hated my clumsy attempts to express my complicated thoughts.

Since the goal of the group was to share authentic feelings, I felt compelled to press on. This was my chance to explain what I was feeling.

"Ironically and paradoxically, the harder I work at being clear, the more complex I sound."

The group burst into laughter. One woman repeated, "ironically and paradoxically," and they all laughed harder. I felt trapped. They all thought I was foolish.

But for the first time, something shifted. Shining through the storm clouds of my fear of being judged, I suddenly saw a glimpse of myself through their eyes. I was amazed to feel my frown give way to a smile. The thought crossed my mind that it would so much easier to just laugh at the situation. And then I did.

Just as the textbook promised, group therapy had exposed a truth about the way people perceived me and the way I perceived myself. The walls that isolated me did not fall immediately, but they trembled.

As the weeks wore on, and I spoke more often, my exchanges with people grew more relaxed. I recognized a pattern I had noticed at other times in my life: As I got to know people, my intensity diminished and my approach softened.

Except for the brief introduction at the start of the first session, Steve gave no lectures, nor would there be any exam. The purpose of the course was right here, in this room. We were there to learn how to relate to one another, and I would succeed or fail based on whether or not I could figure out how to just be me.

You can hide yours

During a pause in the group interaction, Steve said, "Just so you know, I'm Jewish, which is a little unusual here in a Catholic university."

A woman spoke up, "I don't see what our religion has to do with the here and now."

This reflected my own thoughts. Steve said nothing and the conversation died down.

Then Steve broke the silence again. Directing his gaze at one of the two Black women in the group, he asked, "How does it feel being Black in a mostly white class?" They shifted in their seats.

Finally, one of them said, "I don't understand why you're talking about it." Her voice sounded tight with resentment. "I don't think about it. And anyway, I hate all the words that are used to describe me. I'm not Black. And I'm not from Africa, so why do people call me African-American? In fact, my family is from the Caribbean. I wish we could just not talk about it."

The other Black woman nodded her head and murmured, "Me too."

I thought about what Steve was doing. By adding religion and race into the group, he had made these topics available for us to talk about. Even though no one had really responded to his comments, it was now fair game within the "here and now" rules of the group.

On my ride home, I couldn't stop thinking about it. By mentioning his Jewishness, Steve had cleverly made it impossible for me to ignore. His simple statement made me aware, for perhaps the first time in my life, how eager I had been to keep that part of my identity invisible.

Like those Black women, I thought, "Why talk about it? My cultural background is irrelevant." And yet, despite a lifetime of pretending it didn't bother me, my edgy reaction to his comment made me aware that in fact, it did bother me. Apparently, I still felt the pressure to pretend I was just like everyone else.

Our homework was to write a report each week about what had taken place in the group. In my report, I tried to solve this puzzle about why people saw me as distant. Earlier in my life, I had speculated that my awkwardness around people might have to do with my overly intellectual thought process. Or perhaps there was something about me that rebelled against social connections. But neither of these explanations entirely satisfied me.

Perhaps another reason I never felt like I fit in was inherited from my grandparents, who had lived during a time when Jews were actively excluded, hunted, and murdered? Even though I'd never felt animosity specifically directed against me, I wondered how much I'd been affected by my identification with such a foreign culture, with its rituals, its mix of two foreign languages, Yiddish and Hebrew, and its centuries of being reviled as The Other. Since this class was designed to help me see myself in other people's eyes, it seemed like the perfect place to explore further.

At the next session, I said, "I'm Jewish, and I've been hiding it. Frankly it has always made me feel like an outsider." I felt so ashamed and so brave. *Am I really saying this out loud?* It was the first time in my life I volunteered this information in a room full of strangers. One of the Black women looked at me and blurted out, "At least you can hide yours." Our eyes met. Then she shook her head and looked away.

Ever since college, in the aftermath of the civil rights movement, I felt that Jews and Blacks had a natural affinity. We had both experienced the humiliation of being considered less valuable, even less human than the people of the dominant culture. But now, in this moment, I could see her point. I could hide otherness.

I had just learned some new insights into the American melting pot. As a Jew, I could walk amid white people, pretending we were all the same. Her difference was apparent the moment she entered a room.

And yet, like me, she wanted to blend in. We were more alike than I realized. And yet more different.

I had only been in the class for a short time, but as I peeled back the isolation that had haunted me my whole life, I was already discovering profound things about myself, Walls were breaking down: walls of intellect, walls of isolation, and walls of misunderstanding. I wanted people to understand me, and I wanted to understand them. I felt a surge of pride and hope. My effort was paying off. I was preparing for a new chapter in my life, one in which I was more socially aware.

Addictions

My addictions class was the first one in which the chairs faced toward the front of the room. I was glad there would be no self-disclosure here. I wasn't ready to share my own experience with substances.

In college, I'd smoked marijuana most days. While under its influence, I thought the drug added mystery to my life and gave me mastery over my inner world. Many years later, I looked back in horror at how much I'd paid for those perceived benefits. Each joint I smoked reduced my sense of responsibility and heightened my sense of isolation. Strand by strand, the drug frayed the rope that moored me to society and set me adrift into the chaos of my unstructured mind.

Of course, back then, I knew adults didn't approve of my behavior. But I pitied their ignorance. "What do they know about marijuana?" I sneered. I could still hear that mocking laughter echoing among my fellow druggies. We were smart and they were stupid. Nothing "they" said had any value. Now, thirty years later, I hoped this class would enable me to help people avoid some of the mistakes I'd made.

He was a clean-cut, professional looking man dressed in a suit, so I was surprised when he introduced himself as a recovering addict. I couldn't remember anyone ever saying that to me before. Certainly not a professor. But except for one or two stories about his escapades, the class centered on learning the dismal facts about addiction.

We learned about the grab bag of substances people used to alter their consciousness, and about the grim statistics that resulted from this epidemic of self-destruction. When it came to treatment, though, he corroborated my own skepticism. People in his offices often lied, deceived, and minimized in order to deflect attention away from their dependency.

My professor said that in order to break through the shield with which addicts defended themselves, two things were necessary. They had to discover through some profoundly painful personal way that the behavior was no longer sustainable. That was the so-called hitting bottom—I knew it well. Back in Berkeley, if I hadn't changed, I would have died.

And the second thing was believing in something higher than your own consciousness. This also echoed my experience. In that darkest moment, when I was sure I had nothing else to live for, something clicked, and through the fog of my own despair I realized I wasn't alone in the universe. That changed everything. Once I embarked on this new direction, pursuing my connection with a higher power seemed far more important to me than the obviously flawed impulses I'd previously obeyed.

But while I could see the enormous shift in thinking that had helped me, I had no idea how as a therapist, I would ever be able to help others in a similar situation. Finally, he offered the solution. As far as he was concerned the best thing a therapist could do for an addict would be to send them to Twelve Step meetings. Even inpatient rehab programs relied on the Twelve Step system.

Despite being the director of a prestigious addiction treatment center in Philadelphia, my professor still attended Alcoholics Anonymous (AA) Twelve Step meetings every week. He was so devoted to these meetings that he even attended them when traveling to other cities.

To help us understand their value, he told us to go see for ourselves. This was another surprise. I'd heard about the meetings before, but it never occurred to me that I would attend one. These hurting people had their own very personal process to go through, and I knew I would feel like an intruder.

I tried to imagine how I would introduce myself. It had been years since my last smoke of marijuana or sip of alcohol, so I didn't want to lie about my own need for the program. Should I say I'm a therapist-in-training? Wouldn't they think of me as some aloof, clinical observer? Approaching my professor after class, I asked him how to handle these fears.

"You don't need to say anything. You'll be okay," he said. His reassuring tone set me at ease.

In the underlit meeting room in the basement of a church, no one seemed to pay much attention to me. And when we introduced ourselves, by first name only, I realized I could be essentially anonymous along with everyone else. During the meeting, a woman stood up to give a presentation. In heart-wrenching detail, she walked us through her experience as an alcoholic, losing her home, her marriage, her teeth, and finally, in the ultimate blow, her children.

There it was. Rock bottom. I thought about my own experience of giving up my hope, my possessions, my friends and family. I'd even given up my mind. I thought I'd lost just about everything a human being could lose. But I didn't have children. This woman's story terrified me. Losing your children? That cut so deep into the core of what it means to be human.

I looked around the room. Some people nodded. Others seemed disinterested. I wondered what was going through their minds. Would they hear? Would it make a difference?

Whoever they were, and whatever the degree of their problem, they had come to seek a better way to cope. Perhaps attending these groups, with their cautionary tales and their methods for reaching toward a higher power, might help.

Then it hit me. In my other therapy classes, I'd been warming up to the healing power of groups, and here I was again, learning the same principle in an entirely different context. These people in this room had banded together to defeat their common problem.

No wonder therapists sent addicts to Twelve Step meetings. Therapists could offer introspective insights and serve as wise mentors on the journey toward healing. They could even offer hope. But they couldn't accompany their clients out into their lives.

My professor's lifelong commitment to the meetings was more than an interesting bit of information. It was a bold, generous insight into the importance of social support to help him confront his powerful compulsion. He had joined a community of people committed to helping one another aim higher than their substance. And every meeting warmly received him, anywhere, in any town, on just about any day, with no fee, and among peers.

As I looked around the room, I wondered if I could offer words of support based on my twenty-six years of never having touched a drop of alcohol or a puff of marijuana. But I immediately rejected that thought. I didn't really fit in here.

As I sat stewing in self-consciousness, I realized the absurdity of my recurring assumption that I was an outsider. In my therapy group, I'd been afraid I didn't belong because I was too complicated. In academic groups, I feared I wasn't rigorous enough. In a Christian group, I hid my religion. In a Jewish group, I feared being seen as not Jewish enough. In a secular group, I'd be seen as too spiritual. And now, ironically, in a room of addicts, I was too sober. My list of reasons others wouldn't accept me was endless.

No wonder I'd been such a loner. And no wonder I'd felt such relief living in a house with others who explicitly, graciously, and generously accepted me. Now, I could see the same healing power at work in the Twelve Step meetings. They accepted each other as they were and gave each other the respect and group support that would help them grow.

In some ways, the addictions class had confirmed my skepticism. If addicts weren't ready to hear, there was very little therapists could say to make them change. But I was learning the antidote to that discouraging viewpoint. In these modestly furnished rooms, groups of like-minded people could band together to help each other solve problems that seemed impossible to overcome alone.

Leadership and humility

Whenever I asked fellow students about which courses to take, inevitably the answer was "anything taught by Nick Rosa." As one of the founding members of Villanova's counseling program, he had a wealth of insight into the evolution of psychotherapy over the previous couple of decades.

During the several courses I took from him, I learned that he was admired for more than just knowing a lot. His insight into people, his generous nature, and his ability to really listen to his students made me feel like I was growing every time I was in his presence.

One of the more innovative strategies I learned from him was called neuro-linguistic programming (NLP).

"I think I understand the neuro, and the programming," I said at the first lecture. "But why linguistic?"

"Because words are so important for shaping our thoughts and feelings. But that's a bit of a misnomer. NLP also offers lots of visual tools, too. Don't try to understand the whole system just from the name. I think of it as a sprawling collection of techniques."

"When clients come to therapy," he continued, "they will ask you to help them resolve feelings that bubble up from their subconscious. These tools can help them relieve their distress."

In one session, he told us that if a client had a scary memory, they could dispel its negative energy by imagining the events playing in reverse. The instruction sounded so strange, but at the same time, sort of intuitive, in a way.

I tried it out on myself, attempting to reduce my fear of other people. I imagined myself walking into a building and finding myself in the middle of a group that made me feel anxious. Then I tried imagining playing the video in reverse, watching myself go backward out into the parking lot, back to a time when I felt relaxed and safe. I found the exercise to be subtly soothing and filed it away for future reference.

During one class, Nick instructed us to close our eyes and imagine ourselves on the beach or a cabin in the woods or anywhere we felt particularly safe. Following his instruction, I imagined myself sitting comfortably in meditation, with my body and mind completely relaxed. As he suggested, I felt that peace entering into my awareness in the present.

The technique made perfect sense. When remembering a bad scene, I felt agitated. Why not just direct my attention to an uplifting scene in order to feel better? I hoped to take advantage of this method for myself. I wondered if someday in the future, I might be able to suggest such methods to clients.

Nick also taught one of my last courses, Advanced Group Therapy, in which we were supposed to learn how to become group leaders.

Because of my habit of wanting to stay as far from the spotlight as possible, I had always been inept at leading people. So even though I had high hopes for my ability to be a therapist in a one-on-one situation, I doubted I would ever be able to effectively lead a group.

During the leadership class, the professor watched the proceedings through a one-way mirror while we took turns attempting to facilitate the group. I soon forgot him and found myself immersed in that emotionally naked crucible, trying to make conversation in the here and now.

After I made some comment in one session, another student said she didn't believe something I said. This horrified me. Who the hell was she to doubt my honesty? I demanded a retraction. Her silence added to my agitation.

For the rest of the session, I dominated the discussion, trying to gain allies. Through my skillful arguments, I wanted to convince the rest of the group that she was the culprit, and I was a victim. How dare she impugn my integrity?

I left the session feeling self-righteous, determined to prove her wrong. At the start of the next session, I continued my crusade.

Finally, the professor couldn't take it any longer. He burst into the room, looking upset, and said to me, "Say you're angry." At first, I couldn't comprehend what he was saying.

To buy time and get a grip on what I was supposed to do, I just looked at him and stammered, "What?"

He repeated, "Tell her you're angry."

I resisted because admitting I was angry might make me look bad. It was her fault. I was determined to force her to admit it.

But he just stood there, glaring. Finally, I relented. I turned to the student who had offended me and said, "I'm angry." It was like magic. I could almost hear an audible whoosh as my defensive energy drained away. I relaxed.

"When you find the words that describe your emotions, you gain immediate insight," Nick said. "Helping our clients find the words to express their emotions is one of our main jobs as therapists."

I drove home that night embarrassed by my behavior. And yet, I recognized that it was precisely this sense of humiliation that shone light on some of my deepest hang-ups. My pride was far more fragile than I'd realized. This graduate program was supposed to be training me to help other people, but before I could do that, I needed to grow quite a bit myself.

My next career

When selecting courses, I had always skipped over Career Counseling. Even though it was a required course, I feared it would be boring and irrelevant. What could I possibly learn about coaching people to find a job? But as I came closer to completing my degree, I could no longer avoid it.

Much to my surprise, I quickly fell in love with the subject, recognizing so much of my own life in every lesson. Figuring out what to do for a living had been one of the most complex and important decisions of my life. And yet, despite all the job hopping and striving, I often didn't feel like I knew where I was going.

One of my perennial complaints in my conversations with Kathy was about my frustrations at work. I occasionally stopped to apologize for wasting her time with such a mundane topic.

She'd assured me that it was important. "We spend so much of our waking lives at work, we might as well feel good about what we do," she said. Her encouragement to find a satisfying line of work had led me to this graduate program. Here, in a class designed to guide people toward suitable careers, I hoped I could gain further insight into my next step.

One of the highlights of the career counseling curriculum was the topic of avocation—pursuing an activity you find meaningful, but which doesn't earn money. The career counseling research suggested that if you weren't totally fulfilled by your job, an avocation could help round you out.

This advice reminded me of Stephen Covey's self-help suggestion to apply effort to a variety of roles. His emphasis on being more energetic during my spare time had pushed me toward the grad program in the first place. I was thrilled to learn that such popularized ideas had the blessing of professional career counselors. The material about avocation showed me yet another way that therapists could help people live in harmony with their own psychological needs.

Once I completed the coursework, I searched for a counseling facility where I could do my internship. Going down the list provided by the department, I interviewed addiction programs, in-patient rehabs, and general mental health agencies. Some were too far away. Others couldn't accommodate my part-time schedule. But they all gave me a preview of the types of places I might be working after I got my degree.

As a starting therapist, I'd be at the bottom of the ladder, with an abysmal salary, and zero seniority. But during my interviews, I saw a glimpse of a more hopeful future when a cheerful, alert eighty-year-old man inserted himself into the conversation. After he walked away, my interviewer said, "He's the person who founded this whole agency. He still practices counseling here." My eyes opened wide. *That's what I want, too. A job so organically wrapped up in who I am that I never want to stop.*

Some final wisdom

Over the span of a few years, this educational institution had changed my life. I didn't want the learning and the growing to stop. As I neared the end of my program, I went to look up my favorite professors, hoping for a last dose of uplifting wisdom.

My first visit was to Nick, whom I now viewed as a mentor. How fitting, I thought, that the neuro-linguistic programming he taught was based on the importance of emulating mentors.

When I went to his office and knocked, no one responded. Since the door was ajar, I pushed it a little farther, and saw him sitting with his eyes closed. He opened them slowly. "Oh, sorry," he said when he saw me. "I was meditating."

Nick and I chatted pleasantly and he wished me well. While our brief conversation didn't add new insights, his actions did. Seeing him meditating in a university counseling department, and then openly admitting it, provided me with yet another lesson. When I started meditating in the early seventies, focusing attention on your own mind was considered weird and self-involved, so naturally I never admitted I did it. It stunned me to hear Nick say it so freely. Maybe meditation wasn't so weird after all.

My next visit was with Steve, who by admitting he was Jewish, forced me to admit the same thing. In his office, he told me that when he first met me, he didn't think I would make it through the program. "You've grown a lot since then," he said.

"I've always been awkward around new people," I admitted, trying to imagine what a mess I must have seemed when I walked into that first group.

"What are your plans?" he asked.

"I don't really know," I said, hesitating. Then I recalled the fellow grad student who laughingly told me she only wanted to treat clients suffering from midlife crises. It seemed like a safe place to start. I repeated that idea to Steve, half joking.

He didn't laugh. "Don't expect that your new job is going to be easy," he said, in a more serious tone than I expected. "Many of the people who come to see you will be in real pain."

It felt like an ominous warning. I couldn't post a sign limiting my practice to easy cases. I had to open myself to any situation I encountered, no matter the severity of their pain. But even though I'd earned the degree, I wasn't sure I could do much for the most troubled clients. I hoped to solve this dilemma by wading into the shallow end of the pool for a while, and only gradually, as I gained skill and maturity, would I muster the courage to dive into deeper waters.

On-the-job training

Positions for pre-licensed therapy internships were difficult to find, especially since I only intended to work part time on evenings and weekends. Fortunately, after asking for leads, begging for interviews, and going out to visit agencies, I was able to find a position about a half-hour drive from my house. The best thing about the position was that I would regularly meet with a supervisor to discuss my cases.

A couple of evenings a week, I rushed out of my office at the software company, hoping the traffic wouldn't make me late. Dashing past three or four people in the waiting room, wondering which one of them was mine, I'd pick up the charts of the clients I would see that night and run up the stairs to one of the empty offices.

With minutes to spare, I meditated for a moment, trying to unload the tensions of the day, so I could be fully present when my client walked through the door. Then I flipped through their chart to orient myself. Exactly at six p.m., I called down to the receptionist to send up my first client. Like an actor when the curtain goes up, I was onstage.

Each client talked about their lives. Some were depressed; others lonely or confused. My goal was to move their thinking in a constructive direction that would help them escape whatever trap they felt stuck in. To encourage them to speak freely, I asked the kinds of questions I had been taught in school, adding, "Tell me more" and "How did that feel?" Or I reflected their emotions. "You sound angry. You look sad." I was genuinely curious, fascinated by their situations, hopeful that my good intentions combined with my training might empower them to improve their lives.

Every week, I asked my supervisor for advice about my cases. Norm had worked with teenagers all his life as an athletic coach.

When he looked at me, I felt like he was looking at his son. At first this was unnerving, since we were both in our fifties. But I quickly came to appreciate the way he helped me feel more competent and behave more effectively. When I asked him to give me advice, he put the question back to me: "What do you think you should do?"

By inviting me to think more clearly, he was performing the same service for me that I was trying to perform for my clients. This formed a healing circle. After he added his perspective, I was recharged and able to bring renewed hope and confidence to each case.

I hoped my clients were also doing their part in the circle, by applying our talks to the challenges in their lives. However, for some of them, this didn't seem to be happening. One woman who lived in a halfway house had taken anti-psychotic medication for years. Each week she brought in another crisis, usually related to her boyfriend's abusive behavior. I listened and tried to be supportive, wondering how our sessions were helping her.

When my supervisor asked me which type of clients I wanted to see, I said "No angry men and definitely no teenagers." He responded by assigning me a sixteen-year-old boy who had been in trouble with the law. I tried to talk my way out of it.

"I don't even know what it means that he was court-mandated," I said, hoping he'd assign the boy to someone else.

"It just means that a judge required him to see a therapist as part of his sentence or plea bargain."

"But I don't know anything about the court system. I'm not ready for that."

"Don't worry about it," he said. "It's not a big deal. You might occasionally talk to a parole officer on the phone, but otherwise, just work with these clients the way you would with anyone else."

"But what would I say to the parole officer?"

Norm looked at me. "Just try."

If I was ever going to complete the 3,000 hours of experience I needed for my license, I couldn't be so picky about who I was willing to see. I relented, hoping that with his help I could get through this.

At the appointed hour, a thin boy walked into my office and looked around, barely acknowledging my presence. He seemed more distracted and afraid than angry. I greeted him and motioned to the chair. He said he preferred to stand.

I started the interview anyway and asked him why he was here. He grunted and I asked again. He murmured something about being in trouble. I persisted, wanting to know what he enjoyed at school and what he didn't. Some of his answers were shrugs. After a while he lay down on the floor and closed his eyes. At first, I was annoyed by this unorthodox situation. Then I let go of my discomfort and kept talking. His answers became a little more coherent now that he was more comfortable. By the end of the hour, my fear of the boy had been replaced by compassion. *What would become of him?* I wondered. *What system, or agency, or act of God was going to help this boy grow?*

As Norm predicted, a parole officer left a message, asking to speak with me. I noted his tone of respect when he addressed me as "Mr. Waxler.". I was the good guy and we were on the same team. The experience relieved my fears about court-mandated clients. They simply became part of my job.

Unfortunately, that boy, like most of the clients at the agency, showed up a few times and then dropped out. So, I never knew if I had any influence on him.

A few weeks later, my supervisor asked me to see another court-mandated client. Wayne's folder was an inch thick, covering several years of visits. His unkempt graying hair, unshaven face, and stained T-shirt instantly broadcast his lack of concern for social graces. He told me he had been arrested for harassing a neighbor.

"She was a thief. I was just trying to straighten things out." According to him, the only reason he'd been arrested was because the woman knew the police officer. "They're all in cahoots," he said.

I wasn't sure if I should laugh or cry. I told my supervisor no teenagers or angry men, and now he'd given me one of each.

Gradually, I engaged him in discussions about who he was and how he came to these conclusions. He willingly answered my questions. Perhaps his court order was especially compelling, or perhaps he enjoyed telling me about all his problems. For whatever reason, he kept coming back and for the first time, I started to get to know a client.

"When I'm off my meds, I feel like I can do anything," he said. "One time, I decided I knew how to control time and space. I sped through stop signs, believing I could avoid the oncoming traffic. That didn't last long."

"Wow," I said. "Your experiment could have killed you."

"When I'm on my meds, I can see that things like that are bad ideas."

Due to his manic episodes, he lost his job, his house, and his wife. He learned that the only way to control his behavior was to take medication, but occasionally he stopped anyway. His recent arrest was the latest disaster.

Whenever he mentioned hospitals or doctors, his face hardened, and he talked more forcefully, sometimes working himself into a quiet fury as he cursed all caregivers. Since I was a caregiver, I could have taken his tirade as a personal insult, yet I remained calm.

When he called his doctors "those Jews," his voice turned bitter. I winced. Anti-Semitism. There it was. Despite its historical roots, I'd managed to go my whole life without hearing a racial slur directed at me. And here, in this office, I had arrived face-to-face with my own worst nightmare.

What was the right thing to say? This man was not an armed soldier. He was tormented by his own fantasies. He was desperate for someone to understand what he was going through. And my job was to listen and search for ways to help him.

So, I brushed off my feelings and pushed aside the glimmers of horror I felt for all those hurt or even murdered for being on the wrong side of someone's prejudice. I leaned toward him with compassion, allowing him to vent. I spoke gently, steering him back to higher ground.

The week after this outburst, he said, in a soft, apologetic tone. "You're Jewish, aren't you?"

I said I was, and he said that he meant no harm and that he had been upset. I told him I understood.

Whether or not I was helping him was difficult to say. But clearly after only a few months of doing therapy, I had grown past some of my fears of talking to angry men and teenage boys, and steered through a challenge I never expected to face in this lifetime: talking with compassion to a guy who hated Jews.

A workbook of love

A young client named Courtney came in to see me about the problems she was having with her husband.

"Every evening, instead of coming home from work, he stops at the bar. I eat alone while his dinner grows cold. Then, I go to bed angry. When he stumbles in, I either start an argument or keep my eyes closed and hope he'll see how he's hurt me. Neither strategy works."

Her tense voice and sorrowful eyes made it obvious she had run out of solutions. I spent the rest of the session listening to her, and gaining more insights into the situation, but when it came to offering help, I felt lost. My training in grad school was intended to help the client with her own feelings. Yet every time I tried to learn more about those feelings, she redirected the discussion back to her husband's behavior.

I told my supervisor about the situation.

"You need to talk to both of them," he said.

Me, talk to couples? I'd only been trained to counsel individuals. And my own marriage, entangled within the social interactions of a group living situation, wasn't teaching me useful lessons to pass along, either.

"Learning how to work with couples is an important part of your job," my supervisor continued.

Gathering my courage, I looked up at this earnest, helpful man. His fatherly, supportive tone made me feel confident. If he thought I could do it, then I would learn.

"But what do I say?"

"Here. Read this." He handed me a book called *Short-Term Couples Therapy* by Wade Luquet. "It's based on a system called Imago therapy, developed by Harville."

Wow. So grad school didn't teach me everything. I'd have to learn a whole new type of therapy. I flipped through the pages, relieved to see it was designed as a step-by-step workbook.

"At least I can follow along in the book," I said, with a nervous laugh.

"Ask the couple to fill out the worksheets," Norm said, breezing past my dismay. "It will help them get to the root of their issues. Try it, and if you have questions, ask me."

Each chapter introduced a segment of the theory. I loved the case studies, showing examples of how people fall in love with the person who will give them the things they wished they had received from their parents.

When my client introduced her husband, Noah, to me, I was impressed by his manner. Well-dressed and clean cut, his gentle voice and loving gaze toward Courtney established an air of peace and reconciliation.

They both said they were committed to restoring the trust they had in each other. But when she reminded him about his visits to the bar, he said, "Why doesn't she understand I just want to unwind with my friends?" He looked at me as if he thought I could convince her of this simple truth.

Courtney's voice rose in anger. "You've been staying out later and later. I want you to come home. I need you at home."

I worried that I would not be able to keep the two of them speaking civilly.

After she explained her side of the story, Noah said to me, "It's her fault I spend so much time at the bar. After I've had a drink or two, I look at the clock and realize that she's already going to be upset with me. In that moment, I have a choice. Either go home and face her wrath, or continue to hang out with my friends. If she wasn't so angry with me, it would be a lot easier to go home."

I handed them the worksheets and explained what I wanted them to do. "Fill these out and bring them with you next time."

In between sessions, while they were doing their homework, I was doing mine, reading ahead and trying to understand how all this would work.

At their next appointment, we went over their answers about what they wanted from their parents and partners. I instructed them to address each other rather than me.

Courtney turned to Noah and said, "For as long as I can remember, even when I was a young child, my mother relied on me for support. By the time I was ten, I was responsible for running the house. She was so helpless, I felt like I was in charge of her life. If it hadn't been for me, she would have fallen apart. With the whole world on my shoulders, I took everything so seriously. When I met you, Noah, I fell in love with the way you could laugh at anything. You seemed so carefree."

Noah nodded and smiled. Instead of the hostility and anger in the previous session, her voice became soft. Their body language seemed more relaxed. When Noah responded, he seemed to open his heart. In an earnest voice, he turned to Courtney and told her his story.

"From the time I was little, my parents started drinking beer at breakfast and kept drinking for the rest of the day. There was always an open case of beer in the refrigerator, and they often had friends over to join them. They didn't seem to care about anything I did. So, I spent all my time out playing. Then at dinner time, the other kids had to go home to be with their families. But not me. I was jealous. My parents didn't really care where I was. When I met you, Courtney, I fell in love with your sense of authority. You seemed to know exactly what I was supposed to do and when. I was so glad to meet someone who knew how to help me manage my life."

When he spoke, Courtney paid attention, reaching out and touching his shoulder in a supportive gesture. While listening, I noted the similarity between the strains in their marriage and the dynamics predicted by Imago Relationship Therapy. It was as if this couple had stepped out of the pages of the book to give me a demonstration of how this system worked.

According to the workbook, Noah's desire for escape at the bar was a reenactment of going out to play with his childhood friends. When Courtney called him to come home for dinner, instead of simply excusing himself from the bar and going home, he reverted to his childhood behavior of staying out late. In the strange realm of unconscious psychological pressures, perhaps her anger reassured him that someone cared about him and wanted him home, a feeling that was missing from his own childhood. And by his refusal to obey her, he was acting out his teenage anger at his parents.

When Courtney first met Noah, she thought his carefree attitude was exactly what she missed in her own uptight childhood. Perhaps he would be able to help her feel free of the structure she had imposed on herself. But instead of learning freedom from Noah, she reverted to her childhood habit of control. She had been forced to manage her mother. And she was furious with him now, as a reenactment of her suppressed anger toward her mother.

Their marriage was splitting at the seams because they were both reexperiencing the pain of their childhood, in a dysfunctional drama that was hurting both of them. My sense of helplessness about their prospects was replaced by optimism.

For a few weeks, Noah and Courtney did the assignments in the workbook and then came into the office to talk about their progress. Noah was drinking less, and Courtney felt more hopeful. They talked about their renewed love. They laughed.

The effect on me was equally uplifting. Each session encouraged me to believe I was making a positive difference in their lives.

Changing patterns

Before I attended grad school, I only listened to the first halves of sentences. As soon as I guessed the gist of what anyone was saying, I cut them off, as if there was no point wasting time on the rest of the sentence. Through the pressure cooker of group classes in my counseling program, I learned to see the flaws in my approach.

As long as I was guessing what they were going to say, I was only getting to know my version of them. In order to become a therapist, I had to allow myself to be fully present, patient, and quiet, as I waited for the ends of sentences. And as I grew increasingly patient, I even learned to be quiet at the end of a sentence, when I sensed another one might be on the way

During the few years it took me to learn this new behavior, I occasionally slipped up and impatiently said something while another person was talking. I could see the pain in their eyes. They seemed to shrink away from me and ended the conversation as quickly as possible.

Now that I was paying attention, I realized I'd been looking at my loneliness problem the wrong way. The people in front of me wanted me to listen to them. How had I never noticed before?

As I became more adept at shifting my attention from my own thoughts to theirs, I discovered that everything they said was new and interesting. In a strange twist of fate, having been stuck inside my own mind had provided me with the perfect background for a therapist. Since I'd never really listened to people before, I could now exhibit and genuinely feel true fascination with my new discovery that all these people actually had inner lives of their own.

Now, when clients told me their issues, I listened with every fiber of my being in order to imagine what they were going through. And when people recognized my genuine, heartfelt curiosity, they opened up even more.

There was also a downside to never having listened. I had little, if any, practice pondering other people's emotionally complex situations. So when Courtenay and Noah both told me about trying to grow up with alcoholic, neglectful, and self-involved parents, I had no idea how that felt or what to do next.

To stay one chapter ahead of them, I studied the process in the workbook and used my own marriage as a test case. While Ruth and I had not talked much about our relationship, I was curious about our pattern of hovering apart, rarely turning to each other for emotional support.

Reviewing my own childhood, I recalled hardly any alcohol or arguing. Everyone seemed to get along.

But then I looked more closely.

Most days when I came home from school, my mom was at the drugstore helping my dad. Since I didn't play sports, I just went up to my room to read. And when it was time for dinner, Mom still not home, I heated up a frozen meal and ate … alone. The more I thought about it, the colder and more distant it all appeared.

As for Ruth's childhood, she'd told me many stories about how her house was so big, everyone stayed in a separate wing, barely even acknowledging she was there most of the time. I'd witnessed her family's cold, clammy dynamic when we went to visit her parents on holidays.

Wow. It had never occurred to me that my childhood had anything to do with my marriage. In light of Imago therapy, I could see that being alone so much in childhood taught me to expect very little emotional support from my spouse. Ruth was apparently the perfect match for these low expectations. Like finding the right combination and snapping open a padlock, Imago therapy was revealing the secrets of my marriage. I pressed on with renewed confidence.

By this time in their therapy, Courtney and Noah had developed a deeper understanding of their own and each other's childhood needs. But understanding patterns was only the beginning. Next, they needed to establish new ones. That required making fresh commitments to each other based on what they'd learned.

To help Noah feel safe in their home, Courtney promised to let go of her need for control. She agreed to emphasize her gentler, more nurturing side. In return, Noah offered to resist his impulse to flee. He promised to look for relief inside the relationship, instead of at the bar. Each seemed satisfied with the commitments—and I was encouraged by their rapid progress.

Fixing problems was harder

Courtney's face was distorted in anguish and tears spilled from her eyes. What had happened, to bring her to our next appointment in this state? Noah looked calmly at her, seeming to be the sanest, kindest person in the room. Eventually, she was able to choke out the words. He had stayed out late yet another night. When she couldn't wait up for him anymore, she dead-bolted the doors and cried herself to sleep. Her trust had been shattered by yet another broken promise.

Noah didn't look angry or sorry. Instead, he attempted to convince her he meant no harm. "I had a hard day and needed to unwind. What is wrong with that?" he asked, glancing at me as if for reassurance that he was within his rights to stay out as late as he wanted.

What had happened to his commitment, the subject of this week's workbook assignment? I struggled to sort out the next step. Apparently, the pattern he learned from his alcoholic parents, turning to booze as a solution to his own responsibilities, was too strong for him to change. And since he was doing the very thing that drove her crazy, her anger swallowed up her good intentions. Naturally she couldn't control her resentment.

I gently reminded them of their progress and encouraged them to stick to their promises. Despite my coaxing and entreaties, their frustration continued through the session, as Courtney begged for apologies. Noah's behavior, which perhaps he meant as reassuring, seemed to make her even more frantic.

The situation had exceeded my skills so quickly I felt breathless. What just happened? Our conversations had raised such important issues and offered hope for new ways of looking at things. And then their behavior simply repeated, as if nothing we'd said mattered.

The following week, an hour before their evening appointment, Courtney called to say Noah hadn't come home from work yet and wasn't responding to her calls. "I'm going to come alone."

When she arrived, her eyes were wet and puffy. She didn't want to talk about her feelings or patterns. She only wanted him to come home every evening. The following week, she didn't even bother coming to the session.

I told my supervisor what happened.

"I feel awful," I said.

He looked at me with soft eyes and asked in a gentle voice, "Why?"

After a few moments of silence, I realized he seriously wanted me to answer the question.

"I failed," I sputtered. "I'm no good at this."

"Go on," he said.

"First, there was the teenage boy who desperately needed more help than I knew how to provide, then the guy who unraveled as soon as he stopped his meds. Now this couple who can't escape the patterns that are tearing them apart. What could I do for any of them? I let them down. Perhaps if I had been able to give them more …"

"You can't take the responsibility for everything. Do your best. They have to live their own lives."

"I feel miserable," I said.

"Pay attention to these feelings," he said, leaning forward. "As a therapist, you are going to face this problem over and over."

His kindness made me feel a little better in the moment. But it also frightened me. What good was it to become a therapist when people's problems were so deeply entrenched? Like a brand-new lifeguard jumping into the ocean to save a drowning person, I was swimming with all my might, but wondered if I was prepared to save anyone.

Facing into the pain

When I started my grad program, in 1997, I was too busy with school work to think much about the fact that we would soon be entering the third millennium. But as the year 2000 came closer, the ticking clock grew louder and louder, until it sounded like a drum beat. The turn of the new year was either promising or portentous, depending on who you believed.

As a mathematician and computer scientist, my attention was consumed by the Millennium Bug. According to this widely anticipated disaster, tens of thousands of financial systems would fail at midnight, December 31, 1999, causing a ripple effect that would cripple the global economy.

This was the reason I'd pressed so hard to finish my counseling program. At least if the world ended, I'd have my degree.

Then, New Year's Eve came, and instead of global chaos, the weeks after January 1, 2000 were roughly the same as the weeks before. Until, less than a year later, someone in the hallway at work said, "A plane just flew into the World Trade Center."

A few techs hooked up a television they found in the closet. In stunned silence, we witnessed the damage wrought by the first plane. Then, the second.

The twenty-first century had crashed in upon us after all—but instead of being disrupted by a bug in computers, the havoc was caused by a few purposeful men who turned passenger planes into weapons of war, and high-rise office buildings into slaughter houses.

Thanks to the shocking images played over and over and over on the television, the horror of those moments felt as close and vivid as if I had been there myself. There must be something I could do to help. I called the Red Cross but it turned out I wasn't qualified for such a mission. However, one of the agencies I called invited me to attend a workshop that would teach me how to offer psychological support in the wake of future community disasters. I signed up.

A few months later, when the world was climbing back from the rubble of the fallen buildings, I drove to a conference room about an hour from my house in a small town near the Delaware River. During the introductions, I learned that several participants worked in the prison system. Another was an activist who worked with survivors of violent crimes. Almost all had worked in agencies that helped trauma victims.

When it was my turn, struggling to suppress my self-conscious nerves, I said, "I'm a therapist. I'm hoping this class will enable me to volunteer for future emergencies." Afterward, I berated myself for not sounding more relaxed and confident.

The teacher introduced herself as a member of Pennsylvania's emergency response team. "Our organization relies on volunteers to help communities cope with the horror after a school shooting or other traumatic event. By the end of this training, you will all be qualified to administer trauma debriefing in order to bring people out of that first wave of shock and fear.

When she finished speaking, she cut the lights and started a video, which reenacted one of the types of community disasters we could be called in on. In the video, a man walked into a crowded fast-food restaurant and methodically shot diners as they cowered under tables, pleading for their lives. The effect of the video brought back the gut-wrenching feelings I had experienced during the news reporting of the World Trade Center catastrophe.

Apparently, that had been the intent of showing us that horrifying video. We needed to get into the mood.

As we wrapped up that day's discussions, the leader told us that when we returned the next day, we would create a mock trauma debriefing. To make it as real as possible, we should think about some trauma that we had experienced ourselves.

I went home that night feeling drained by this focus on suffering. I was also nervous about my participation. What could I say to these people? I'd lived such an ordinary life. When I woke up the next morning, I remembered the time I'd been mugged in college. It was the first time I'd thought about it in many years.

When it was time for the group session, we pulled our chairs into a circle. One person told of feeling violated when her house was robbed. Another had lost her son, who had been a passenger on the airplane that had exploded over Lockerbie Scotland. Then it was my turn.

"When I was around twenty years old, I was walking on my college campus, sporting the long hair that identified me as a war protestor. A carload of young boys jumped out of their car, punched me, threw me to the ground, and kicked me. The violation I felt during that incident kept me on edge for the rest of the summer." I looked around the circle and saw their concern. "This is the first time I've ever talked about the incident, even with close friends."

After a few minutes, the group moved on to the next person's story, but I could barely hear. For the rest of the session, my mind was racing, remembering how the intimidation I felt the night of my attack had settled over me like a shroud. In the aftermath I had remained silent, so ashamed of the event I never even told my parents. Back then, there were no psychological services, at least none that I knew about. So I pretended it never happened, allowing the shock to sink deep into the background where it stayed until this training workshop pulled it out of me.

After all the introspective work I'd done throughout adulthood, writing in a journal, meditating, and speaking with a therapist, I had never noticed this intense memory, buried deep in the bowels of my past. This forgetfulness challenged all I knew about introspection and self-awareness. Trauma seemed to play by its own rules.

In the years following my mugging, I made a string of incredibly bad decisions, as if my internal compass had been broken. Until this practice session of trauma-debriefing, it had never occurred to me that being attacked had had any influence on my behavior at all.

How much would my life have played out differently if, back then, someone with a deeper understanding of trauma had offered me a path to safety? What if I could become such a person, offering help to others? It seemed a noble calling.

I recalled my final interview with Steve, my counseling professor, when I told him my plan was to be a therapist only for easy cases. I could see how my flippant comment was essentially an admission that I had not yet grasped the significance of becoming a therapist. This was serious stuff. And my recent discovery of my earlier trauma provided further proof that I still had a long way to go.

At the end of the week, the emergency response team spelled out the details of volunteering. When a catastrophe struck anywhere in the state, volunteers had only a few hours to pack their bags, disengage from their other responsibilities, and travel to the scene, where they might stay for days in any available accommodations. The trainer said she'd spent many such nights sleeping on a sofa in someone's living room. I admired the superhuman flexibility such volunteers must achieve in order to participate in this way. I just couldn't picture myself doing it. I declined.

And yet, the week had been far from wasted. I learned so much about the people who fearlessly show up to help others in their time of need. And in my attempt to become one of them, I had uncovered valuable information about myself, which would in turn require more processing and healing.

I sighed. This path I had chosen seemed to demand self-improvement without end. Was there enough time left in my life to complete everything I'd set out to do?

And what if there wasn't? The only other option was to give up, and that wasn't an option at all.

Continuing my crawl to credentialing

In order to accumulate my needed 3,000 hours of supervised clinical experience, at least half of which had to be actually sitting with clients, I had to squeeze in a few hours each week, in the evenings after I finished at my computer job.

I was fortunate to be hired by the same agency where I'd done my internship, and they were willing to work with my limited schedule. But after I'd been there for a few more months, Pennsylvania sharply curtailed financial support for mental health counseling. The mood at the agency changed. Rules became more intense, and urgent meetings were held. It wasn't long before they let me go.

Desperate to keep moving toward certification, I called Curt, my first therapist, to ask if he could offer any advice. He said if I wanted to join him in private practice, he would supervise me. I could rent an office in his building and work as many or as few hours as I wanted.

I loved the new arrangement. The drive to my new office was considerably shorter, so I didn't need to waste much time in the car. And I had no agency rules to worry about. I hung my diploma on the wall of my new office, and posted a "Jerry Waxler" sign on the door. I envisioned my practice growing to the point that I would eventually have enough clients to justify quitting my job and moving to full-time counseling,

Several clients from my previous counseling agency followed me to the new location, so for the first few weeks, everything seemed perfect. But just as I'd resisted the inconvenience of driving thirty minutes south to my former location, my clients didn't want to drive north. They soon dropped out.

Then I hit a new snag. Since I wasn't licensed yet, I couldn't take payments from insurance companies. I discovered that insurance referrals were the primary means to find therapy clients. I was left with a degree and an office, but no clients.

The building was on a commuter road. If even one of every thousand, or even ten thousand, knew I was there, I would be able to continue. Collaborating with Curt, we posted a large sign by the road. Yet, week after week, then month after month, the cars kept cruising right past the sign. No one stopped or called.

From hoping for a thriving and growing practice, I set my sights on having enough client income to pay my office rent. Most weeks, I didn't have a single client. It looked like I would be working at my day job longer than I expected.

I asked Curt what he thought I should do.

"People don't know you yet. You have to get your name out there. You should advertise."

His suggestion scared me. Perhaps after I'd gotten my 3,000 hours and achieved state licensing, I'd be willing to let people know about my services. But for now, despite having an advanced degree, I couldn't shake a deep sense of dread. When I tried to say "I'm a therapist," I felt like a liar.

Trying to embrace my new role

Curt and I were too closely associated as business associates, so I wanted to find another therapist with whom to share my insecurities. That led me to Lyndra.

Despite being a full-fledged medical doctor, Lyndra had an excellent reputation as a talk therapist. I'd been curious about her for years, at least in part because of the coincidence that her office used to be in the same building in which I was now practicing.

When I met her, her dog sat nearby, a gentle presence in the room. While I explained my background, her dog's tail thumped lazily against the floor.

"When I was in high school," I told her, "my brother was already in medical school, and I expected to follow in his footsteps. By the time I left college, he was a doctor but I had failed miserably."

"Tell me more," she said.

I tried to stammer out a few incidents about those tumultuous years but the words tumbled out in a confusing sequence.

"Have you ever written all that down?"

"I've filled dozens of journals with my current thoughts and feelings but it never occurred to me to write about the past."

"You can learn all sorts of things about yourself by writing the major events and transitions in chronological order."

At home, I started a computer file and tried to write what I remembered.

1965, I moved from Philadelphia to Madison, Wisconsin, full of hope about becoming a doctor.

1967, big war protest and riot.

1969, moved to Berkeley, California, and instantly fell in love. After that emotional train wreck, I felt lost, stranded, nothing worth living for.

1971, planned to move to Central America to live on the beach and eat fruit.

At the next session, I showed her my timeline. "I've been in therapy for years and this is the first time I've ever seen the sequence of events laid out so clearly."

At the end of our discussion about my timeline, she gave me an assignment. "Keep it up. Add more details for each year. You can learn a lot about yourself this way."

Then we circled back to the problem I had come here to solve: how to overcome my reluctance to call myself a therapist. In one conversation, I mentioned that crowds made me nervous, especially when I thought they might focus on me. She asked me to give an example.

"Okay, here's one. As I pulled into the parking lot at work, I saw a few people huddled around the front door. To get into the office, I had to walk past them. My mind went into a frenzy–what would they think about me, what would I say or not say, should I look at them, and so on."

As I shared these thoughts with Lyndra, the embarrassment rose up through my neck and face, but I didn't hold back. I wanted her to know everything. The whole point of being here was to get help. I just wished I didn't sound like such an emotional idiot.

"That's a lot of anxiety," she said compassionately. "Does it happen often?"

I paused scanning my memory and trying to put my thoughts into words. Finally, I said, "These episodes have bothered me my whole life, but they make me feel so vulnerable and embarrassed, I've never described them to anyone–I probably never even described it to myself."

"Social anxiety," she said, jotting something down in her notes. It sounded like a good research topic for me to look into later. However, none of these insights broke through my reluctance to announce myself as a therapist.

"I want to try EMDR with you," she said to me at one session.

"What is that?"

"Eye movement desensitization and reprocessing. It typically involves moving your eyes back and forth. But I like a variation on the technique, in which I alternately tap each knee. It's a modified form of hypnotism that helps link the two sides of your brain."

She told me to close my eyes, which I did.

Then she asked me to think about how I wanted to resolve my fears of calling myself a therapist. I opened my eyes. "But I don't know the solution."

"Just think about how you are now and how you want to be. The goal is to see what comes to mind."

She tapped on my knees, right, left, right, left. The rhythmic tapping put me into a mildly altered state. While I imagined calling myself a therapist, I had a vision of my older brother Ed.

He was such a profoundly respectful person. In those few times I saw him in the last year of his life, even though he was dying, his love seemed to include me in a warm embrace. I could feel that loving kindness lifting me out of my self-doubts.

In the vision, he smiled warmly and told me how proud he was of me for going back to school to learn how to help people. His kindness and support felt so real.

I came out of the trance feeling that Ed had validated my new role. Reassured by his blessing, my fears lost their power and I walked out of the office eager to let people know I wanted to help.

Unravelling

While walking a fellow student out to her car after one of my counseling classes, she said, "My marriage is falling apart." I was shaken by the abruptness of her delivery. She seemed disoriented, as though she couldn't quite grasp what was happening to her.

I wasn't sure how to respond. I had a stable marriage. In fact, I was a little smug about it. "Oh, no. That's too bad," I managed.

She said that when she'd told one of our professors about her marriage problems, he wasn't surprised. He'd heard similar stories from other students. "According to him, counseling grad school inspires so much personal development that some partnerships become lopsided and stop working."

At least I don't have that problem, I thought. After all my years of loneliness, I had no interest in facing life without this marriage.

Now, just a year after that self-assured assessment, I discovered my relationship was not as secure as I thought. Despite my own confidence that everything was fine, my wife had been feeling less and less support from me. Finally, she went in another direction. Suddenly, my relationship went from a sure thing to no thing at all.

Without my marriage to sustain me, my emotions went into free fall. The dark depression that crushed me in my twenties descended like an avalanche. The sheer pain of it was unbearable.

What happened? I thought. *How had I failed?*

As the dissolution progressed, it became obvious that in our new, fractured state, one or the other of us would need to move out of the house. A second disaster! How could I leave the house that had given me safety and support after the debacle of the sixties? Such a move was unthinkable. Twenty-five years earlier, this house had saved me from myself. I was sure that if I tried to live on my own, I'd slide down into the pit of self-involvement from which I'd emerged all those years ago.

But it was just as impossible for her to imagine moving. It soon became obvious that I was the one who would have to muster the courage and make the plans. But where would I go? Even trying to imagine a next step felt like I was planning my own execution. Did I really have to go out and fend for myself? What would become of me?

What goes down must come up

In my new, single state, I could hardly remember how to be me. Fortunately, our bonds in the group were so solid both Ruth and I continued to feel connected and supported by our friends. Just without each other.

One of our friends, Janet, had been part of my life for years, involved in the group and the software company. She even boarded her horse at the same barn as Ruth, so while hanging out in a pasture or stall, she'd been telling me about her woes in the relationship department. Now it was my turn to share my sorrow with her.

She turned out to be as good a listener as she was a talker, and I found it easy to talk to her about almost everything. While at first, we looked at each other as friends, it didn't take long for me to start thinking about her all the time. Miraculously, fate had installed a fast-forward button in my life.

After only a few months, we were looking into each other's eyes amazed at how lucky we both felt. We laughed at almost any excuse. And most mysteriously, when I took something the wrong way, she managed to twist it around so in moments I was laughing at myself.

Soon, I was joining her on regular visits to her family. These visits were nothing like the stiff, awkward formality I'd always felt around my first wife's family. With Janet's extended family, I played cards and laughed for hours, as though we had known one another our whole lives.

As our relationship continued to evolve, I discovered a remarkable thing. Whatever mental damage had made romance dangerous when I was younger had apparently been repaired. I was madly in love and I enjoyed every minute.

The fact that we felt so comfortable together also resolved my living situation. After living in a group for twenty-five years, I was afraid I didn't know how to live any other way. In my new relationship, the problem simply evaporated. When Janet and I moved in together, I enjoyed being with her so much, I had all the company I needed.

The dizzying speed of these changes felt as though I was living in a Broadway show whose set and backdrop had been switched out between acts.

My wishes for a loving relationship and a place to call home granted, I couldn't help but hope that my third wish—a new professional life— would come together with similar grace and speed.

I placed a classified ad in the local paper. "Therapist will help you improve feelings and effectiveness." The day the paper was published, I touched my phone expectantly. What if I missed a call because I was busy? What if I received more calls than I could handle? Would I sound confident enough?

I waited. And waited. Finally, after a few days, my phone rang. The caller said she was giving herself a gift for her fiftieth birthday. I made the appointment, excited to have figured out how to find clients.

We talked about how she would find more fulfillment as she moved into this period. I gave her my full attention in exchange for a modest fee, which was exactly enough to pay for the ad.

When I ran the ad again the following week, I didn't get a single call. Fortunately, the woman who had seen me the week before returned for a second visit. But when it was time for a third appointment, she said she couldn't afford it. I was back to zero.

"Now what?" I asked Curt. "Getting clients is difficult and keeping them is even harder."

"There's a health fair at the high school every year. Just go and sit at a table, and let people know you're available."

Panic rose in my chest. My mind threw up a hundred objections. I couldn't take time off from work. I wouldn't know what to say. I was still working up the confidence to sit with one other person and offer my services. Sitting in a meeting room, in a swirl of parents, teachers, and students? No way. I sank lower in my chair.

Meanwhile Curt fished through a pile of papers on his desk. When he found what he was looking for, he handed me a flier. I looked at it blankly. It said something about the Chamber of Commerce. "Here's another option. Go to this meeting and shake some hands. You can even give a short speech introducing yourself and telling them what you do."

"I don't understand what good that will do." His suggestion seemed preposterous.

"Some might need your services."

I started to sweat. I knew with certainty I would never, ever be able to speak to a group. If building a practice required public speaking, I was doomed.

I expected him to see my discomfort. Surely, he would sympathize with the sheer impossibility of this option and offer some other method for finding clients.

Instead, he said, "Have you ever heard of Toastmasters?"

I had not.

"It's an international organization that helps people overcome the fear of public speaking."

I thanked him and walked out into the parking lot, just a few yards away from the stream of cars passing by the office. "Stop and look at the sign," I wanted to shout. But no one stopped. To continue as a therapist, I had to learn how to attract their attention in a more active, energetic, personal way. I didn't see myself ever doing that.

This felt like the end of the line. Perhaps I would always be a computer guy, after all. It wasn't a bad life. It's just that I had hoped to do so much more.

Trying to speak above a whisper

I parked my car, screwed up my courage, and walked toward the door of the hall where my local Toastmasters met. In the front lobby, I encountered about twenty people, hovering near the coffee pot, and a tray of cookies. My usual surge of self-consciousness sloshed over me. They all looked so comfortable, gesturing with their cups and laughing as if they'd all known one another for years. After a few minutes, I timidly approached a woman who looked friendly. I said I was new here and had spoken on the phone to someone named Arlene. The woman smiled and called to another woman nearby.

Arlene turned around to greet me. She was well-dressed, as if she had come straight from work. I told her I wasn't sure if I was going to stay. I just wanted to see what it was like.

"I'm glad you could make it." She smiled. I smiled back.

Okay, at least there was one person I knew.

From the front of the room, a man bellowed a five-minute warning and everyone drifted to their seats. I sat at one of the tables and poured myself a glass of water, hoping to settle my nerves. Then, the sergeant at arms banged his gavel to call the meeting to order.

The sound, which I associated with robed judges in television courtrooms, was oddly reassuring—as if the organizers knew what they were doing, and were going to tell us exactly what we should be doing, too.

Once the room quieted down, Arlene spoke. She was cheerful and upbeat, and freakishly comfortable cracking jokes in front of the group. I would never be able to do that.

She asked if there were any visitors. I raised my hand and felt sweat form on my upper lip as I stood. I spoke in a clipped voice. "My name is Jerry Waxler. I'm trying to improve my speaking skills." I sat, heart racing, but reasonably satisfied with my two sentences.

Arlene then introduced the master of ceremonies, who would be in charge of running the rest of the meeting. Alan stepped forward and introduced what he called his team.

One of his team members stood and said he was the "ah-and-um counter." "Verbal fillers steal energy from your talk. Whenever you hear someone say 'ah' or 'um,' please squeeze the squeaky toy or ding the bell on the table in front of you. By calling attention to these fillers, you will help your fellow Toastmaster break these bad habits." Another person said she was responsible for timing the talk to ensure it stayed within the prescribed limit.

Then the actual speeches began. The first speaker had run for President of the United States on some alternate party ticket. I tried to make sense of the enormity of what he was saying. His talk gave me a glimpse into pockets of politics I never even knew existed. I admired his courage. He seemed nervous, though, which perhaps explained why he lost.

The next speaker was a young woman who grew up in Russia near Chernobyl during the nuclear disaster. Through her strongly accented words, I realized that in this little club a few miles from my home, I was listening to a first-person account of one of the greatest nuclear tragedies of my lifetime. I was impressed both by her story of survival as well as her courage to speak in spite of the fact that English was her second language

In the next segment of the well-choreographed meeting, a volunteer stood up to provide feedback about what each speaker had done well and how they could improve next time.

One evaluator suggested the speaker's voice lacked dynamic range. This concerned me. I knew my voice often sounded flat and wondered if I'd ever be able to speak with more energy. The other evaluator commented that the speaker should not have held a piece of paper in her hand, because even just a quick glance down at the paper reduced the connection between speaker and audience. This was more bad news for me. I was pretty sure I would be able to write a decent speech, but I didn't see how I could deliver it from memory.

After the meeting was over, I approached a man a few years older than me, fishing for reassurance that this program would help me.

"I'm so nervous about speaking in public. I don't know if I'll ever be able to do it."

"I felt the same way when I started," he said. "Now I'm completely comfortable. Toastmasters is like magic."

His testimonial gave me hope. Even though I lacked the nerve as well as the skill to deliver a good speech I'd managed to find a club that offered to solve both problems. Their systematic approach seemed to work for others. Perhaps it would work for me.

At the next meeting, I joined the club. The meeting after that, I volunteered to be the 'ah-and-um counter," which required that I stand and give a two-sentence "speech" encouraging people to ring a bell when they heard an "ah" or an "um." The following week, I volunteered for yet another minor role in the meeting.

But the real challenge, the one I still wasn't so sure I could pull off, was giving a speech.

How could I speak when I could barely breathe?

The Ice Breaker was the chilling name of the first formal speech new Toastmaster members were supposed to present. This first talk would introduce you to the group. They claimed that because it was about yourself, this talk should be easy to construct. Ha! Maybe that was true for other people, but not for me. I hated talking about myself, even when speaking individually to one person. It would be a lot harder in front of a room full of strangers, all focused on me.

In high school, when facing an impossible situation, we boys quoted a poem, "Charge of the Light Brigade" by Alfred Lord Tennyson. "Into the valley of death rode the six hundred." Like Tennyson's doomed soldiers, we had no choice. We had to show up for the difficult exam. Now, while preparing for my Toastmaster's talk, I often found myself repeating that line. "Into the valley of death." It helped me lighten the mood so I could keep pushing forward.

Each morning I chipped away. First, I gathered moments of my life. Then I put the bits in order, trying to hit the major issues. To make it easier to follow, I used the analogy of a book, presenting each segment of my life as a chapter. I needed an ending, and I thought of a tricky device. I would say the book was unfinished, and I couldn't wait to read the next chapter.

As the speech took shape, I started to like it. It flowed nicely, achieved the purpose of explaining my life, and I liked the clever snap at the end. My confidence grew. *I can write a speech that fits into the Toastmasters system. This is going to work.*

Except for one problem. In the Toastmaster meetings, whenever a speaker referred to notes, or even simply held a piece of paper, they were criticized. The evaluator would say something about how a real Toastmaster doesn't need to refer to notes. Each time I heard this advice, I cringed.

I had no experience memorizing an entire speech. It didn't even seem possible. I felt trapped. Even if I delivered it perfectly, they would certainly point out my incorrect use of notes. Just imagining being criticized in public made me feel awful. I dreaded this whole experience.

And yet I really wanted to do this.

At coffee breaks I asked other members for advice. They all assured me that many beginners are afraid to let go of their paper, but with practice they all move beyond the fear and give the speech with empty hands.

I couldn't imagine how others moved past these deep fears, but I was sure that I never would. My only hope was to deliver the speech with such sincerity, they would congratulate me for being the first person they'd ever known who could hold onto a piece of paper and still deliver a convincing speech.

All I had to do was rehearse a lot. I read it aloud a few times, but I couldn't figure out how to practice in front of an audience. Even with friends, I was too nervous to read it aloud, and I couldn't expect anyone to sit and listen to it several times.

I found a captive audience: our two cockatiels. Once or twice a day, I stood in front of their cage and recited my speech, with feeling. To my amazement, the little gray-and-white birds, which weighed all of three ounces each, appeared to be paying attention. They didn't criticize me for holding paper, and occasionally chirped or preened while I spoke.

After a couple of weeks of daily rehearsing, I still wasn't convinced that I would be able to perform with enough energy. I asked around to see if anyone could recommend a speech coach. A friend knew a drama professor at a local university who coached actors. He agreed to see me. His fee was breathtakingly high, but I felt this would be an investment in my future, a worthwhile step on my journey to become a therapist.

I went to his home and explained my predicament. He said, "To speak in a way that will move your audience, be aware of the emotions you want to evoke in them. Every time you speak, you need to think about which emotion you are communicating."

"But I'm just trying to explain who I am." I looked at my speech and couldn't see any emotion in it at all. I pointed to a line. "What's the emotion here?"

"You tell me. Do you intend to make them sad, happy, afraid, or anxious?"

"I have no idea. I'm just trying to explain my life."

"Okay," he said, appearing flustered. "You want to convey information, so you want to evoke the emotion of curiosity."

I tried to absorb what he was saying. "What about this line?"

"Same thing. It's information, so you are evoking curiosity."

It seemed he was trying to improve my script in ways I didn't understand. That wasn't what I came here for. I knew what I wanted to say. I just wanted him to show me how to deliver it. My expensive hour was slipping away, and I didn't feel any more confident than when I started.

"What else can you suggest?" I felt a little desperate.

"Breathing is very important," he said. He showed me how to pull air all the way down to the bottom of my lungs and use it to power a voice with strength and authority. I already knew about the importance of breathing from choir and yoga, but I appreciated the reminder.

"What else?"

"Your mouth is your instrument. You need to warm it up before you go on stage. Here's an easy exercise you can learn in a few seconds."

He held up three fingers, then jammed them between his teeth to force his mouth open. When he read a few lines of my speech, he sounded garbled. I laughed nervously. He didn't laugh back.

He pulled his fingers out of his mouth. "Now you try it." I jammed my mouth open with three fingers and read a paragraph from my script. My tongue and jaw muscles strained against the unfamiliar obstacle and my words sounded distorted.

"That's it," he said. "Now take your hand out of your mouth and speak normally."

After pulling my fingers out of my mouth, to my great surprise, my voice sounded stronger and more confident.

He wished me luck. Our time was up.

Before the next Toastmasters meeting, I sat in my car for a few minutes, pulling air down into my diaphragm. Then I stuck my hand in my mouth and spoke a few sentences. Finally, when I couldn't stall any longer, I got out and walked to the door. My body felt disconnected, a disoriented feeling I get when I am extremely nervous.

They called my name and I strode to the front of the room. When I pulled out my paper, I saw audience members frown. *They already think I'm a failure.* Looking down at the paper, distracted by shaky legs, I pressed on. But I was horrified to discover that my speech sounded much less impressive here than when I presented it to the cockatiels.

Everything slowed to a crawl. I tried to make eye contact, but lost my place while trying to read the expression on each person's face. They were judging me–and worse, I was judging myself. My eyes fell back to the page and stayed there. I wanted so badly to express emotion, but I no longer had any inkling of how I was supposed to do it. My voice grew fainter, until it sounded like I was gasping out an airy whisper. When I reached the end of the speech, I slunk back to my seat, drenched in sweat.

My eyes focused on my lap, I braced myself for the evaluation.

They went through the formal praise they always gave to first time speakers. But the only thing I heard were the dreaded words, "You would do a lot better if you weren't holding that paper."

It was the final blow. Despite weeks of crafting a speech, and more weeks practicing it aloud, my delivery had been a disaster. I found myself at an impasse. I couldn't speak without the paper. And to my horror, I couldn't even speak while holding it.

If the future of my counseling practice depended on me speaking in public, then I was lost.

Another way to reach the world

Even if I was willing to stand up in front of a group, the quaking mess I would present to them would be unlikely to attract new clients. Writing seemed like the obvious solution. I could write articles during my early morning study time, then send my words out into the world while I remained safely hidden. One challenge I had to overcome was that since I'd never taken any writing courses, I didn't really know what I was doing.

One of the courses in grad school offered a novel solution to this problem. According to neuro-linguistic programming (NLP), to succeed in any field, study the psychology of people already successful in that field. The book that explained that system was informative, and easy to read. It occurred to me that its author, Joseph O'Connor, would be the perfect person to emulate, in order to become a writer.

Exploring O'Connor's website, I found that he offered a mail-order writing course on precisely this topic. What a perfect person to learn from—a writing teacher who specializes in teaching complex, subtle psychological skills.

The first lesson arrived in email, a few skimpy pages riddled with typos and grammatical errors. But I had already paid, and I knew this guy was smart. Hopefully, beneath this messy exterior, I would find a few gems.

Just as he'd promised, the lessons were directed not toward the craft of writing, but the psychology of being a writer. Because society places such high regard on literature, many of us think of writers as demi-gods and fear there is no way we can ever reach those lofty heights. It would be foolish to move toward a goal without believing it was attainable. According to O'Connor, the first task for anyone who wants to become a writer is to get comfortable with the notion of becoming one.

I knew exactly what he meant. I'd had a similar discomfort when I tried to call myself a therapist. Apparently, seeing myself in a new role created a surprising amount of fear and insecurity.

O'Connor offered a brilliant suggestion for becoming more comfortable calling myself a writer. Instead of seeing myself sitting alone in a room typing on a computer, I should concoct a more dynamic visualization.

After playing around with a number of images, I settled on seeing myself as a "warrior-messenger" running from village to village, dressed in scanty native garb, carrying important messages that would help people prepare for the challenges of life. When I sent my homework to O'Connpor, he praised my image and suggested I make it my own.

He sent me another lesson, and I eagerly read through it, ignoring the typos and rough formatting. This little mail order course was exactly what I needed, inviting me to think slowly and deeply about my ambition to reach people through my writing. I savored each lesson, sometimes taking weeks before sending him my responses.

Thanks to these wonderful insights, I felt increasing confidence in my ability to become a writer. But one fundamental question remained. Other than knowing I wanted to reach people, I didn't know what I was going to write. I sent O'Connor an email and asked him for guidance.

He responded that in order to become a writer, I needed to focus on some particular project. In response to that suggestion, I pictured the body of knowledge I'd learned in grad school, as well as all the strategies I'd picked up during my years studying self-help. If I could offer it all in an easily accessible style, I could promote the many ideas about mental health that had helped me.

I began to develop a series of pieces about problems such as depression and anxiety. Other articles covered types of therapy, such as couples therapy, cognitive therapy, and NLP. I also wrote about self-help methods such as breathing, positive self-talk, and meditation.

I worked for months, generating dozens of these articles. But these pieces remained in my computer. I needed to get them out in front of other people. Perhaps they would someday helpe me attract new therapy clients.

At my day job, I had recently learned how to create a website. Learning things like this was one of the perks of working with computers. I asked a friend to help design a logo and set up some graphic elements. I named my website the *Mental Health Survival Guide.* I hoped that someday it would help a lot of people, and if it brought me a few clients, that would be good, too.

I posted an article on my website and waited for the calls. But not a single person reached out to me for more information. I posted a few more, and had the same reaction. Article after article resulted in dead silence.

Despite the lack of feedback, I could feel the stirring of a grand idea–to offer uplifting strategies that would help others feel good about themselves, too. So even if I didn't help clients in my office, perhaps writing helpful articles might be my new calling.

Joining forces with fellow writers

Despite my ongoing effort to write articles for my website, I still wasn't getting any nibbles for my therapy practice. Perhaps one reason no one had contacted me was the lackluster quality of my writing.

A search for a writing class near my home revealed an organization called the Writers Room in Doylestown, Pennsylvania. I phoned and left a message. The founder, Foster Winans, called back.

"What is this place?" I asked.

"I modeled it after the Writers Room in New York City, where writers could relieve their loneliness by writing together. We offer shared office space, classes, and critique groups, and we publish a literary review."

"That sounds perfect," I said. "I need help with my writing."

"We're starting a nonfiction group this month. Come and join us."

I hadn't done so well with the first writing group I'd tried, thirty-some years earlier. Hanging around the University of California at Berkeley in 1970, I attended a meeting of a poetry club. Even though I had hardly any training or experience, I assumed they would find my poems full of deep meaning. When they offered constructive criticism, I felt so angry and humiliated. How dare they comment on my precious words? I vowed to never solicit feedback about my writing again.

That vow seemed ludicrous to me now, an artifact of a much less emotionally competent version of myself. At least that was my hope. There was only one way to find out if I'd grown.

I entered the small office suite, where eight people sat in a circle. Except for Foster and me, they were all women.

Each of us introduced ourselves. Most of them had written for newspapers and magazines. One woman told us she had published articles in magazines for a dollar a word, and she was looking to bump up to three dollars a word. Her voice was tense, her face drawn tight. She sat on the edge of the chair. She had come here with high hopes. This was going to be a serious group.

After the introductions, Foster left and we were on our own. The intense woman laid out how our meetings would be structured. She added, with extra emphasis, "During the critiquing, it is crucial that the person who wrote the piece remains absolutely silent." At the next meeting, mine was one of four pieces to be critiqued. I felt flushed, worrying about what they would say. One of them asked, "What is this?" I thought I detected a sarcastic tone, but I looked around the room and saw heads nodding. The others agreed they didn't know what it was. I started to explain, but our serious moderator spoke sharply.

"Please. While you're being critiqued, don't talk."

I swallowed hard, already feeling a bit shaky. I didn't want to break the rules, because I desperately wanted their help. But I couldn't get my mind to shut up.

"Excuse me," I blurted. "How can you understand my piece if you won't let me explain it?"

She gave me a hard look. "The writing must speak for itself. You won't be standing next to every reader to explain. The purpose of the critique group is to comment on the writing. Let us do our work."

"That makes sense." I shrugged my shoulders in a gesture of reluctant submission.

One of the other women said, in a gentler tone, "Just remember that our critiques are simply each individual's opinion. So, there's no point in debating. If you try to defend your writing, it stifles our feedback. You'll see," she said with a smile.

One writer pointed, "It's not really an article. You could never publish it in a magazine."

Another said, "Perhaps it's a brochure?"

Several women liked that possibility, and they went on to talk among themselves about how I could print them on trifold paper and place them on racks in my office or hand them to clients.

This was not what I wanted to hear. Brochures in my office would be useless if no one came in. To attract clients, I needed to write for a larger audience—the whole world, if possible.

These women were accomplished magazine writers and according to them, my pieces did not fit into their publications. Instead of feeling wounded, as I had done years ago, I saw that they had pinpointed my main challenge. I didn't know how to make my writing interesting to readers. That became my necessary next step. And thanks to the Writers Room, I wouldn't have to take that step alone.

Writing meant opening to strangers

The articles on my website could be accessed anywhere in the world, but to turn readers into clients, I needed to find people within driving distance. Newspapers were the obvious choice. Every town had one. If I could write articles for one of these papers, perhaps a reader or two might look me up.

But as soon as I thought about it, I was racked by fear. Newspapers relied on their own staff writers, didn't they? Even if they were open to freelancers, I had no journalism background and no connections.

This whole round of objections sounded suspiciously similar to the inner debate that prevented me from calling myself a therapist. Writing articles didn't seem like something worth discussing with my therapist but these waves of fears seemed appropriate.

At my next therapy session I told Lyndra about wanting to write an article, and then, broke off from my hopeful plan with a litany of reasons why I could never succeed.

Unfazed by my fears, she told me she liked the idea. "Local papers are much more open to new writers."

"But I've never written a newspaper article before," I said, in case she didn't hear me the first time. "And anyway, they want news, right? My psychological advice is too broad."

This was the way I exhausted myself: raising so many objections to a new idea that by the time I sat down to actually do it, I'd dissipated all the excitement that had energized me.

Lyndra's dog lay on the floor, lazily thumping her tail as if to say, "Take it easy. There's nothing to worry about."

"Thanksgiving is coming up," Lyndra said. "Newspapers are always looking for articles about the holiday season."

Her comment brought back the family holidays of my youth. After I helped Dad insert the leaves, our dining table was so long it barely fit in the room. As my grandparents, aunts, uncles, and cousins arrived, I watched my mom desperately trying to please her own mother. The anxiety I felt for my mom dominated my feelings. No wonder I stuffed myself with food until my stomach hurt.

I smiled at Lyndra as relief washed through me. "You're right. I could say a lot about surviving the holidays. And I can see how the seasonal slant would make a psychological topic relevant to a newspaper. But Thanksgiving is only once a year. What else would I write about?"

"Emotional issues arise throughout the year," she said. "There is Christmas, New Year's, winter doldrums. Give it a try."

As usual, I left Lyndra's office more hopeful and braver than when I entered.

For the next couple of weeks, I wrote about how differently people behave when they come together under one roof. I wrote about honoring those who were missing, and about really listening to repetitive stories while trying to find new insights.

I enjoyed the unfamiliar challenge of trying to describe the scene at a holiday dinner. And I hoped that by including some personal anecdotes and a few self-help suggestions, I could make it interesting. And if it didn't hit the mark, my critique partners would have no problem telling me.

At my next writing group, I nervously read the draft of my article. Their feedback gave me some ideas about how to improve it.

I then asked them for permission to ask a question. The intense woman pursed her lips and looked at her watch, but the others nodded.

"If you think this would work for a newspaper," I said, "can you suggest one that might be interested?"

"I could see this working as a column," Brenda said. "I know the editor of the local newspaper. He's a great guy. Why don't you give him a call?"

Her personal recommendation bolstered my courage. The next day, I stood in front of the phone, took a few deep breaths, told myself "you can do it," and then dialed the number.

"I want to write articles that will help people cope with life," I said to the editor. "Do you print anything like that?"

"I've never done it before, but I'm willing to start," he said. I hesitated, waiting for some further objection. Apparently, though, no further convincing was required. He actually was offering to print my columns.

I gushed out a relieved thank you, thrilled to be getting a "yes" on my first try. After ascertaining the length of the article and how to submit it, I hung up the phone, elated at my good fortune. An article in the local paper seemed like the perfect next step.

All those seemingly insurmountable fears and objections were behind me, thanks to the encouragement, support, and suggestions from Lyndra and my fellow writers. I wasn't sure it was possible to be in love with a whole community, but if it was, I was in love with them.

And I was moving forward.

Climbing up the writing mountain

I sent my first 500-word column to the editor of the *Doylestown Patriot* and waited for the edits. When I didn't hear back, I imagined the worst: He'd lost interest. The following week, when I flipped through a copy of the newspaper, there was my article–exactly as I'd submitted it.

Apparently, he'd deemed it worthy of his readers, and now I was a published writer. It should have been a cause for celebration, but my main goal in writing the article had been to attract clients. And for that, I'd hoped the sentence at the bottom. "Jerry Waxler is a therapist in Quakertown" might prod people to look me up.

At first my biggest concern was that my phone would ring during my working hours. Phone calls from strangers made me nervous no matter where I was. In the office, they made me even more anxious. I would need to answer the phone in a discrete whisper, which would create a terrible first impression on a prospective client. To prevent such an awkward first impression, I'd have to dash out the back door of the building the moment the phone rang so I could speak in a more natural tone of voice.

However, none of those problems arose. I didn't receive a single phone call. I needed to lower my expectations and be more patient. I would write more articles. It would take time for people to get to know about me from the column.

With December coming, I continued the seasonal slant by writing about the pressure of giving gifts. My newspaper editor published this one, too. No questions asked. For January, I wrote about how to sustain New Year's resolutions. In February I'd focus on Valentine's Day, or, since I knew so little about romance, perhaps I could talk about a subject that I knew much better: getting through the winter doldrums.

If I kept this up once or twice a month, I was confident that over time, I would get all the calls I would need to keep my practice going. However, months flew by without generating a single call.

As my dreams of a thriving counseling practice faded, I noticed I was becoming increasingly confident as a self-help writer. I wanted these articles to grow, and possibly to find other publications.

Every time I had to run an errand in a nearby town, I grabbed a local newspaper, assuming each one would include guidelines about submitting articles. I was surprised to discover that hardly any of them offered such information. To pitch my column to these papers, I would need to actually speak to an editor, one of those social-outreach tasks I was so good at avoiding.

One local paper seemed promising, and was far enough away that it wouldn't be competing with my Doylestown paper, but still within driving distance of my office. I sent an email pitching my column, and waited. Weeks later, I still had not heard back.

This was going to be harder than I thought. Perhaps my first success was just a fluke. Perhaps if I kept improving the quality of my writing, other opportunities would appear.

I brought more articles to my critique group and paid close attention to their feedback. Most suggestions were helpful, but in one session, a tiny, wizened woman said, "I have nothing to say about this piece. I hate this type of writing." She seemed angry. And for some reason, she felt entitled to let me feel the full brunt of it, as if she needed to put me in my place.

I suppressed my panic and tried to talk myself down. *Stay calm, Jer. She apparently takes pride in saying whatever comes to her mind.* Despite feeling wounded, I smiled and thanked her.

Later my panic subsided and I realized I had learned an important lesson: Not everyone was going to like what I wrote. I only needed to learn how to please the people who were in my target audience; in other words, people who "liked this kind of writing" and needed its message.

After a few more months in the critique group, the same woman who'd given me that gruff feedback said, "This one is different. I really like it." I felt especially lifted, and not just because she liked the writing. I was proud of myself for staying calm and creating enough trust to let her open up and express appreciation.

Another guy, who used to be a reporter for a major newspaper, said the quality of my writing was good enough for a much bigger publication. If there is one thing better than being praised, it's being praised in a group. If he only could be my agent, my problems would be solved.

Inspired by his enthusiasm, I kept writing.

Since my editor seemed intent on publishing anything I sent, I branched out beyond seasonal tie-ins. I wrote columns about positive thinking, becoming aware of addiction, and other self-improvement topics. My mornings were filled with productive, engaging work, and each day added validation for my growing identity as a real, published author.

But the endeavor never earned me a single therapy client.

One door closes

My hope for a career as a therapist slipped away. To some extent, my difficulties had been created by my own decisions. Most graduates of the program jump-started their clinical careers by working in agencies. But I already earned a decent paycheck at the computer company and couldn't afford to give that up and start all the way down at the bottom of the pay scale.

It wasn't just the drop in earning capacity that concerned me about working in an agency. I didn't think I was emotionally prepared to see clients all day every day. I needed to grow into this new career gradually.

When the office rent came due each month, the futility of continuing in this direction came into sharp focus. Looking to the future, I could see that achieving 3,000 hours of supervised clinical experience had also come to a standstill. At the present rate, I would die long before I would reach that goal.

Finally, I accepted the obvious and told Curt I needed to give up the office.

"You could keep going part time," he suggested. "You're welcome to schedule an hour here when a room is available."

"That's generous of you," I said, silently doubting I would find even one person who might come in and see me.

"What are you going to do now?" Curt asked.

"Keep working my day job," I said, gulping back disappointment. "Maybe I'll be able to resume my journey toward counseling after I retire." This wasn't much consolation, since I had no idea when that might be.

I felt an ache in my soul as I removed my diploma from the wall. Had I really failed? I'd worked so hard for so long to escape my cubicle. No doubt, I'd made some mistakes, and perhaps I'd been overly ambitious. Still, it didn't seem fair. Shouldn't the universe be willing to meet me half way?

But complaints and regrets wouldn't solve anything. Instead of griping about what didn't work, I shifted my focus to all I'd learned. Putting myself into this position as a novice therapist had set me further on a path of understanding than I could have ever anticipated. I couldn't stop now. I wanted to keep growing.

Curt's question echoed in my mind. What next? What next?

In order to push the failure of my therapy practice out of my mind, I turned my attention toward improving the rough draft of an article I'd been writing. Even though I no longer expected my newspaper column to win clients, my motivation to write had taken on a life of its own. My encounters at the Writers Room had been like opening a door partway. I wanted to find out what I might find if I walked through.

Earning a place among my new peers

Just as I was getting ready to fall apart in Berkeley, in 1970, I made one last desperate attempt to resuscitate my dream of becoming a doctor. I enrolled in a grueling lineup of pre-med courses at the University of California. Once the courses started, though, my physical and mental health plummeted, and I quickly failed out.

As if I was following some inner impulse, which I'd never even noticed before, it dawned on me that becoming a writer would be an interesting alternate life path. I wrote a couple of pieces for the UC Berkeley campus newspaper and wrote an article for a small local literary journal. But just as I didn't have the consistency and concentration needed to become a doctor, I was similarly unable to sustain my ambition to be a writer.

Now, in 2002, I was once again reaching toward writing as an alternate path. This time, though, I was starting from a much different place. I had stability, friends, a job, and lots of tricks to help me stay focused and energized. And I had a secret weapon: the Writers Room.

I had always thought of writing as a loner activity. The Writers Room brought us together to explore our shared desire to communicate. Surrounded by writers, it dawned on me that the books I'd been reading all my life had been written by people who, just like me, wanted to grab what was going on in their minds and put it on the page. Now, I could hang out with them. I could even start to consider myself one of them. And it was available less than a half-hour drive from my house.

Parking was a pain, but after driving around the block a few times, I usually found a good spot up on the hill near the courthouse. The only bad thing was that on the walk down to the Writers Room, I had to deal with a cacophony of feelings unleashed by the sight of war protestors.

The US had recently invaded Iraq, and a small group of hardy souls stood quietly in front of the county courthouse holding peace signs. Seeing them brought back memories of that October day in 1967 when my attempt to hurl my body in front of the war machine left me with tread marks etched into my soul.

On one of the most violent days of my life, standing arm-in-arm with fellow protestors, I watched in horror as a policeman brutally beat the girl next to me. In that instant, I went from being an idealist, intent on expressing my beliefs, to a cynic, convinced nothing would ever change.

Shaking off those confusing memories, I brought my attention back to the present. Perhaps by learning to write well, I could spread some hope, joy, or even peace.

I continued down the trendy street, past the chocolatier, the boutique dress shop, and then reverentially paused in front of the independent bookstore. *Beloved books*, I thought, as I read the titles in the window display. I pushed myself to keep moving, though, because I didn't want to be late for the writing class.

As I neared the office suite of the Writers Room, I looked through the window at the people standing inside. My anxiety escalated. Many times over the years, I had stopped at the entryway to some gathering, turned around, and walked away. At the Writers Room, so much of what I wanted to achieve in this stage of my life shone like a beacon from inside that room. I used my self-talk techniques. *Come on Jer. You're going to have a great time. These people won't hurt you.* And then I took a deep breath and entered.

Inside, as I heard everyone talking about writing, I relaxed. We had so much in common. Once the event got started, I relaxed even more.

Introductions revealed that they'd come from as far as Philadelphia, New Jersey, and the Poconos.

One woman in her thirties told a story that reflected the magnetic attraction this place had exerted on those of us in the room. "After I graduated from Sarah Lawrence," she said, "I got a dream job working in a big publishing company in New York City. I couldn't imagine living anywhere else. After the terrifying World Trade Center attacks, we drove through Bucks County, where we saw the sign for the Writers Room. I turned to my husband and said, 'We're moving here.'"

Week after week, I attended meetings and classes, learning about writing, and just as important, learning about writers. As I got to know them, I realized that in addition to us all wanting the same thing, we also shared many similar problems.

One of them said, "I've always loved writing but I hate allowing people to read what I've written." Another said, "I hate rejection so much, I hide the writing in my drawer." Others said, "I don't have time," or "I am going to write more, someday." I'd spent years experimenting with methods to overcome all these problems.

During my morning time in front of the lights, I began to compile a list of techniques that had helped me feel and act like a writer. For example, over the years, I'd increasingly come to appreciate the value of positive self-talk, which had been critical for helping me overcoming self-doubt. Another method I'd used extensively was to write as if I was talking to kind, curious, receptive listeners.

Two of my most important ideas came from Stephen Covey's *The 7 Habits of Highly Effective People.* First, as the title suggested, he'd instilled tremendous respect for the power of constructive habits. And his idea about focusing effort toward other roles was a crucial for beginning writers who had to ply their craft while earning a living doing something entirely different. Kathy's suggestions had provided me with two more fundamental tools. Writing in a journal gave me practice allowing words to flow easily from mind to page, and then her introduction to the morning therapy lights had provided the time each day when I could ply my craft.

As my collection grew, I became increasingly confident that my suggestions might be useful to the other club members. I thought with a laugh how my goals had changed over the years. From thinking I could help all of humanity by stopping all wars, to helping a few fellow writers overcome their problems. My new goal was far less ambitious than earlier one, but also far more likely to succeed.

Emerging from silence

Most of the time, when I was around people, I hoped no one would notice me. And yet I couldn't stop thinking about teaching. This could only happen if I could overcome these terrible fears of being seen.

I needed help, and I already knew where I could get that help. Toastmasters, that quirky group with its formal, almost silly, rules was designed to address such feelings. When I ran away from them the previous year, I'd abandoned an important goal. Now I'd have to start over, but I could not face the same people in front of whom I had humiliated myself so badly. Fortunately, there were a half-dozen other chapters near me. One of them met early in the morning, my favorite time of the day.

At seven a.m., I pulled into the parking garage and found my way to the brilliantly lit meeting room, where fifteen or twenty people chattered noisily. They were morning people, like me. I felt lifted by their vigor and curiosity, in sharp contrast to my bad nerves, fatigue, and self-consciousness at last year's evening meetings.

One of the members came over and introduced himself. After shaking hands and trading names, I repeated my lingering concern. "I don't think I could ever give a speech without holding notes."

The man said, "I used to feel the same way. But after trying it, I realized I felt more confident without the notes than with them."

"That must have been nice for you," I said. "But I don't expect to ever be able to do it even once. I'm terrible at memorizing. I would never be able to get the words right."

"Oh god, I don't memorize either," he replied. "I just remember the gist."

"What?" I said, my voice rising an octave. "How does that work?"

"I practice over and over, but each time, the words come out a little different. That way when I actually deliver the speech, I feel fresh and energized, as if I'm speaking it for the first time. In a way, I guess I am."

His explanation instantly shifted my perspective. If, instead of memorizing the exact words, I could just practice the approximate speech, that would change everything. Hope broke through the hard shell of my fear.

Armed with this new attitude, I signed up to give a talk, setting a deadline for myself of just six weeks.

I figured I would deliver roughly the same personal introduction I composed last year. I dug up my notes, and for each paragraph, I wrote the basic idea on a 3x5 index card. When I practiced, I would glance at the card, quickly load the idea into my mind, and then speak freely about those ideas for a few sentences.

To ensure the cards stayed in order, I punched a hole in the corner of each one and inserted a ring through the holes. This created a deck I could easily flip through. I practiced the talk while flipping through the cards, figuring that the more I spoke it aloud, the more I would build the memory into my body.

Occasionally, when my energy was high, I could give the whole talk from memory, without the cards at all. But I wasn't ready to give them up altogether. For this first talk, I would keep the cards in my hand in case I forgot something.

On the drive to the meeting, I gave the entire talk aloud so I'd have it fresh in my mind. When I finished, I was amused to note that I'd run through the whole thing without looking at the notes. I wondered if I could give the actual talk the same way. But that would be asking too much. I decided I would definitely hold them, even if it meant that someone would surely criticize me for it.

After I parked, I walked over to the meeting room and reached into my pocket for the cards. They weren't there. I knelt down and rifled through my backpack. Again nothing. I must have left them in the car. I had a few minutes, so I ran to the parking lot and slid my hand under the seat. Still nothing. After all this work, was I going to fail again?

I paused and closed my eyes. I already knew I could give my talk without notes. I just had to do it again... in front of people. When it was my turn, I walked to the front of the room, my heart throbbing in my chest. I faced the audience and began.

Dear fellow Toastmasters, the Ice Breaker is an opportunity to tell you about me, in a five- to seven-minute speech. I want to cover a lot of ground, so let me start out with a couple of highlights.

My own voice sounded strong and confident. I couldn't believe I was really doing this.

On my thirtieth birthday, I got off the plane in Cairo, Egypt. It was late in the day, and after the long flight, I was tired. But I wanted to do one thing before sunset. To see the Great Pyramid at Giza. Arriving at Giza under the setting sun just minutes before the guards were preparing to close for the night, I bounded up the great stone blocks to the entrance of one of the greatest works in the history of civilization. Just as this monument symbolized the crowning attainment of humans on earth, I felt in my heart that reaching this doorway on my thirtieth birthday in some way symbolized a meaningful journey for my own life.

After practicing with the cards, I could easily visualize the gist of each segment of the talk. I kept going.

Now flash forward a year. It's my thirty-first birthday. I'm working in a sand-casting foundry in Pennsylvania. If you've ever been in a sand-casting foundry, you know about the black sand everywhere. The smoke and flames belching from the furnaces. For ventilation, massive overhead doors stand open so it's blazing hot in the summer and freezing cold in the winter. On that particular day, my boss asked me to assist the plumber, who had come to clear a clogged septic system. There I was on my birthday, dodging splashes and struggling to hold down lunch. I wonder what that symbolized.

As I neared my closing line, I felt increasingly confident.

So, what's the next chapter? I apologize fellow Toastmasters. I can't tell you. As I flip to the next page, it's blank, waiting to be filled in. But there is one hint. At the top of the blank page appears an inscription. It says, "Welcome, my friend, to the show that never ends."

Jerry Waxler

This time, instead of assuming the audience's applause was only done out of courtesy, I opened my heart to it and felt lifted. I imagined that some of them genuinely liked the talk. I know I did.

A few minutes later, a club member stood up to offer feedback. I listened carefully. One comment was that I don't look people in the eye enough while speaking. This didn't surprise me. I've always had trouble maintaining eye contact when I'm thinking. He also said I didn't move around enough at the front of the room. This was a standard Toastmaster reminder. Someday, I would learn the knack of moving while speaking. For today, I was happy enough that I'd been able to move my lips.

And then the reviewer said, "And Jerry did it all without referring to paper." I felt flushed—but this time, instead of from embarrassment, it was from pride.

Begging at the gate

Once I was able to speak to a room full of people without fainting, I was ready to implement my plan. All I needed was a nod from Foster. He seemed like a nice guy, but asking anyone for anything terrified me, so I had to prepare carefully.

To catch Foster alone, I took a long lunch break and drove over to Doylestown. During the drive I rehearsed my pitch. Just as I'd hoped, he was alone in his office. I stood at the open door and tapped softly. When he turned around, I said, "Hi Foster, could I talk to you for minute?"

He smiled. I took a deep breath.

"I notice there are no courses on overcoming psychological obstacles to writing. I'd like to teach such a workshop."

"If you're referring to writer's block," he said, "when I want to write, nothing gets in my way." I held my breath. Just because he can write whenever he wants, does he think that everyone can?

In a way, I sympathized with Foster's skepticism about writer's block. The solution must have seemed so trivial to him. But I had met many people for whom the act of writing continued to slip out of their grasp. I could help them overcome their reluctance by teaching them how to overcome procrastination one step at a time.

My future rested on approval from this man, and he didn't like the idea. The whole thing had fallen apart before it even began. But I noticed a hesitation.

Then he said, "We do get calls from people asking for help with writer's block. In fact, I just received one this week."

Another pause. Only this time, his body language softened. Was he changing his mind in mid-thought?

"Sure, let's try it. You can give it at Workshop Wednesday."

His initial skepticism had melted away, and by the end of his sentence he sounded downright enthusiastic. I loved this guy. He was sitting there, with all the power. And he had just promoted me from an attendee to a teacher.

"Thank you so much," I gushed. "I'll do a good job."

On my way home, I wondered where I'd found the nerve. If he'd asked me more about my background, I would have had to confess I'd never done anything like this before. But I took a chance, and so did he. I vowed to prove myself worthy of his trust.

Each morning, I shaped my tips into modules in the workshop. All the while, I was imagining how it would sound to the attendees. With growing excitement, I realized that I was employing one of the best pieces of writing advice I had ever received: "To write well, imagine you are speaking to a trusted friend." When pulling together the material for my workshop, I was imagining not one friend but a gathering of them. Writing as if I was in front of a group of writers increased my commitment even more. I was not just doing this for myself, or for Foster. I was doing it for them.

Despite my heart-thumping desire to teach this class, my mind occasionally fought back. "What if they don't like it? What if they don't like me?"

Hearing these negative thoughts made me completely nuts. I knew very well that saying such things to myself would deflate my mood. And I'd gotten pretty good at applying the surprisingly simple solution of intentionally saying encouraging things to myself. The problem was that at the very moments when I needed these positive statements, I'd forget to say them.

I had a solution to that problem too. I kept a few 3x5 cards in my pocket, on which I'd written positive statements. When feeling down, all I needed to do was pull out the cards and flip through them.

Another trick I'd learned was to rehearse a lot. The more times I spoke the words in the privacy of my home, the more confident I felt during the actual performance. So every time I developed a segment of the workshop, I repeated it aloud to an imaginary audience.

After each rehearsal, I tweaked the handouts to match my latest insights. A few days before the event, I reluctantly stopped making changes. It was time to finalize what I had done so far. I printed twenty-five copies of my twenty-page handout.

Rehearsing the entire talk was tedious, but I forced myself to do it a couple more times, just to get a feeling for how the whole thing would sound.

Occasionally, I would feel certain I was going to fail or that no one would care about it or no one would come. When I found myself sinking into such discouraging thoughts, I applied the very techniques I was going to teach. I breathed deeply, focused on positive self-talk, and imagined a kind receptive audience. And then I kept going.

Teaching self-help in the mirror

As I approached the Writers Room that evening, the room was dark. I couldn't recall ever seeing it empty before. Foster had given me the combination to the front door, in case he wasn't there, but he hadn't warned me to bring a flashlight. I fumbled in the dark. "Please don't let me mess this up," I prayed silently, afraid this simple obstacle could wreck my night. On the second try, the lock sprung open. I realized I'd been holding my breath.

In the empty suite, I fumbled for the switch. When the light came on, I imagined the room like an empty theater. It would soon fill with people and I would be on the stage. To keep my nerves in check, I scanned my 3x5 cards. The first one said, "Love God." I thought about it for a moment. The next one said, "Love people." I thought about that, too. Then, the single word, "Breathe." I relaxed my shoulders, pulled air deep into my diaphragm and expanded my chest. Then released it with a sigh.

As people entered, I greeted as many as I could, soothing my nerves by exchanging names and smiles. Foster still wasn't there to introduce me. *What if he didn't show up?* Just when it was time to start, Foster breezed in.

To get everyone's attention, he said, "How about those chickpeas. They are not chicks and they're not peas." He chuckled contentedly at the absurdity of his own comment. How could he be so relaxed and unafraid? I wondered if someday I could stand in front of groups with such ease. For now, I hoped my audience would forgive me for the tension I was struggling to keep under control.

When I opened my mouth, instead of the whispered squeak I anticipated, I heard the authoritative, confident voice of a teacher. I couldn't believe it. I had come so far!

Taking a deep breath, I plunged into the material. "The very first step to increase motivation is to identify something you really want to write about. If your topic excites you, naturally you feel energized." To help them apply the lesson, I asked them what topic might carry them into the future. Heads went down, and only the sound of pen or pencil scratching marred the silence.

While they were writing, I glanced at my notes, and prepared for the next points. After a few of them put down their pens, I asked everyone to wrap up.

"So, tell me what you've written."

Hands went up, and as they rattled off their ideas, I was thoroughly entertained by the variety. "That's great," I said. "All those topics are there waiting to be expressed. For our purposes today, let's consider the things that might get in your way. Most of us assume the worst obstacle is a lack of skill. I'd like you to take a closer look at an even worse problem: self-doubt. It drains your energy and leads to loss of momentum, which in turn leads to procrastination. You can't write well if you don't write at all."

I paused here, and was gratified by a few chuckles and murmurs of agreement. I continued.

"One of the best methods for overcoming self-doubt is positive self-talk, which emerged from the well-researched methods of cognitive psychology. Its fundamental premise is that positive thoughts will make you feel better than negative ones. That might seem like I'm stating the obvious. But the thing most people seem to forget is that they can influence their own thoughts. Instead of accepting whatever thought your mind dishes up, consciously insert a more positive one."

Even while I was telling them these uplifting methods, I worried that people might not be impressed by my suggestions. I looked down at my notes for a moment, not to remember what I wanted to say, but to remind myself to stay positive and to focus on the receptive ones. Certainly, some people in the group might be admiring what I said.

When I asked them to offer examples of their own self-talk, their enthusiastic answers reassured me that I had no need to worry. They'd been engaged all along.

I recognized the absurdity of having self-doubts while teaching how to improve one's thoughts. But I had no illusions that I could ever completely stop my negative thoughts. Naturally I wanted to keep improving, but I also knew I'd always need to deal with my own imperfections. I made a note to myself to add a module in future versions of this course about self-forgiveness and self-compassion.

Moving on to my next topic, I asked them if they resisted calling themselves writers. Many of them nodded. I knew from my own reluctance to call myself a therapist that such imposter anxiety could be incredibly demoralizing.

"The problem with calling yourself a writer is that it's not very glamorous to think of just sitting at a keyboard moving your fingers. I'll give you a couple of minutes to think of a more picturesque metaphor to help you visualize yourself in this role."

While they were writing their responses, I pulled out my own pad of paper. Doing an exercise along with the class made me feel connected to them, and I hoped it might teach me more about myself.

While trying to think of a new metaphor to apply to my own life as a writer, I realized I didn't have to look very far. Picturing myself teaching a group was a perfect image that could energize me while writing self-help articles. When the time was up, I set aside my own mental model, eager to hear theirs.

One woman said she would visualize herself as a clown at a circus. Her description included outlandish shoes, a big red nose, and playing to crowds of children by falling down and bouncing back up again. She made me laugh, which was quite a relief, considering that a few hours before I had been fighting waves of panic.

This pattern of teaching a lesson, asking them to write their thoughts, and then listening to a few responses made the two hours fly. I hoped others enjoyed the experience as much as I did. I would soon find out. They'd all filled out evaluation forms.

The pile of evaluation forms handed in at the end of my session sat before me, still untouched. Wanting every single attendee to like me was absurd. In my presentation, I'd even warned writers to avoid this trap.

It's impossible to please everyone. Some people will always like you more than others. And some less. It's human nature.

I struggled to hold onto this perspective. But another voice warned, "What if someone told Foster I did a bad job? I would be finished."

Fending off my anxiety, I dug into the pile of forms, at first scanning through for the good or bad news. Then slowing down to read more details.

By the end of the pile, I breathed a sigh of relief. The feedback was generally positive. I had done it. I'd pulled off one of the boldest forays out of my private bunker that I had ever attempted.

Because of the large attendance and positive feedback, Foster gave me free rein to present as many workshops as I wanted. The Writers Room had such a large following, I decided to give the same workshop again, hoping for a new batch of attendees.

When preparing the second presentation, I found dozens of opportunities to add or clarify various points in the handouts. And having taught it once, I could anticipate which parts would work and which needed improvement.

I found myself becoming even more excited about the project. I was learning to teach, and in addition, was fulfilling some of the same goals I'd wanted to achieve as a therapist. Instead of the personal connections with individual clients, I would be offering self-help tools to a room full of writers.

The next time I taught the class, my self-doubts had quieted substantially, and again, several people enthusiastically thanked me at the end of the session, reinforcing my budding confidence. Afterward, I scoured the evaluation forms more eagerly, absorbing any tips that would help me provide a better experience.

I thought about that other transformative moment when I stood in front of a class. In my first few weeks in high school, after I wrote a correct equation on the board, my algebra teacher's praise made me feel euphoric. But the years I'd spent trying to sustain that euphoria ended in failure. It turned out my only potential admirers were mathematicians who were so caught up in solving their own puzzles they didn't have much interest in mine.

As a teacher, I was seeking an entirely different source of satisfaction from the students sitting in front of me. Instead of hoping they would see me as smart, I wanted them to see themselves as good writers. When I succeeded even a little bit, I felt connected with them in some sublime way. I wondered if I'd invented a new self-help strategy: by teaching others, I was able to feel better about myself.

Teaching at the Writers Room embodied the sense of love and belonging I had been seeking my whole life. In this modest office suite, with others who had been attracted here for the same purpose, my separation from strangers appeared to be crumbling. Together we were searching for our voices, and in the process, I was developing talents that I never even realized I had. I was so glad I'd found this group. I wanted to continue to participate in it forever.

Please give a talk

My gratitude for the Writers Room must have been apparent, because one morning Foster phoned me and said, "There's a board meeting this weekend and I was hoping you would come by and say a few words in praise of the organization."

"I've never done anything like this before," I said, my heart fluttering. "What would I say?"

"Just share your personal observations of what the Writers Room means to you. The board members rarely attend our events and I wanted them to hear from a member."

"I'd hate to let you down," I said.

"You'll do fine. Be yourself. Wow them with your big smile and calm voice. And don't take too long. Figure on speaking about six minutes."

I was flattered that Foster would trust me with this task. I set to work writing notes on 3x5 cards. On some, I listed the benefits of the Writers Room to me. On others, I wrote benefits to the community, and tried to remember anecdotes that would support my points. I arranged the cards in the most compelling order, and searched for a good beginning and ending. Then I rehearsed.

It was handy that he had given me six minutes, since that was about how long the talks were at Toastmasters. I tried to fit all my thoughts into exactly that period, but every time I rehearsed, I went a few seconds over the limit. I just had to remember to talk fast.

The night of the meeting, there were ten or twelve people at the Writers Room office, none of whom I'd met before. They seemed friendly enough, and after talking about some business issues, Foster gestured to me and said, "I've asked Jerry to say a few words. He'll only take two minutes." He turned to me and in a low voice repeated, "only two minutes."

His introduction knocked me off balance. Was I supposed to trim the talk by more than half? As I stood up, I thought, "What are they going to do, stop me in mid-sentence?" I decided to ignore his warning and stick to our original agreement.

I introduced myself and told them how the organization had brought me out of isolation and connected me with other writers. After a few sentences, my attention shifted from my nervous stomach to the people in front of me. Everyone in the room was looking at me with soft, receptive expressions. Growing more confident, I recounted stories about other people who also experienced this transformation, such as the couple from New York who moved here after 9/11, convinced by the Writers Room that they had found a new home. Another woman said that volunteering at the organization had given meaning to her life after she lost her job.

After these details, I jumped to a wider viewpoint. "In a world that constantly tends toward chaos, we're offering one of the best antidotes. Community and culture are pillars of civilization. Here in the Writers Room, we're building both, giving writers a place to come together and help each other create stories."

Then I launched into my finale, invoking one of the icons of the sixties. "Ken Kesey and his Merry Pranksters drove a bus around the country to spread the message that individuals, through creative passion, could do anything they want to do. Well, we aren't dressing up and doing street theater, nor are we dropping acid, but we are showing the world how people can band together and help each other turn words into culture. Someday we will be known as the little group that started a big movement."

When I was finished, my audience stood and applauded. I basked in that unexpected, utterly enchanted feeling. Of course, I hoped I'd impressed them with the Writers Room's numerous community benefits. But I was even more thrilled with the effect the experience had on me. I couldn't detect a trace of my usual flurry of self-doubts. In that moment, my social anxiety had simply vanished.

Speaking about writing was turning out to be every bit as fulfilling as writing itself. I couldn't imagine any way I could possibly feel more involved in this group, but if there was a way to go higher, I wanted to find it.

Writers are heroes, too

One of the charming features of the Writers Room was that they never asked me for money. Since I attended many of the workshops for free and never heard anyone mention dues or fees, I had no idea how the organization survived, financially. One of the people who had been there since the beginning told me that Foster had taken a mortgage out on his house in order to raise the money to start the place.

He was clearly the driving force behind the operation, constantly organizing events and interacting with the members. Then one day, Foster stepped down. What did this mean?

Rumors flew that he had been forced out by his own board of directors. But hadn't Foster designed and started this place? Hadn't he given his own money to keep it going? Foster devoted so much attention to the group, I feared without him the place would fall apart.

I was wrong.

Jonathan Maberry assumed the responsibility with the enthusiasm of a captain whose ship was under threat of being boarded by pirates. If the Writers Room was in trouble, his background provided him with a formidable set of tools to save it.

As a former bodyguard and martial artist, he brought a larger-than-life presence to the job. And as a writing teacher, he quickly earned our respect. No matter what type of writing we needed advice about, he was willing to stop what he was doing and give us his full attention. His willful, enthusiastic passion about writing lit up the room.

In one of his classes, someone asked him why he put so much energy into helping us. He said that by cooperating, we would all benefit. He explained why writers banding together is a good idea.

"Every time one writer succeeds, it increases the value of good writing, which translates into more readers for the rest of us."

One thing about the Writers Room that did not change under Jonathan's leadership was its lackadaisical attitude toward money. After the shift in leadership, I still never heard about a membership fee. All I had to do in order to be part of this group was to show up.

A boost into the big time

Jonathan let us know that he was going to establish a Writers Room contest that would pit teams of writers against one another – like a reality television show, but without the cameras. Each team of writers would propose a topic for a book. The proposals would be submitted to Jonathan's New York agent. The one she selected for publication would be the winner.

While Jonathan had organized the project and arranged all the activities, and coached us when we needed direction, the entire plan cost nothing. The volunteerism of the whole thing added to its magic. Another thing that made the experience so pleasurable were the members of my team. Even though we were grouped together by picking a number out of a hat, Kerry, Don, Keith, Jeannette, and I bonded as if we had been best friends for years.

Our only instruction was to write a proposal for a book that could be sold to a traditional publisher. When we pressed for more guidance, Jonathan said we could select any topic. He made it sound easy. "Research the book market, see which types of books were successful, and then write a book that will fit into that niche."

"Write a book? That could take years."

Jonathan patiently explained that no one writes a nonfiction book until after they get a contract.

"How do they get the contract if they haven't written the book?" I asked.

"All you have to do is sell the idea of the book." He then explained how to write a book proposal, which would include a marketing plan, how many people we expected to buy it, and the sales figures for other similar books. If the publisher felt the proposal was worth considering, they might suggest changes before agreeing to proceed.

Creating a sales and marketing plan for a book that didn't exist sounded outrageous. "Those business people don't understand the creative process," I protested.

"There's no point in fighting it," he replied. "I imagine the business people complain that writers have no idea how to make money. The fact is, it's a partnership. Our job is to give them a product they can sell."

We all had come to the group ready to do whatever we could in order to become writers, and Jonathan was providing us a path to follow. Every one of us agreed we would give it everything we had.

At each meeting, we brought our best, most creative selves, pitching and brainstorming all sorts of crazy ideas. Our open-ended approach led to a wild, electric flurry of possibilities. Then, using whatever intuition we could muster, we rejected some suggestions and clarified others.

The topic that survived this thrashing related to the massive changes caused by the Internet. It was 2006, and everywhere we turned, the Internet was disrupting patterns. I threw out the phrase, "Social Tsunami" and everyone felt it fit. We were excited to report on the tidal wave that was sweeping through our culture.

At first, we intended to write a book in which each chapter would be about one aspect of the changes caused by the Internet. For example, there might be a chapter on Internet banking, one for Internet shopping, another for Internet marketing, and so on. But when Jonathan floated that idea past his agent, she said it was too broad. She suggested we pick just one of these ideas.

At our next meeting we reviewed our original proposal. When we got to the chapter about the explosion of online dating, someone said, "Sex sells"—and everyone nodded in agreement.

I felt like the project was dragging me away from my desire to help people grow and toward writing a book for commercial purposes only. But everyone was so excited, and I wanted to be a part of that. When someone said "Are we all in?" I raised my hand and shouted hoo-hah with the rest of them.

Jonathan had taught us that in order to ensure a nonfiction book made sense to readers, or more important, to bookstore owners, we were supposed to decide which section it should be shelved in.

The research sent me to my beloved bookstore, which carried no books on Internet dating. I wasn't sure if this meant we had the perfect topic because we were the first to think of it, or we had a terrible topic because bookstore owners had decided it was unsellable.

Another thing our group identified that could help sell books was fame. If we could find a celebrity willing to associate their name with the project, we would be more likely to get a deal. Even though my sister-in-law's sister was world famous, asking her to back a book on dating seemed unseemly. There was no way I could help with that one.

But at the next meeting, Don shared that without even telling us, he had called the founder of one of the big online dating services. She told him she was interested in participating in the project. I was blown away at his chutzpah. It began to dawn on me that we might really have a chance.

Occasionally I worried that if the proposal was accepted, I might be spending the coming year writing a book about dating. I was happily married, and when I had dated, the experience felt little better than torture.

After thinking it through, though, I decided such a project could open me to the emotional complexities of human relationships. The others were all in. Only a few days later, Don had another surprise for us. He had gone home that weekend and cranked out an entire book proposal, including marketing plans, comparisons with existing books, a list of proposed chapters, and so on.

We all gasped in astonishment. How could a writer be so energized about business? But Don, whose day job was in sales and marketing, shrugged. "That's what I do."

We all read the document and added our suggestions. When the proposal was complete, we submitted it to Jonathan's agent and prayed, wondering if our lives were about to change.

The project might not be too bad. Working together would surely be a blast. Having a publishing credential would be a lovely step toward my goal to become a writer. And perhaps I would even learn something about romance.

Nothing ventured, nothing gained

During the next couple of weeks, we took a break from meetings. There was nothing to talk about or do until we received word.

Finally, Jonathan sent us an email and said he had news.

When we convened, he said, "Look guys. My agent's not interested. You did a great job, and I was really hoping she would work with us, but she said it's just not for her."

"Did she give any tips about what we could do better?" I asked. "If it's just a question of tinkering with some details, we could perhaps keep pushing."

"I don't think so," he said. "The topic just didn't capture her interest. You'd have to come up with an entirely new project."

Groans filled the small office. Someone said, "But this has taken all summer. I don't have the energy to do this again." We all nodded.

Jonathan said, "If you want to reach out to other agents, I'm okay with that."

But that would mean resuming weekly meetings, proposing and debating the merits of each new book topic, doing more research, and then eventually writing another proposal. None of us could imagine continuing this process. After more discussion, we agreed the project was over.

In the end, none of the writing teams submitted a sellable book proposal. In a sense we all lost. But in other ways we all won.

Jonathan's crazy writing challenge had turned into a free master class on pitching and publishing a book. During the class, I had bonded more than ever with a group of fellow writers, reinforcing my belief that traveling the long road to successful writing was best done with companions. And I had even survived the terrors of rejection without dying.

Now that our little clan of intrepid writers had disbanded, I was no longer driven by the frenetic pressure of a contest. In this more contemplative mood, I decided that if I was going to pour years of my life into writing a book, it would be on a topic that excited me. And my measure of success would not be merely that I could publish it. I wanted to write a book that would pass along some of the insights I had learned, just as countless authors had informed and lifted me.

Could I serve the world with a book?

Every time I prepared to teach my self-help-for-writers course, I revised the existing handouts and added more material. Then I printed reams of pages for everyone who attended. Before Jonathan's publishing contest, I would never have considered turning this material into a book. But after learning so much from that trial run, I imagined I might be ready for the real thing.

I asked Jonathan what he thought about my plan. "That's a great idea," he said. "As soon as you get a draft ready, I'll send it to my agent."

His offer was far more generous than I'd imagined. A direct line to an agent would bypass all the heartache and endless begging that most authors undergo. Once again, I fantasized about joining the camp of published writers.

Bringing myself back to earth, I realized that the introduction was only a first step. I needed to give her a book that would sell lots of copies. Having never written a book before, I knew I needed help.

In one of our free Workshop Wednesdays, I met editor Diane O'Connell, who had come down from her New York City publishing job to conduct a workshop. Her talk helped me understand that even professional writers rely on the assistance of an editor. After her presentation, I told her about my project.

"I've worked on a number of nonfiction books," she said, handing me her business card. "I would be happy to work with you."

I sent her the consolidated collection of handouts, which by then were quite extensive. When we spoke on the phone, she got right to the point.

"You have so much material here, it's difficult for me to understand what you are trying to teach."

Hadn't she read it? I had a lot of important ideas to convey, and it was all in there. What did she mean she didn't understand?

After a long pause, I said, "But all the topics are interrelated." I heard the pathetic tone in my voice. "If someone wants to understand what it's about, they have to read the whole thing."

Her only response was silence.

"Do you see what I mean?" I asked, desperate for her to ease up and allow me to make my book just as complicated as I wanted.

Finally, she said, "But I did read the whole thing. And I'm still not sure what you are trying to achieve. The way you have presented it feels like a collection. Help me visualize some order through it."

"I guess my image was that readers would jump in anywhere and get what they could."

"But people buy books because they trust the author to lead them on an interesting journey. Your title needs to tell your readers where you are going to take them."

"Can I call it *Self-help for Writers*? That's what it is. It's a compilation of all the material I've read and studied about how to grow as a writer."

"The word self-help is over-used. And it's too generic. Calling it a compilation sounds like you are offering a bunch of stuff. Your title needs to convince them that you are going to take them on a well-constructed journey."

"People understand what I'm doing when they come to my workshops," I whined.

"People who come to a workshop can see you, hear your explanations, and can ask questions. Someone who sees your book cover will have none of those reassurances. You need to appeal to them in just a few words."

I started to sweat. "I don't think I know how to do this."

"Picture someone seeing your book title," she said in her kind, enthusiastic voice. I wondered if all her clients were as dense as I was about these basic facts of publishing. If so, how did she manage to remain so patient?

"If the title sounds boring," she continued, "most customers will skip right past it. If the title piques their interest, they might pick it up, glance at the cover, and then perhaps read the blurb. At every step, they need to feel drawn into your material."

I silently groaned. *There it is again. I explain things in the most complex way. Then, I'm surprised when no one understands me.*

But my frustration with the complexity of my thinking was mixed in with pride. Gathering all these tips into one book had been a triumph of my desire to help others. It wasn't the same as sitting in an office with a client, but I felt I was fulfilling some of that same desire to serve.

It might take a reader the better part of a lifetime to implement all these methods. That's how long it had taken me. But for anyone who wanted to try it, the book would be a great resource. And gaining the emotional capability of becoming a writer seemed to me to be a worthwhile goal. So much of what makes a good writer also makes a good person.

But in order to get even one person to buy the thing, I needed to condense its message in a title.

When teaching my workshops, I had been arranging the material in four parts, each one emphasizing a different aspect of self-help. Now that I was trying to title a book, I needed a brief, easily understandable metaphor that could simplify the four-part organization. Was it four parts of the brain? Four parts of the mind? Four parts of the journey? None of these seemed catchy enough.

Years earlier, as part of Kathy's Tarot project, I felt intrigued by the alchemical notion of four elements: earth, air, fire, and water. Perhaps I could match each of the four sections in my material with one of the elements. I mentioned this to Diane.

"Yes, you're on the right track," she said. "The metaphor will help prospective readers visualize how the parts fit together."

My project now had a tentative title: *Four Elements for Writers*.

Out of respect for the gatekeepers

I spent months arranging, rearranging, and polishing the material in my manuscript, but after more than a decade as a technical writer, I knew my style was still stodgy. A husband and wife editing team I met at the Writers Room helped me add some zest, but it still fell short of my expectations.

I was also skeptical of my credibility as a subject matter expert, considering that many self-help authors had doctoral degrees and headed up academic research departments. Others, like Tony Robbins, made up for their skimpy academic credentials with the kind of charisma that could fill a sports stadium with eager fans. How could I expect to compete?

Jonathan was far more encouraging to me than I was to myself. Overriding my self-doubts, he offered to take a look at it. I gave him a copy, grateful for his interest. A few weeks later, he got back to me. "This is a good book. I read it twice. I'm going to send it to my agent."

His offer gave me hope. The old expression, "It's not what you know, it's who you know," seemed to apply. I handed over the manuscript, hoping it would find its way out into the world.

A few weeks later, Jonathan asked if he could talk to me. When I met him, he was holding my manuscript. "She said she's not having much success with books about writing."

Saddened by the setback, I didn't know what to say.

"I thought your book had a good chance," he said, his voice softening.

"It is so cool that you gave me an introduction like this. Thank you."

"Sorry it didn't work out," he said.

I walked away, hopes dashed. That was my best shot. Some writers spent years developing pitch letters and business proposals in order to find a traditional publisher. I was not drawn to this option. It seemed like such a huge expenditure of time and energy, especially when even then, there was no guarantee it would succeed.

I just wanted to write. Not look for an agent. Not look for a publisher. I didn't want to become a marketing whiz or convince people of anything. But if I didn't, then who was ever going to read my book?

Ironically, this was exactly the kind of emotional hurdle I wrote about in my book. The situation provided a perfect laboratory experiment to test my own advice and use positive thoughts to prevent me from falling into despair.

But what positive thoughts could I think? At the moment, I couldn't see how anything positive could possibly come from this. How could I move forward when I wasn't even sure what "forward" looked like?

Between waves of discouragement, I tried to think about the situation rationally. If I wasn't willing to look for another agent or small publisher, I would have to give up altogether. Yet giving up also held no appeal. I had gathered all this good self-help material. It didn't make any sense to stop now. I wanted to share it.

While the Writers Room had always been oriented toward commercial publishing, there was another option that had fascinated me since the seventies, when I read *The Publish It Yourself Handbook* from Pushcart Press. The book featured dozens of success stories of writers who chose to bypass the publishing industry and go directly to readers.

I couldn't remember why I had been so interested in self-publishing way back then. I had not written a book and didn't even have an idea for one. Like some slumbering compulsion tucked away in a back room of my mind, this idea seemed like it had been waiting for the right time. I knew I'd need some help with cover designing, editing, and proofreading. I asked around at the Writers Room for help finding these specialists. If one person didn't know the answer, they referred me to someone who might.

As my book moved closer to completion, one fear haunted me. I felt as though I owed my entire intellectual life to the publishing industry. I worried that self-publishing my book might anger the people whose products continued to enrich me.

I asked Jonathan if he thought self-publishing would poison my chances of ever publishing traditionally.

"I think you're okay if you publish it to support your workshops. My agent is coming down to speak at this year's Philadelphia Writers' Conference. Why don't you ask her yourself?"

Directly approaching such a powerful person would have never occurred to me on my own, but with Jonathan's encouragement, I decided to try.

I attended the conference, held only a few blocks from Old City Philadelphia, where the nation was born. That history always filled me with hope and courage. During the agent panel, I was so preoccupied with my own question I barely heard the proceedings.

After the panel ended, Jonathan's agent lingered alone. This was my chance. Too shy to climb the few stairs to the stage where she sat, I stood beneath her looking up, as though I was having an audience with royalty.

I nervously introduced myself, mentioning that Jonathan had shown her my manuscript. "Do you think if I self-publish this as a workbook for writers, I would tarnish my reputation and make myself less attractive for future publications?"

She gave me a soft, courteous look. "I don't think that would be a problem."

I floated back to my seat as if I had just received a pronouncement from a spokesperson for the whole industry. I no longer needed to beg for a seat at their table. I could set up my own table, and hope a few people might come over to ask for advice or support.

Published my first book!

Editing, cover design, professional proofreading—the cost of publishing my own book kept growing, but I was willing to invest in a goal that had been calling to me for decades. After hiring yet another member of the Writers Room to design the interior layout, I was ready.

I found a company in Ohio that would print a hundred copies. I sent the file, and a month later, several heavy boxes arrived on my porch. Cutting one open, I lifted out my book. It was so shiny. So substantial. What a journey.

All my life, I had been so grateful for all that authors had done for me. Finally, I'd contributed a book of my own. And since my book was intended to help other people become book writers, perhaps it would have a multiplier effect.

Crowning my sense of accomplishment was Jonathan's request to hang a picture of the book cover on the wall of the Writers Room.

"You are one of our success stories," he said.

Seeing my book cover every time I entered the Writers Room gave me more confidence than I ever thought I would have in this life. Even if I couldn't sell many, at least I could replace the sheaf of loose handouts that accompanied my workshops with a beautiful, bound book. And if anyone wanted to send me a check, I could mail them a copy. Despite that limited availability, I loved the sense that I'd crossed some sort of threshold. The Writers Room was continuing to change my life.

I was now a book author and a publisher.

Looking for the main highway

After publishing my book, the obvious next step would be to sell more copies. To learn how to do this, as usual, I asked Jonathan for advice. He said I needed to build a circle of followers. "Write more books. Give talks. Join groups."

The idea of writing another book was interesting, but not very practical. I didn't even know what I'd write about. Following that piece of advice might be useful in the future.

By contrast, his idea about joining groups and giving talks sounded immediate and exciting. My enthusiasm for giving such talks struck me as funny, considering that a couple of years earlier, the prospect of speaking to a group made me want to hide under a table.

However, I wasn't sure I would be qualified. As the author of one book, would anyone want to listen to me?

Then Jonathan gave me another boost. He'd been volunteering at the Philadelphia Writers' Conference, where I'd met his agent. When he invited me to join the board of directors, I enthusiastically accepted. This nonprofit group had been hosting big annual writing gatherings for decades, so being involved in the organization placed me at the hub of the regional writing community–with one caveat. Board members weren't permitted to teach classes at the annual conference. So even though I helped plan the annual event, when the crowds arrived, I had to watch from the sidelines.

However, I soon discovered that one of the board members, Sean, had been arranging small writing events throughout the year in order to publicize the organization. The rule that barred board members from speaking at the big event didn't apply to these smaller ones. I asked Sean if he needed help, and he welcomed my offer. Once he discovered how passionate I was about arranging these small informal events, he told me he'd been thinking of taking a break and asked me if I wanted to take over.

As a representative of the well-known conference, it was easy to find local colleges where we could meet. Sometimes I gave the talks myself, and sometimes I'd invite other teachers or writers who wanted to present a free workshop. Everything was voluntary, with no fee from the audience and no payment for the speakers. Even the rooms were free.

The best part of this operation was that I didn't need to do any publicity. The same people who spread the word about the annual conference graciously offered to promote these smaller sessions. In a sense, Sean had handed me the keys to a speaker's bureau for writers. Since I enjoyed speaking and meeting writers, it felt more like a playground than a business.

Then I got my big break. Due to a last-minute speaker cancellation at the big annual event, they waived their rule and asked me to give a talk. Because of a quirk in the scheduling, my session was the only one offered during that time slot. While I stood in front of the room, preparing my notes, people poured in, filling every available seat and then standing shoulder to shoulder in the back.

Riding a surge of excitement, I launched into my explanation of how writers could use each part of their brain in service of their desire to write. When someone in the audience asked a question, I felt as though I was having a dialog with a hundred people.

At the end of that talk, a man approached and said, "This self-help stuff never made sense to me before. But now I see how it works. I'm the CEO of a company, and when I want my people to do their best, I need to give them the right tools. You're doing that for writers, giving us the tools we need in order to succeed." I was elated by his comment. Not only had he given me a much-appreciated compliment. He'd also offered another cool metaphor I could use to bolster my own ambition to help people write.

After the three-day event ended, I was back at my cubicle, earning a paycheck and scheming to find my next speaking opportunity. By the next year, I'd spoken at every writing conference within a twenty-mile radius of my home. That was the good news. It was also bad news. I wasn't being invited back, and it looked like I'd run out of venues.

These speaking opportunities had given me a wonderful sense of fulfillment. I didn't want to stop. But since I had no interest in traveling outside my region, I had to figure out how to earn more invitations. Most speakers at these writing conferences had a list of publications far more impressive than mine. So to increase my value as a speaker, I would need to write more and write better.

Small message, big impact

Jonathan had always been willing to offer advice to anyone who asked, so one day I caught him on his way out the door. "Jonathan, do you have a minute to look at this?" I held out a copy of one of the self-help articles I had been working on.

"Sure," he said. He glanced through it briefly.

Handing it back, he said, "Your ideas are too abstract. They sound like they dropped from the sky. Put more of yourself in the essay." He walked away, leaving me stunned.

In this one, brief comment, Jonathan had solved a puzzle that had been confusing me for my whole life. Ever since I was a teenager, I'd expounded on heady topics like science, history and literature. Since I loved what I was saying I expected my listeners would, too.

But over and over, instead of seeing the glow of appreciation in their eyes, I'd see blank stares. Worse yet, I occasionally detected a stressed response, like I'd made them uncomfortable. I'd always felt bewildered by this radical difference between my expectations and their reactions.

Studying therapy, joining Toastmasters, even coming to the writing group had been designed to help me reach people. And it had all culminated in the momentous insight I'd just received from a seemingly innocent comment about my writing.

I could suddenly see that while I'd been working so hard to describe my intricate thoughts, I must have come across as someone who was struggling to stay out of sight. The discomfort in my listener's eyes had resulted from the utter absence of any communication about me or my feelings. And now, Jonathan was the first person to actually give me the feedback I needed to hear.

As if a hole had been punched through a dam, a cascade of insights poured through my mind. I had just wanted to improve my writing style, but Jonathan's comment went straight to the core of my identity.

My reluctance to advertise my counseling business, my difficulty showing enthusiasm during my public speaking, even my fear of talking to girls, all resulted from the fact that I was terrified to let others see me.

Jonathan's comment not only identified the source of my isolation. He'd put his finger on the solution. If I could improve my writing in accordance with his suggestion, my readers would see that my ideas emerged from an actual person.

Self-disclosure 101

Three of us sat in Foster Winans' memoir class, to learn what a memoir is and some suggestions about how to write one. I'd never considered writing about myself before, but it seemed like it might be a good way for me to learn how to open up.

Foster had already played such an important role in my life by creating this writing community. So taking the class would also give me a chance to get to know him better. I already knew he had been a columnist at the *Wall Street Journal*. But in the class, he revealed he had been in jail for selling insider information about stocks. Founding the Writers Room was his way of giving back to the community.

He'd written a memoir, *Trading Secrets,* about the escapade. If he had the courage to write a book about such a shameful event, who better to teach me about revealing my own heart?

Surprisingly, Foster didn't have much to say about overcoming his public reputation as a felon. He wanted to share a much more private, emotionally wrenching effect the book had on his relationship with his mother.

When he finished his first draft, his mother asked if she could read it. He resisted, telling her she wouldn't like the parts where he harshly criticized her for being too pushy and over-involved. She insisted. He gave it to her and went upstairs to bed.

In the morning, she was still sitting in the same place. She cried when she saw him and asked, "Was I really that bad of a mother?" Foster and his mom talked for hours. Out of those talks came a softening and maturing of their relationship.

That story of a breakthrough between an adult and his parent sent shivers through my body. This was my very first exposure to the healing potential of memoir writing. It had never occurred to me that sharing a story in this way could open people up to deeper levels of connection.

For homework, he told us to write about an important experience. I hoped I could find the courage to reveal something about myself that might make an interesting story. The incident that came to mind was one of the most raw and vulnerable in my life.

I had recently taken finals at the end of my senior year in college, and then, on an impulse, drove 2,000 miles from Madison, Wisconsin out to Berkeley, California. During the first week there, I fell madly in love with a tall, athletic dancer. In the silence of my own mind, this story had always been darkened by the misery of our painful breakup.

But in the story I crafted for the group, for the first time ever, I reached past the pain to remember the pleasure. I described the crowded dance floor where I met her. It was in the basement of a professor's house in the hills above the university. A few days later we went for a romantic swim. The lake was probably crowded, but in my memory it felt like we were alone.

I never understood why she returned my affection. Perhaps it was the case of a sunny Californian attracted to a dour, dark Pennsylvanian. But for whatever reason, she didn't run away like all the others, and I was in heaven.

As I pulled these memories out of hiding, I burned with embarrassment. Never having shared the story with anyone in my life, I hated how the episode made me sound so human. But mixed in with my reluctance, I also felt curious. How would it feel to let strangers see this side of myself? I decided to go for it. I would share it and simply watch what happened.

The following week, when I read my story aloud in class, I was surprised that instead of hearing it as a heavy tale of sorrow, they responded to it as the zany outpouring of unbridled age-appropriate passion. Their cheerful response broke the brittle crust that had always encased my memories of California, transforming my bitter failure into an upbeat, sharable anecdote about a normal rite of passage.

One guy came up to me afterward and said my story reminded him of his first love. His eagerness to tell me his own memories made me forget all about my social anxiety. We chatted comfortably, about his past and mine, all because of a shared story.

I was shocked to observe that I enjoyed being the center of attention for those moments while I was reading aloud. As for my misery about that painful breakup, some mysterious alchemy had taken place. After liberating it from its crypt, it had taken on a new life. Out here, in the light of day, my romantic story didn't look anywhere near as disturbing as it had when it sat gloomily in the dungeons of my mind. It might even become part of my future, as I strived to turn more stories of my past into an energetic connection with my fellow writers.

Collecting memories

Following Foster's advice about gathering scenes from my life, I wrote another anecdote during my morning writing session. When I searched my computer to find the best place to store it, I came upon a file I'd written several years earlier in response to a request by my therapist, Lyndra.

The file contained descriptions of a few key events, such as "went to college, 1965," "big anti-war riot 1967," "moved to California, 1969." The events were lined up along a timeline. Clearly, I'd been intending to fill in more details, and then had become distracted and had forgotten all about it. That file became a starting point, to which I added many more incidents in the coming months.

I made more progress when I contacted my sister, Marilyn, and asked her if she would be willing to share some of the stories she remembered about growing up. I arranged to meet her for lunch at the restaurant in the train station in Jenkintown, just a few miles away from where we grew up. After we ordered, she said she'd always been jealous of the way our father had let my brother and then me go off to the school of our choosing. "Dad wouldn't even consider letting me leave home to go to college." I knew she'd commuted, but I'd assumed it was her choice.

"It never occurred to me that they were treating you so differently." Unsure what else to say, I told her I was sorry.

She shrugged and looked away.

Hoping to soften the mood, I pointed out that having that additional privilege had not been as wonderful as she might have thought. "Attending college a thousand miles away was a disaster."

I told her how, after I moved to Wisconsin, I became increasingly untethered, first from my family, and then from myself. "When I moved to California it got worse. After a couple of years trying to be a hippie, I decided I needed to live in the jungle like a chimpanzee."

I tried to chuckle but it came out sounding closer to a sob.

"I knew you were hurting but I didn't know it was that bad," she said, "I wish there had been some way I could help. I'm sorry."

When I'd told this story before, most people laughed out loud. But in her eyes, I could see she understood how serious the situation had been. "Yes," I silently shouted, "I'd really been that alone. Yes it really hurt like hell." Aloud, I thanked her for caring.

Back in 1971, during the worst of it, she'd come out to live near me in Berkeley for a few months, so I assumed she knew what I was going through. But I'd been so disconnected from my own feelings, I probably looked like I was enjoying the hippie lifestyle.

Our conversation at that restaurant was the first time we had ever talked openly about our emotional challenges. Our honesty about those times opened a trust between us I had never felt before. Already, my memoir project was providing emotional healing, a remarkable achievement considering I had barely started writing it.

With a renewed appreciation for the benefits of this research, I looked up people who had been in my high school class. One guy not only remembered our pressured intellectual competition, but in his edgy responses, I recognized echoes of those earlier insecurities. He seemed to be stuck in the past. The uncomfortable exchange provided me with valuable validation of my memories. I thanked him and moved on.

To corroborate my own sense of isolation in college, I tracked down Marty, my roommate in my sophomore year. He played a memorable role in my life, because he'd nominated me to run in a student election, an adventure so far outside my self-image I could barely believe it really happened. He seemed happy to speak with me. I asked what he thought of me at that time—and was surprised to hear him express genuine affection.

John was another guy I'd bonded with more than others. In my senior year he helped me pick out a motorcycle, and that spring we rode together through the country roads outside Madison. When I reconnected with him, I told him I feared that everyone from back then hated me. He laughed. He said we were friends and my intensity didn't bother him. He thought I was a nice guy.

The positive feedback from Marty and John suggested I may have had skewed perceptions about that period. I looked forward to revealing additional surprises hidden amid my fragmented memories.

One day my sister phoned to tell me about a memoir writing class sponsored by the historic Laurel Hill Cemetery near Philadelphia. Coincidentally, this was the cemetery where my brother Ed was buried. She asked if I wanted to take the class with her. We entered the somber building, greeted the whisper-quiet receptionist, and entered a large room typically used for funerals. Some twenty people had assembled to unearth memories that had been long buried.

An energetic teacher greeted us and told us how much she loved memoirs. At the end of the first session, she gave us a writing prompt to stir our creative juices. When Marilyn and I brought our stories back and read them aloud in the second session, they touched on our relationships with our parents, as well as with my older brother Ed. His early demise from cancer meant that neither my sister nor I had much opportunity to get to know him as an adult.

Marilyn suggested we visit the grave, but I declined. Even though his body had been buried here, I couldn't force myself to think of this as his final resting place. Because of my belief in life after life, I was far more comfortable visualizing him actively involved in the next chapter of his journey.

Ed may also have believed in his ongoing existence. He'd composed his own epitaph, engraved on his tombstone, which included the phrase, *Ad Astra Per Aspera*—Latin for "to the stars through hardship." I thought with pride how fitting that was, and I hoped he had found his way much closer to the stars.

After I hugged Marilyn goodbye and walked to my car, I realized that we were healing some of the angry wounds I'd created when I left home. Back then, I'd tried so hard to cut myself off from my family.

Since returning, I'd gradually reestablished those bonds. But until I started researching my memoir, it never occurred to me that I could reclaim the years I'd lost. Now, as Marilyn and I embarked on this effort to write about the past, I realized that we were engaging in a different type of reincarnation. We were bringing our family journey back to life through stories.

From writer to storyteller

When I first attempted to write about the events of my early life–high school math, college protests, my marijuana use, and subsequent collapse of purpose–they felt crusted with thick layers of confusion, anxiety, and forgetting. Sharing these awkward incidents in memoir groups broke through the crust and breathed new life into dead parts of myself. What began as hazy distant memories became more accessible. More … me.

But while my memories were gradually coming into focus, linking them into a compelling story had barely begun. I had so much to learn: how to build scenes, develop characters, and generate dramatic tension. Fortunately, the Writers Room provided the perfect environment for acquiring these various skills.

Many of the talks at the Writers Room introduced story-crafting topics. So, I signed up and began the journey. But I quickly ran into a problem. The examples and discussions in all these classes centered on imaginary people in imaginary worlds in imaginary situations.

When I told one teacher that I wanted to write a memoir, he said, "Only famous people write memoirs." Foster had already convinced me that this old barrier no longer applied.

In my search for more instruction, I learned that a book I'd read back in the eighties might provide important clues. The *New York Times* bestseller, *The Soul of a New Machine* by Tracy Kidder described the invention of a new computer. While my original excitement about the book related to its content, I now focused on the book's style. Kidder was pioneering a new literary movement called creative nonfiction.

The one book I found about creative nonfiction explained that Kidder had used elements from story writing in order to bring his topic to life. This was horrible news. Even though I'd been reading and watching stories my whole life, I couldn't put my finger on how they actually worked.

Back at the bookstore, I found a massive tome called *Story*, by Robert McKee. It was supposed to be for screenwriters, but desperate as I was to break down the structure of this exact subject, I brought the book home and waded in.

Skimming past the instructions about camera angles and dollies, useful only for those who were producing movies, I slowed down when I encountered explanations of dialog, plot, and pacing. By visualizing how all these elements came together into a compelling movie, I began to visualize how storytellers in any medium generate dramatic tension in the hearts and minds of readers.

I kept thinking of the central question asked by the drama coach I hired to help me tell stories at Toastmasters: *What was the emotion I was trying to inspire in my audience?* Back then, his question seemed as unanswerable as a Zen koan.

But now the student was ready. McKee confirmed what that drama coach had been getting at. The storyteller's job was to take the audience on an emotional journey. The notion fit into my mind like a key into a lock. My mind opened to the intention of the storyteller–and I was convinced that I could learn how to write one.

What is a memoir hero?

As I searched for more guidelines to help me write about my life, I circled back to Joseph Campbell's mind-boggling assertion that human beings have relied on stories since the beginning of time. And not just any story. According to him, a particular structure ran like a golden thread through the eons.

To learn more about that model, I turned to Campbell's own writings, but quickly found myself drowning in endless examples of ancient myths. Hoping for more practical advice, I visited the titles about story writing at my local bookstore. To see the shelves more clearly, I had to drop to my knees as if kneeling at the altar, praying to the book gods to let me into their arcane arts. As if in answer to my plea, I spotted a volume that seemed perfect: *The Writer's Journey: Mythic Structure for Writers* by Chris Vogler.

Vogler had ventured into Campbell's dense forest of mythological lore and emerged with a simple set of instructions that could be followed by modern storytellers.

To demonstrate how this could work in popular fiction, Vogler showed the similarities between two radically different movie heroes: Luke Skywalker in *Star Wars* and Dorothy in the *Wizard of Oz*. By focusing on the underlying structure of the stories, he explained how they both traveled the hero's journey.

These straightforward explanations opened my eyes to heroes' journeys in all sorts of novels and movies. At the beginning of each story, the characters were unfulfilled. Many of them seemed entirely ordinary at first. But some pressure forced those characters to grow. They had to pass tests, fight armies, and face their deepest fears.

Vogler had handed me a roadmap through the thicket introduced by Joseph Campbell. Now all I had to do was to learn how to apply that roadmap to the story of my own life.

There was just one obstacle, and it was a biggie: Vogler had directed his instruction toward fiction writers. But fiction writers could invent and exaggerate anytime they wanted. Someone attacks you with a knife and you must fend off the attack and counter it. To create tension in the story of my life, I couldn't just insert exaggerated drama. I had to find the drama amid my actual experiences.

Did this mean that memoirs could only be written by people who had spectacularly interesting lives? I didn't believe that was the case. There must be some other way to look at storytelling, and I needed to understand that other way.

For deeper understanding, I went to the source. I devoted myself to reading dozens of published memoirs, allowing my imagination to be swept along on the magic carpet of the author's experience. After completing each one, I paused to think about what I'd just felt, where I'd been, how things turned out. Then, I dwelled on it in depth.

From these studies and observations, I learned that there was something fundamentally hopeful about the genre. In every author's life story, a hardship suffered at the beginning set in motion a series of efforts that resulted in an uplifting conclusion at the end.

The conclusions were not about the perfect resolution of outer circumstances. Because memoirs were focused on the character's inner life, the successful conclusion of a memoir was about the author's inner peace and contentment. At the end of a grieving memoir, the character had returned to a sense of purpose, ready to carry on with life. At the end of a coming-of-age memoir, the character was preparing to enter adulthood.

After I'd read many memoirs, I was able to put in words why I loved these endings so much. By emphasizing the main character's inner world, memoirs had shone a spotlight on the courage and wisdom that result when people try to grow toward their higher potential.

But it wasn't as easy to see how to organize my own life along such uplifting lines. All I could see in memory were random, chaotic scenes. I ached to assemble them in a way that would reveal to me why I'd made so many bad choices.

Intuitively, I believed what Socrates had said thousands of years ago, that an unexamined life is not worth living. Certainly, in order to write my story, I'd be forced to do a lot of examining. If I did a good job, I might eventually be able to see the whole mess in terms I could tolerate without wanting to scream.

Even better, as the story came together, I hoped to see myself as a character on a purposeful journey toward some better, higher truth. Ultimately, like the characters I had admired my whole life, I wanted to be the hero of my own tale.

In the process of writing the story, I hoped to achieve some of that universal wisdom, strength and "worth" that Socrates considered so important, and perhaps I could even pass some of that value along to others.

People of the book

Throughout my foray into memoir writing, I'd kept up a dialog with my sister, occasionally attempting to reminisce about the dim, almost invisible years before the age of fifteen. I'd heard many horror stories of siblings disagreeing or even arguing about differing memories. In our case, we were totally aligned. Neither of us could remember much.

Perhaps we inherited our amnesia from our parents. Mom never talked about her childhood. Dad was even worse. Anytime the past came up, he either changed the subject altogether or simply looked helpless as if there was nothing to say.

His unwillingness to reminisce was so predictable that even when we asked him a direct question, my sister and I were already rolling our eyes, prepared for his usual evasion. Once, at a lunch celebrating his eightieth birthday, we were throwing out questions, hoping for any morsel. "What about raising Jerry?" my sister asked. "What do you remember about him as a young man?"

Dad paused for a moment. Then he surprised us with an actual answer. "I took Jerry to a ball game once. He had a book with him, which he read the whole time. I never took him again."

Even though he delivered this memory with a smile, I felt a sting of disappointment. After all the years I worked for him in the drugstore, the only thing worth mentioning about our relationship was his disappointment about one missed opportunity for bonding? And now, fifty years later, this was the first time he said anything to me about it?

As a memoir writer, I sought to bring back to life this scene at a ballpark, straining to send my mind back to my state of mind at the time. Why had the world inside the book been more interesting than the men throwing a ball out on the field? More important, why had the book been more interesting than talking to my dad?

As I jotted notes about the importance of books, I saw that throughout my childhood, I'd almost literally been taught to worship them. Every Saturday morning at synagogue, the highlight of the service was the reading from the Torah, a scrolled book that was stored in an ornately decorated vault.

Before removing the sacred object from storage, the congregation chanted and prayed, as though the room and everyone in it first needed to be in a holy state of mind. When our minds had been sufficiently prepared, the scrolls were brought out, followed by more prayers and rituals before it could actually be read. When it was time to restore it to its place of honor, this process was reversed.

This ritualized training, which had been drilled into me from such an early age, naturally heightened the importance of reading books. However, the book that commanded all this attention was written in Hebrew. To find books I could actually understand, I went to the public library, which was directly across the street. There I became a devotee of the science fiction shelves, immersing myself in novels about men roaming the universe in spaceships.

I carried around books by Isaac Asimov, Robert Heinlein, and A.E. van Vogt, sneaking in a few pages on the trolley, at the dinner table at home, and on my lap when we went out to eat in restaurants. These authors took me to other worlds, where their heroes would emerge victorious no matter how many obstacles they encountered.

One day, when visiting the local penny candy store after school, my eyes were drawn to the books lining a small shelf in the back corner. Each volume had a picture of two mysterious-looking boys on the front cover. From my savings, I bought my first Hardy Boys book and fell in love with the way these young sleuths could decipher the behavior of other people. I felt such strength in the way the two brothers supported each other. With my own brother having recently moved away to college, their adventures right here on planet earth alleviated my aloneness. For my next birthday, I requested more Hardy Boys mysteries.

When Dad handed me my gift, though, I worried that it was too thin. *Hadn't I made it clear that I wanted more than one?* When I tore off the wrapping paper, the book's plain cover said *Robinson Crusoe* by Daniel Defoe. I felt betrayed and made no effort to hide it. "Please," I pleaded, before running to my room and slamming the door. Eventually he bought me a Hardy Boys book on the condition that I also read *Robinson Crusoe.*

After I recovered from the shock of not getting my way, I began to read. As I adjusted to the old-fashioned language, I grew curious about this lonely hero. Stranded on an island, he had to figure out how to survive. Soon, the character's resourcefulness completely captured my imagination.

My literary adventures continued every week with books by Charles Dickens, Mark Twain, and Alexandre Dumas. In their pages, I could interact with English dukes and French counts, country estates and small American towns. In addition to extending my world beyond the narrow, predictable range portrayed in mysteries and science fiction, these authors were stretching my reading muscles. I poured myself into fictional worlds so vigorously I felt as though I was really there.

In retrospect I could see that tearing off the wrapping paper of that birthday gift revealed a new way to explore the world. And yet, it also revealed a puzzle. Dad's desire that I read this particular book seemed disconnected from anything I'd known about him. I'd never seen him reading classical novels. He just went to work early in the morning and came home late at night. Why his sudden interest in what I read? And why had he offered this story about a castaway trying to survive alone on an island?

I now saw parallels between Dad and Crusoe. Dad certainly didn't talk much, so even after I'd stocked the shelves, rang up a sale, or mopped the floor at the end of the night, I never expected him to express approval. He was too preoccupied with running the business to spend time speaking with me. Even though we were together, I still felt alone.

Perhaps he viewed the drugstore as his own island. Perhaps his insistence that I read this particular book was his subconscious way of letting me see what it felt like to be him, all day every day at the store alone.

Extreme reading

Dad's recollection of me reading in the ballpark continued to raise a slew of memories: my excursions into Center City to visit huge second-hand bookstores; my reverential awe when walking into the majestic main library; the intoxicating smell of fresh ink and paper in the new bookstore near my school. But when I tried gathering all these scenes into a story, the task seemed overwhelming.

I decided to follow the basic principle of storytelling: Start from the beginning and then proceed from there. But I couldn't figure out how to sort them in order, because throughout those high school years, every week was almost exactly the same as the one before. Each Friday, after the relentless competition with my smart classmates, I began my weekend job at my dad's drugstore.

In every one of those scenes, though, I was holding a book. Inside its covers, my humdrum life transformed into a series of exciting adventures. In the early years, I might become the captain of a spaceship, trying to avert catastrophe. When I turned to serious literature, I was more likely to assume the role of a British lad navigating the moral and financial quandaries of nineteenth-century London.

When I graduated high school and flew a thousand miles into the heartland, my routine was demolished. I had no drugstore to hide in, and instead of competing with grade-hungry boys, I was set loose in a mob of eager young men and women whose social realities bore no resemblance to mine.

Confused by my inability to relate, I retreated to my apartment and lost myself in my extensive record collection. For verbal companionship I turned to books.

Sitting alone, holed up against the long, howling Wisconsin winter, I read books like George Orwell's *1984* and Franz Kafka's *The Trial* whose main characters lived in an oppressive world. No matter how hard they tried, they still felt helpless. Thanks to my ability to lose myself in stories, I accompanied each one of them on their futile quests. By the end of each despairing novel, the heroes had given up–and so had I.

My devotion to these foreboding stories made me feel smart, hip, in the know. Combined with marijuana and the futility of my anti-war stance, my literary heroes beckoned me into a deep depression. By the end of my years at college, the damage had been done. I felt so lost and confused that I was able to sustain my despair without any additional reinforcement from books.

In my mid-twenties, books about spirituality led me to higher ground. A few years later, self-help books also inspired me to find a better version of myself. When I read for entertainment, I gravitated to detective novels. The chaos at the beginning of the story always ended with a satisfying resolution. The good guys caught the killer and restored order to the world.

Once I discovered memoirs, I noticed a similar effect. No matter how miserable the author felt at the beginning, by the end they felt better and had gained insight into their own lives.

Was there really a memoir in my future?

The more I worked on my memoir project, the more I liked it. But I also began to grasp its sheer magnitude. At the present rate, I worried that creating a meaningful book-length story might take as long as it had taken me to amass the original experiences.

When I heard that Jonathan was teaching a course called "Write Your Novel in Nine Months," I was excited. A course like this could bring it all together. But most of the workshops at the Writers Room were directed toward fiction writers. I feared this new workshop would be no different. And yet, if I could attend anyway, perhaps I would gather useful insights.

I met Jonathan at a coffee shop and above the loud buzz of chatter from the crowded room, I explained my situation and asked if he thought I would benefit.

"You'd fit right in," he said. "My course is not about the content of your book but about urging you forward, so you can finish."

"But I'm not even sure what the point of my memoir is yet."

"Look. You can't fix it if you don't write it. The class will guide you through the process of completing that all important first draft."

As I expected, I was the only nonfiction writer in the group. And yet, it quickly became clear that the training applied to my situation as much as theirs. "To write your book," Jonathan said. "Write every day, and aim low. Make it achievable. Even a page a day would give you a book in less than a year."

Taking his advice, I began to turn my rough notes into the manuscript of a coherent, book-length story. The material was raw, but I relied on the universally agreed writer's guideline that first drafts stink. Adapting his suggestion to "aim low," I intended to write two pages every day. But once I completed my daily minimum, I didn't want to stop. I often wrote twice as much.

Individual anecdotes blossomed into full-fledged scenes, which gradually accumulated into a manuscript. I felt like a forensic scientist, collecting, restoring, and ordering archeological artifacts.

Before beginning to write a memoir, my college years felt murky, as if hidden behind a curtain of marijuana smoke. Looking back through memory, all I could see was a young man who began college full of hope, and a master of the challenges of academia. Then instead of taking advantage of this important step toward adulthood, he industriously demolished everything he'd ever achieved, striding inexorably toward the edge of a cliff.

Now that I was writing a memoir, I had to sweep away the layers of regret and attempt to describe what actually happened. This gave me a radically new way to view those years. Out of that disorganized pile of misery I would try to find the story.

As I described my arrival at a college campus, in an environment unlike anything I had experienced before, I marveled at how poorly I was prepared to cope. Lacking the social skills that would permit me to make small talk or establish simple friendships, I could only watch my fellow students from afar. Embittered by my own loneliness, and further inflamed by anger against the war and the draft, my intellectual ambition curdled into fury, against society, and secretly even against myself. Through the eyes of a storyteller, I could see how desperately I tried to cling to sanity each day while losing sight of tomorrow. Without a compass, a map, or even a true north, I was lost.

As the manuscript developed, I watched this guy use his intelligence to move in directions that would only make him feel worse. "Stop!" I wanted to shout to him. "Go back. You will suffer from these choices."

But despite the suffering that unfolded on the page, what kept me writing was my eager anticipation of the moment when my younger self realized that love was everywhere, if only he knew where to look.

Writing that first memoir also deepened my appreciation for other characters in my life. Seeing myself at the drugstore had already shown me more about my relationship to my father than I'd seen before. My mother also came to life. As a child, I had resented her because I didn't think she was smart. As she emerged on the pages of my memoir, I expanded my view of her to include her playfulness, her curiosity about literature and the arts, and her constant willingness to learn and grow later in life.

One of the difficulties about turning all of this into a compelling story was that I couldn't make sense of this young man's goal. He wanted to be a doctor. No, forget that. He wanted to stop all wars. No. Wait. After the violent confrontation he realized the futility of protest, and he came to a complete stop. So now what? How do you write a good story about a character who doesn't know what he wants?

His motivation was a scrambled mess, and he had no way to move forward until he understood what "forward" meant. When a spiritual system brought him back into focus, he was finally able to identify the mission of his life—to find a coherent understanding of his place in the world.

By the end of the nine-month class, I'd created a book-length narrative, Seeing my life unfold in the shape of a story shed light on my own complex path toward adulthood. I was breathless with excitement about my achievement. And yet, there was no time to celebrate. I was already planning the next leg of my journey. I had so much to learn in order to turn this messy manuscript into a good read.

Horror

In the fall, Jonathan announced that the Writers Room would celebrate Halloween by holding a horror-writing contest. Since he was an expert in this genre, I should have been thrilled by yet another opportunity to learn from him. Except for one thing: I had no use for horror. My life had been horrific enough, to the point that when I read even a few pages of a horror novel or saw a few minutes of a movie, the misery of my younger days closed in like a dark cloud. I avoided such stories and certainly had no interest in writing one.

When I told him I was disappointed to miss out on his latest writing event, Jonathan told me, in that upbeat manner that never failed to inspire, that the contest included a nonfiction category.

"How does a horror contest have a nonfiction category?"

"There are a lot of ways you could approach this topic from a nonfiction point of view," he said. "In fact, I got my start in horror by interviewing anthropology professors about the folklore of vampires."

I came up with the idea to write a short piece in the style of a nonfiction essay, in which I would explain why I hated reading horror. I told of waking up after falling asleep with a book open on my chest. A demon had crossed out of the fictional world of the book and into my physical world. Was I really awake, or was it a dream? I wasn't sure but in either case, I vowed to never allow another horror book or movie into my mind.

Writing the essay stretched my writing muscles into unfamiliar territory, and gave me the exhilarating opportunity to express complex emotions through a simple story. I won second place in nonfiction. I recognized the possibility that there were only two entries in that category. Even so, I enjoyed writing it, and enjoyed the thrill of winning something.

Only a couple of months later, though, horror really did emerge into my reality. I heard from a friend that the Writers Room was shutting down. I tried calling the office, praying this was only a rumor. No one answered. But that in itself didn't mean anything. It could just be one of those times when no one was available to pick up the phone.

Then I ran into another member who had heard a similar story. It was impossible to imagine. If they were out of money, surely some generous benefactor would come and resurrect the place. But there was no magical solution. The machinery of the nonprofit organization had apparently come undone, and once broken, there didn't seem to be any way to make it whole again.

I felt as if I'd just lost a best friend in a car crash. I had built my dreams for the next chapter of my life on participating in this community of writers. It was the place where we could always hang out and talk about writing, where teens could come after school to hone new skills, where aspiring writers could glimpse the author's life.

This place taught me about overcoming reluctance, procrastination, fear of readers, and all the other psychological obstacles that block writing. The Writers Room had given me license to thrive.

And now this creative union was dead, along with the community, my plan, and the hopes of many other people who had seen the place as an incubator for their creative energy. Just as I had become accustomed to seeing light in people's eyes when they expressed their appreciation for the Writers Room, I now saw darkness.

Just to torture myself, I drove past the office building where we all used to gather. The awning still said "Writers Room," but the doors were locked, cruel reminders of all the creative joy we had lost.

A few of us got together at a private home for one last meeting. One woman in her seventies had intended to write about her life as a painter. She said, "I was looking to the Writers Room to help me find the words to describe my life in art. I can't believe it's gone. I don't know how I'm going to carry on."

She looked at me as if she was going to cry. We stood there in silence. I too had run out of words.

Finding readers in faraway places

Losing the Writers Room was a devastating blow to my plans. Nowhere to teach. Nowhere to learn. But at least by writing columns at the local newspaper, and seeing my byline in print a couple of times a month, I could feel that I was participating in the regional writing scene. Then, the newspaper suddenly went out of business. What seemed like the on ramp to a career as a writer had turned into another dead end. I had no idea what to do next.

One day I received an email from someone I never met, who said he had read my self-help book and that he'd posted a review of it online. I clicked the link he sent me and for the first time, saw praise for my own book. It felt like magic. I wanted it to happen more. I sent this stranger a note, thanking him for his kind words, and asking him where he heard about my book. Obviously, it wasn't from a bookstore. I was only selling them to attendees of my workshops.

He said he had won my book as a door prize at the Philadelphia Writers Conference. I recalled donating a few copies to the organization, but I never imagined I would hear anything more about it. The fact that he posted a review seemed like a message from the universe, pointing me to a possible next step.

I wrote him back. "You said that you posted the review on a blog. What's a blog?"

"It's a new way to post articles online."

"But how do you get readers?" I asked.

"I don't know," he said. "Somehow they find me by browsing on the Internet. It has something to do with search engines. Without even doing anything, I'm already getting fifty visitors a day."

The previous year, working on the group book proposal had opened my eyes to the massive changes being caused by the Internet.

Already, two such changes were affecting my life—online advertising was contributing to the demise of local newspapers, and at the same time, the Internet had made it easier for writers to reach readers. Writing a blog seemed like a great way to stay on top of this wave rather than being swept beneath it.

I remembered in one of Jonathan's workshops, he told us, "Every writer needs to develop an online following." He called it our "platform." Starting a blog sounded like a step in that direction, helping me become not just a writer, but a modern writer, able to thrive in the Internet-driven world.

To create a blog, I needed to find more than just a few individual topics. I wanted to follow a theme that would provide an ongoing, interesting source of material. Since I'd become increasingly interested in memoirs, I decided to focus on them.

Every time I read a memoir, I tried to think of worthwhile things to say about it. Framing these insights took far longer than reading the book in the first place. Every week or two, I finished an essay and posted it. Then several times a day I checked to see how many people had visited over the last few hours. I felt a little obsessive about checking so often, but that didn't stop me from doing it.

Early on, there were only a few visitors, but over time the numbers grew. In addition to sheer numbers, I craved comments. People offered opinions, or even occasionally, praise for one of my essays. Still grieving the loss of the Writers Room, I hoped that through posting and answering comments, I would somehow create my own community.

And since these people were reading my blog because of their specialized interest in memoirs, I hoped to increase my connection with the memoir writers of the world.

For variety, instead of only writing about books, I occasionally reported on something I learned at a writing conference, or some thoughts I had about memoirs in general. And I often included a writing prompt, so that blog readers could try writing their own material.

When I heard about a memoir author publicizing his book in Philadelphia, I had another idea. In addition to writing about the books, I could write about their authors.

I drove down to see Tommie Smith, the Olympic athlete who raised his fist in protest at the winner's podium of the 1968 Olympics. Tommie Smith was a hero of the Black resistance for those few brief moments. The glossy, memorable photo of his fist in the air haunted a generation. But until I read the memoir, I didn't realize how much his courage cost him. After his brief fame, he'd been ruthlessly shut out from competitions and coaching jobs and stripped of potential earnings from endorsements.

That evening in Philadelphia, in his presence, I felt I was honoring a man who had boldly placed his reputation on the line in order to express his conscience. I was touching history, and by writing about it, I had become a news reporter. In my blog, I explored the way a memoir lets readers into the heart and mind of a man who played a role in shaping our world.

I soon discovered that other memoir authors, eager for publicity, were often willing to give me an interview. In this way, I was able to interact with many of the people whose stories had inspired me. And through my blog, I was able to give a few authors access to potential readers.

Who will support my emotional evolution?

Since, for me, emotions were a foreign language, the only way I could know if I'd said something correctly was to ask someone how my writing made them feel. After the Writers Room collapsed, I was desperate to find a new source of feedback. I assumed it would only be a matter of time before some of the former members would clump together into small groups. I watched and waited for announcements, but at first, no such meetings appeared.

Finally, I did hear about one such group, but when I attended the meeting, I was disappointed by their lively debates about how to make a fictitious character sound more believable. I couldn't see the purpose of solving that problem when there were so many real people I needed to understand.

Eventually I tracked down a few memoir writers who'd be willing to get together, if I scheduled and led the meetings. At first, I balked. I had no interest in arranging such get-togethers. I wanted to write, not coax people to show up. But if I didn't do it, it wasn't going to happen.

Once I began, my fears were confirmed. The endless churning of schedules and emails really was a hassle. And yet with patience we agreed on a time that worked.

Searching for places to meet turned out to be another responsibility I'd inadvertently accepted. Several libraries said they were full or didn't do this sort of thing. How I missed just showing up at the Writers Room. Eventually I found a coffee shop willing to host groups like ours. It was a little noisy, but once we got together and settled into the creative work of sharing stories, the hubbub of the place faded into the background.

When it was my turn, I read a scene from my California hippie days. I felt reassured by my listeners' nods and smiles. When they praised some aspect of the writing, I felt even better. However, suggestions for possible improvement stirred up waves of agitation, like being on a lake in a canoe after a speed boat just blew past. My mind crouched into a defensive posture. "They don't know what they are talking about. They don't really understand my point," I wanted to shout.

Then my self-soothing tools took hold. "Hang in there, Jerry. Slow down and breathe. They are just trying to help." Finally, my nerves settled and I laughed at myself. "Obviously, if they don't understand what I'm trying to say then I need to write it more clearly."

Month after month, my reviewers pushed me to dig deeper. Once I was able to accept their gentle, supportive comments, I could see how important it was to understand my writing from their point of view.

By continuing to write stories about myself, and then absorb feedback from my fellow writers, I kept learning lessons about how people speak and listen to one another. Back in my youth, I never bothered to check if my listeners knew what I was talking about. And except for a few insights I'd gained from my grad school encounter groups, no one had explained to me, "This is why we don't understand you."

Now, as a writer, I'd found an endless source of feedback about how to express myself built right into the system. The contract in every memoir group went something like this: "I'm going to try my best to describe some intricate emotional situation, and I appreciate your thoughts about how I could say it better."

Then, when it was my turn to listen to their pieces, I had to see in my mind's eye what they were describing in each scene. More important, as I entered the scene with them, I had to feel what they were feeling.

I realized that I'd always allowed myself to be swept up in stories. But in my younger days, I was reading about fictional characters, usually men, and usually limited in their emotional range.

These critique groups exposed me to the vast variety of emotions experienced by real people, and because we were together in real life, it also provided a master class where I could learn to attune myself to the way people respond to their experiences.

All this intense listening converted me from a passive listener of other people's journeys to an active participant. As I listened to each story with every morsel of my awareness, I felt myself opening up to emotions that I'd not been aware of earlier in my life. My emotional vocabulary was growing.

When one of us was unable to attend, instead of letting them miss the meeting, I rescheduled to a time that worked for everyone. These negotiations demanded more effort, but because I valued the interaction and recognized its contribution to my quality of life, I was willing to do it.

Accepting the responsibility to keep these tiny groups together had a powerful emotional benefit: I was going to keep growing as a writer even after the demise of the Writers Room.

Teach what you love

While I had figured out how to find readers without the newspaper, and to find mutual support and feedback without the Writers Room, I still had not replaced the opportunity to teach classes. For that, I was going to need to find writers.

I did find a few groups that met in libraries once a month, but nothing even close to the magnificent scale to which I'd been accustomed. Writers like me tend to be introverts, which means that unless someone actively herds us together, we'll stay alone. The Writers Room had been unique in that it provided an environment that drew us out of our homes and into one another's presence.

The largest, best-established group I found was the Greater Lehigh Valley Writers Group. Like most such groups it was focused mainly on fiction, but when I pitched a memoir class, they were willing to stretch outside their comfort zone.

I didn't mention to them that all my previous teaching had been about self-help for writers. I was excited by my new topic, and looked forward to preparing a curriculum and handouts.

By the time I taught the class, I'd already rehearsed it in my mind many times, basing my methods on my own experience. Once I was in front of actual human beings, their questions stirred up my thinking and created fresh perspectives. It reminded me of the old wisdom that the best way to learn is to teach.

The magical bonus to teaching a class about memoir writing was that by sharing stories, everyone in the room got to know one another better. It was the ultimate social tool. After all the years I had struggled to relate to people, I had stumbled on a remarkably effective way to do just that.

The positive student reviews provided me with much needed encouragement for my new curriculum. I looked forward to doing it again—if I could find more students.

Early in my journey to become a writer, I read a book titled *If You Want to Write* by Brenda Ueland, which exuberantly claimed anyone can write. It was a heady notion. If you can speak, you can write. It encouraged me to extend myself toward the writing life. Perhaps I could test Ueland's hypothesis, and find other non-writers who wanted to record their own stories.

One day, I noticed a sign for a small art studio which had recently opened near my home. Perhaps I could convince some of these artistically inclined people to represent their lives through the medium of a story.

I went to meet the director, who was in her glory at a potter's wheel, surrounded by a riot of art supplies, paint splotches, and partially completed pottery. I gave her the pitch I had prepared, which straddled the two worlds of visual arts and life story. I told her I would call the workshop, "How to add writing and storylines to a scrapbook."

She liked my idea and listed it in her schedule. While waiting for the class to materialize, I enrolled in a beginner's drawing class. In the first session, the instructor set an egg on a table and told us to draw it.

The task defied reason. How could anyone draw that white object armed only with a lead pencil and an eraser? But by learning the techniques, accepting guidance, and with liberal use of the eraser, I did end up with a drawing that gave some sense of curvature and depth.

Trying to represent this three-dimensional shape on two-dimensional paper struck me as a perfect metaphor for writing a memoir. Like artists, memoir writers represent the complexities of life with squiggles on the page. At first, we too think it's impossible to represent real life with words. And then, gradually, with a scene here and a chapter there, with some training here and revision there, the story begins to resemble the original experience.

When it came time to teach my memoir class to artists, though, the owner of the studio was the only one who showed up. I conducted the whole thing just for her, then crossed art studios off my list.

Thanks to my blog, occasionally people found me. That's how I received an invitation to teach a class at a nondenominational church.

Based on my complex journey to find God, I assumed that many who attended church would want to write about their spiritual sagas. I repurposed my notes once again to be appropriate for that environment. In the class, I discovered that I'd had no need to modify my curriculum. Like people everywhere, the five students who showed up were attempting to reconstruct the stories of their lives. Spirituality, if it came up at all, was just one aspect.

Once again, though, the church failed to provide an ongoing stream of learners. They'd only invited me to share my observations about memoirs, but had no interest in hosting a class.

Still grieving the lost opportunities offered by the Writers Room, I circled back to the Lehigh Valley group. They'd hit on an interesting strategy: To fill their annual conference, they sent writers out into the community to speak at public libraries.

Since I wanted to keep getting in front of groups to tout the amazing benefits of writing, I volunteered.

It was a fun full-circle moment, as libraries had been such an important part of my youth. Despite a few successful events, though, libraries didn't appear to offer a sustainable venue. I would always just be a visitor, a roving minstrel with no home.

Sometimes, after I gave a talk, I asked attendees to recommend other places to speak. One man invited me to speak at his Rotary Club. The Rotary mission to serve others was a great match, since I already believed memoir writing is an opportunity to serve the community. The audience listened with bright, attentive eyes, but as soon as the meeting adjourned, they dashed out the door to face the day.

One of my most prestigious opportunities was an interview on a local public radio program. This was a neat experience, sitting in a control room, in front of a microphone, on the sending side of the radio after all these years on the receiving end.

My search to find a sustainable venue for teaching might at times seem like a failure. And yet, inch by inch, I was gaining confidence to speak about writing, and to respond to the questions and needs of those who wished to write a memoir.

A dowser looking for underground water

The only time I visited Rosemont College's campus on Philadelphia's Main Line, with its majestic trees, and historic architecture was when I was invited to speak as a member of the nonfiction panel at their annual writer's conference. Sitting in front of a group of writers was one of my favorite places to be in the world. And I'd be alongside some highly respected Philadelphia writers.

When it was my turn to speak, I shared my quirky, opinionated, and passionate observations that the memoir genre is a window into our collective soul. Since I had neither written a memoir, nor had an advanced degree in creative writing, I considered this opportunity to share my views to be a validation of all that I'd been trying to achieve.

After the session, I felt so energized I couldn't wait to line up another teaching or speaking gig. When I spotted Christine, the event organizer who had invited me to speak on the nonfiction panel, I wondered if she could help. I walked over to her, said hi, and then asked her if she might have need for a memoir teacher.

"We're going to put together some workshops early next year and this might be a good topic," she said. "Tell me what you have in mind."

She stood there, waiting to hear more. I froze. I hadn't planned any specifics. Quickly reviewing my options, I hoped she wouldn't notice that I'd broken into a sweat.

"I've got enough material for about eight hours, but if we do it in four sections, it will require too much driving back and forth. How about doing the whole thing in one all-day event?"

"Sounds interesting," she said. "How about early March? That gives us plenty of time to market it."

Just then, someone stepped closer to get her attention. She turned away. That was the end of our discussion. I couldn't believe what had just happened. "Ask and you shall receive," flashed through my mind.

Fifteen minutes earlier such a great opportunity would have been a pipe dream. Now I had to figure out how I was going to pull it off.

Over the next couple of months, I mapped out a step-by-step curriculum that would keep people engaged all day. As the date approached, I was feeling increasingly confident that I'd know exactly how to orchestrate such an event. But when I checked with Christine, only four people had signed up. I had assumed her far-reaching connections would result in a more robust attendance.

"Let's keep trying," she said.

I felt caught between two powerful desires. In one direction, I wanted to teach students how to write a memoir. And opposed to that desire, I felt an equally strong revulsion at having to promote myself. When I took an honest look at my hesitation, I recognized it as a resurfacing of my lifelong tendency toward isolation. This class presented a perfect test to see if I could push past it.

I knew, at least in theory, that the sales process could be an act of love. My wife Janet's career as a salesperson helped me see that reaching out and ignoring the risk of rejection took real courage. It was only now that I realized my first wife, Ruth, had also earned her living in marketing. Had I been attracted to these two women because I was looking for someone who could save me from my fears?

From their point of view, it was silly to shrink away from promoting this class. How could I think it was wrong, when in my heart and soul, I believed I was offering people an enriching experience?

I set aside my worries and contacted all the writing groups, organizations, and individuals I could think of. I didn't know if I was cured of my selling phobia, but I was happy to take advantage of this crack in my armor. When I told Christine what I was doing, she matched my enthusiasm, offering to send even more emails and listings.

One day Ruth phoned me. It had been almost ten years since we divorced. Somewhere during those intervening years, the bitterness of our broken bond had softened, and we had gradually eased back into a gentle friendship. She saw one of my announcements for the course. "Would my presence make you feel awkward?" she asked.

I hesitated, wondering if I would be able to handle the emotional complexity my ex-wife sitting among a classroom full of writers. My first impulse was to wish I had been less energetic in announcing the class. But that was my old, withdrawn self talking.

Why not invite her to the party? Perhaps showing her how to write about her life might provide a bridge that could help us normalize and update our relationship.

"I'd love to see you writing again. It's such an awesome hobby," I said. Then taking a deep breath, I said, "We can even drive down together."

When the final number came in, twenty-three people had signed up. I had achieved another peak life experience, helping to pull together a bunch of writers from the thin air of the Internet. It was hard, but possible.

Just when I should have been celebrating, another fear arose. What if I'd been too ambitious? So many people… All day… Would I really be able to handle it?

I laughed. Too late now. The wheels were in motion. I had been preparing for years. I would do everything in my power to give them a great experience.

Shepherding a room full of truth seekers

At six a.m. that Saturday in March, I hustled to load my books and handouts into the car. When Ruth showed up, she and my wife Janet, her fellow equestrian, hugged and made plans to meet at the barn later.

As we pulled out of the driveway, Ruth said, "So tell me what we'll be doing again?"

I groaned. "You're going to be immersed in it all day. Do you really want me to tell you what I'm going to tell you?"

"Sure," she said. "It will help me get into the mood."

"Now that you mention it, it will help me get into the right frame of mind, too," I said. As I rambled on about memoir writing, the drive flew by, and soon we arrived at the address in Manayunk.

At first the place looked just like any row home. But walking down the driveway, we found ourselves in front of an outbuilding. "Perhaps it used to be a carriage house," Ruth said. A lovely mural painted on its side instantly changed the vibe, as if to announce "artists welcome here."

Inside, bright track lights illuminated oil paintings hung on the walls. Their festive landscapes, portraits, and colorful abstractions instantly dispelled the darkness of the overcast day.

As the individuals trickled in, I noticed I wasn't particularly nervous. On the contrary, I found myself thinking, *What a perfect day to teach a writing class.*

When we started, I invited them to see the day ahead through the metaphor of a journey. "Every journey starts with some desire. Let's start the class with yours. Let's divide into groups of three and discuss what desire brought you here today."

As they clustered together, I felt the energy in the room rise. By the time I tried to get their attention, they didn't want to stop talking. *Memoir writing is magic*, I thought. *I just gave them the tiniest nudge, and they've already started sharing.*

Once I regained the floor, I said, "Let's start from the beginning. For our first writing exercise, list the rooms in one of the houses you lived in before the age of, say, eighteen. If you feel the urge, extend your imagination to the front porch or backyard, or your school playground. By visualizing the locations of your early life, you will begin to catch glimpses of events which had an emotional impact on you. When a scene jumps out, jump in."

Their attention shifted from me to the page. The only sounds were pens scratching and pages turning. After they shared what they'd written, one woman said, "I hadn't thought about that home in years." Heads nodded. I loved these bits of feedback and body language from the class, which turned teaching from a monologue into a conversation.

"Next you have to raise dramatic tension. Do that in the next exercise, by writing about a time when you were blocked from achieving some goal."

Their stories revealed a variety of traumas such as death, near-death, abandonment, unwanted teen pregnancy, failed marriage. Even an international kidnapping and a baby abandoned at birth.

Someone spoke up. "Is it normal for people to have so many problems?"

"Yes," I said. "Under our facades we all contain extraordinary events, tremendous courage and suffering and unique achievements. Writing memoir is a chance to confront our hidden worlds head on."

During the lunch break, I passed a guy staring intently at a canvas on the wall of our makeshift classroom. He stopped me with some urgency. "See that inn?" he said, pointing to the painting. "I used to be a chef there."

I squinted at the painterly scene, trying to make out the shapes that had stirred so much nostalgia. "What a cool coincidence," I said. "And what a great way to awaken memories."

While I quietly ate my sandwich, I mused that if I could design a perfect memoir classroom, the walls would be adorned with paintings related to every student's past.

After lunch, and facing another four hours, I felt my energy drain. To distract myself from my own fatigue, I decided to share it.

"Consider the story of our day together in this workshop. We started with desire. Then we embarked on the journey. Now, we have entered our own long middle, and we have to make it past the afternoon slump." Their laughter provided the hoped-for energy boost.

"While obstacles block you from satisfying your desire, you also need to write about successes. For the next exercise, write about a scene in which you overcame an obstacle."

After ten minutes of writing, we went around the room again. By recounting a scene of heroism or success, each person had begun to transform their nightmarish betrayals and disappointments into the foundation of a good story.

This was the lesson I most wanted them to grasp: that when they saw their lives through memory, the downbeat experiences often dominated; but when fashioning their lives into a story, the ups gained importance.

In fact, I was eager to see how some of that wisdom might apply to my own history with Ruth. When we got to her story, I held my breath.

In her previous piece, the veterinarian had told her that her horse's intestines were blocked and without a major operation, he would be dead within hours. She continued the story in the second exercise. The operation had succeeded. Despite the dire warnings of Mac's imminent death, by the next evening, he was on his feet.

No one else in the room knew that Ruth's husband during this experience was teaching the class, and that in his mind, she had just brought that day roaring back to life. Mac was like her child, and we were both traumatized by his brush with death. But I had to wrestle myself back from my own thoughts and offer a comment that would be helpful to her and could give the group closure so we could move on. Recognizing Mac's almost miraculous recovery, I said, "Resurrection… Facing the jaws of death and then returning. Your horse proved that you don't have to die in order to be reborn. You just need to come close."

As we completed this round of sharing, some of them had begun gathering their things. We were all ready to go home. But I wanted to add a few more words to wrap up the day.

"During the class, you've gained insights into how a character must proceed from a low point, through obstacles, to reach a conclusion. Now that you have experienced a day's journey into that process, I encourage you to go back into the world, continue to fill in the blanks, pull together more anecdotes, and flesh in the character arc. It's a long journey. But the fact that we went through it together will provide you with a model of courage and stamina."

For those of you who continue to travel on this journey, there is an elegant surprise waiting for you. By discovering the best way to give your readers closure for having read it, you will provide yourself with a sense of closure for having lived it."

While each of them had been learning how to find their stories, I had been on a journey, too. I had taken a giant leap in my experience as a teacher. I'd conveyed the entire basic framework in one day, guided a large group to find their individual stories, and fostered the empathy that transformed strangers into a tribe for a day, whose sole purpose was to help one another grow.

Till death do us part

On the drive home from my marathon memoir class, Ruth said, "That was great, Jer. Everyone seemed to enjoy it. I know I did."

"Since the first time I taught these classes, I've been struck by the way each person, by sharing their story, welcomes us into their hearts. And during each reading, everyone listens carefully. I feel like I'm a DJ or party host or something, and the gathering is a celebration of shared humanity. It's such a beautiful experience."

The pace of our conversation was punctuated by long pauses, both of us tired and thoughtful after a long day.

"It's wonderful to see how you have grown, Jer. You're so passionate."

"I'm pretty surprised by it myself. Sometimes when I say something in a class that makes people laugh, I ask myself, 'Who is this guy who could teach classes and joke with strangers?' A few years ago, I would have trembled with fear. How did I shift from trying to be invisible around strangers to being entirely comfortable in front of them?"

"You've become the person I always saw," she said.

I felt flattered by the kind way she spoke about me. "The connection with writers is a big part of what brought me out of my shell. Associating with people who are willing to slow down and explain their lives through stories makes me feel safe. Like I'm around friends."

"I wouldn't have guessed writing would have such a big influence on you," she said.

"Me either," I said. "And yet from the first evening when I walked into the Writers Room all those years ago, I felt like I'd come home. I still get that feeling when I'm around any group of people who are trying to write."

"Can you explain it?" she said. "I don't know if I've ever heard of anything like that before. It's as if writing is your religion." We both burst out laughing.

"The only image I can think of to explain it is that nursery rhyme of Humpty Dumpty, who broke into pieces and couldn't be put back together. I used to feel fragmented in that way, like every different part of me was disconnected from every other part. I used to love to dance. I used to love physics. I used to be so shy I hated the sensation of anyone even looking at me. Writing my story has given me a way to knit the parts into a healthy whole. And I guess I just feel comfortable around people who are trying to do the same thing. "

The ride home was along a highway I had traveled hundreds of times. Each morning I drove down this road to go to work, and then each evening I came home, pretty much the same guy, except ten hours older than when I left, and a little more tired.

Today was different. I was returning at the end of the day having been on a journey, not just by myself, but with a room full of other lifetimes.

"I think memoir writing could help a lot of people," I continued. "We're all swimming in an ocean of stories, anyway. But so much of what happens to us stays hidden. In these classes, there is a type of radical sharing. When people allow themselves to be authentically seen, everyone learns so much."

Ruth thought for a moment. "What about your life, though? Did you feel left out by the fact that you weren't sharing your own story?"

"Hmm," I said. "I didn't feel left out. By inviting them to speak, I feel like I was an intimate participant in every conversation, embraced by the love flowing in the room."

Musing about how memoirs and memoir classes bring people together, I realized the day showered some of its magic on Ruth and me. We had never talked about the end of our marriage. By sharing stories today, we had tied up some loose ends. I felt more comfortable with her than I had in years.

When we arrived home, Janet welcomed us. Then the two of them drove off together to care for and ride their horses.

Even though I had never blamed myself for the breakup of my first marriage, I often had to swat away feelings of failure that accompanied our divorce. I feared I had betrayed a sacred promise. But hearing the way she'd written about an event that we'd shared, and that had impacted her so powerfully reminded me of the importance of our relationship. We'd been through so much together already and in this new phase of our lives we were still working toward mutual support and understanding.

In this respect, perhaps my vow to support her "until death do us part" was true after all.

Old people!

Pulling together an all-day training session in partnership with the director of Rosemont's writing program and the publisher of Philadelphia Stories was like winning the cultural community lottery: not likely to be replicated any time soon. I returned to my strategy of putting out feelers and then waiting.

One such offer, arising as if by magic, came from a woman who invited me to speak at a senior living expo. She said they would be running full page ads, including an announcement for my talk. "Last year 6,000 people attended," she said.

Before this moment, I'd always thought of seniors as being mixed in with the rest of the population. For the first time, I anticipated walking into a whole exhibit hall full of them. With all their life experiences and free time, surely they would be able to tell amazing stories.

When I entered the large meeting hall, my outsized expectations were quickly deflated. Companies were promoting reverse mortgages, in-home elevators, assisted-living communities and handicap-accessible bathrooms. There wasn't a single exhibit geared to writing and sharing stories, or for that matter, any other methods for creative aging.

I asked a friendly looking woman at one of the booths, "Where are all the boomers?"

"They're at work." I could relate to that. I had to take a vacation day to attend.

When I gave my talk, about fifteen people showed up at the appointed corner of the big room. There wasn't a wall or even a curtain to separate us, so I had to shout out my pitch about the healing power of gathering memories. I asked them to write for a few minutes.

When they read their pieces aloud, everyone leaned closer. As we concentrated intently on one another's stories, the crowd faded into the background. The session must have moved this little band of storytellers in some way, because at the end they stood to applaud. Their enthusiasm felt like it validated my belief that life stories bring people together.

To follow up on the possibility that seniors might be my natural audience, I found a local center that offered educational programs. I called the director to pitch a four-session class. "Sure, we could do that," she said. "Send me a blurb."

"I'd have to offer the course in the evening. Would that be okay?"

She paused. "We can certainly try it, but I have to warn you. Most of our members are only here during the day."

I hoped she was wrong. When the date arrived, eight people had signed up. My optimism surged. Senior centers could provide the steady source of aspiring memoir writers I'd been looking for.

The youngest was in her sixties and the oldest almost ninety. They shared fascinating stories from World War II and the extreme poverty of the Great Depression. Several of them reminisced about the ways they had to entertain themselves before the universal acceptance of television. By plucking memories from before I was born, they brought history alive for me.

Each time I heard one of these glimpses that had occurred just before my time, I felt as though I'd been given some sort of magical vision, as if they were standing on a taller hill, seeing farther into the past than I could see.

Then it hit me. I'd had access to this historical insight from my elders all along. During college, when I desperately struggled to understand the agony and culture of the world, it never occurred to me to ask my own parents, aunts, uncles, or grandparents. My high school teachers had all lived through the upheaval earlier in the century, yet I couldn't recall asking a single one of them to tell me about their own direct experience.

I felt a wave of regret, recognizing how blind I'd been. Taking a deep breath, I reeled myself back to the present. I couldn't change my past behavior, but I could be present right here, in this room, listening to these elders.

Even though some leaned on canes and others listened through hearing aids, when they told their stories, it was easy to imagine the teenagers and young adults they used to be. Teaching these classes populated my imagination with curious, interesting seniors. Together we were reshaping our elder status from being yesterday's news to tomorrow's thought leaders.

Emotional intelligence in action

When I offered another class at the center, no one signed up. I asked the program director her thoughts about this downturn in fortune. She replied, "You were lucky the first time." I hoped to repeat my lucky break elsewhere, but I failed to discover any other senior centers in my area that offered continuing education programs in the evening. Stuck again.

Like a pioneer trying to move a covered wagon through a dense forest, I frequently had to stop to clear the path. Even though I wasn't sure where I was going, I hoped I'd know when I got there.

Each time I found a teaching or speaking opportunity, its source could usually be traced back to feelers I'd put out the year before. While I was shy about many things, I was never shy about finding places to teach.

One day, I bumped into an author I'd known at the Writers Room who told me she'd landed a part-time job, teaching at a local university.

"I wish I could do that," I said, "but I don't have an advanced degree in English literature."

"The program I'm in, Adult Enrichment, has no such requirement. Your master's degree in counseling should be fine."

I found a program similar to the one she described and sent an application which included a copy of my self-help book. When I received no response, I assumed it was a dead end. Months after I forgot about having applied, Northampton Community College invited me to teach.

The following semester, I was proud to see my course listed in their catalog. I was a college instructor. At the first class, students introduced themselves. I'd been wrong to emphasize older writers.

Plenty of young people were also interested in learning about the genre.

At the beginning of the class, I delivered what had by now become my standard introduction to the wonders of memoir writing. And even though I'd delivered it over and over, I felt energized, offering my enthusiasm about the healthy, important journey they'd be taking by engaging in this project.

After my motivational pitch, I offered specific suggestions for writing a first short piece, and then gave them ten minutes to write. After the time was up, I asked them to read their pieces aloud.

As we listened to one such story, the reader broke down and sobbed, talking about the recent loss of his wife to cancer. Other members of the group nodded, with moist eyes and patient silence, offering brief expressions of support. I realized how familiar I'd grown to such outpourings of emotion. Memoir groups tapped into mutual connection unlike anything I'd experienced since my grad school group therapy days.

My role as a facilitator was crucial to this process. While the feelings of each reading dominated our attention, at the end of the reader's allotted time, I had to gently shift our focus to the next reader. Much to my amazement, no matter how deep the emotions or how torn up the reader, when their turn was up, we were able to collect ourselves and move on.

Rather than feeling dragged down by the speaker's vulnerability, other attendees seemed to be emboldened by it. Once they realized that their powerful emotions could be conveyed in this way, they also opened up and revealed their own hidden places.

I marveled at my ability to facilitate these sharings. Through most of my life, I shielded myself from expressions of raw emotion. Now, in my new personality, the guy who had learned to listen, I stayed in my heart while they were reading, fully present to their feelings.

If, at the beginning of my grad program, someone bet me I would ever be able to coordinate such emotionally rich interactions, I would not have taken the bet. And yet, here I was, at the front of a room in which people felt safe enough to share their most traumatic moments.

Since the classes were held as a series, each week everyone in attendance would learn a little more about one another, a little more about themselves, and a lot more about the journey of writing a memoir. When the series was over, I felt satisfaction, grateful for the opportunity to share my excitement about memoir writing.

The following semester the college offered the course again. For the first time since my initial experience at the Writers Room, instead of wondering where I'd be teaching next, I could focus on improving my delivery, gaining confidence and adapting to the patterns of writing and mutual support.

You should write another book

I was excited to receive an invitation to attend a memoir group hosted by a book editor who had previously worked at a commercial publishing company in New York City. I viewed the meeting in the old Allentown rowhome through a romantic prism, as though it harkened back to days of literary salons and urban culture.

I hoped this invitation signaled the beginning of a new hub of memoir activity, one that I wouldn't have to keep aloft on my own.

Each of us at the gathering had a chance to say why we had come, what we wanted to write, and how far along we were. When it was my turn, instead of talking about myself, I spoke about why memoirs are so important and how they are changing the world.

"In just a few years," I exclaimed, "the prevailing attitude toward writing a story about an ordinary life has morphed from 'no one would ever want to read about me' to 'I would love to share my story.' This has offered us a whole new way to connect."

My body crackled with energy, as if I was a preacher, inviting people to celebrate their own stories.

At the end of the session, a few of us lingered to help clean up. By the time I was pulling on my coat, everyone else had gone. My host thanked me for my presentation and said to me, "Why not write a book about your big ideas?"

"What do you mean by big ideas?"

"The things you say about the importance of memoirs, why they have become so prevalent, and how writing one can help a person feel better about themselves."

"You think that would make an interesting book?"

"Not only do I think so. I want to talk to my business partner. I think we can publish it."

I had been camping at the gates of the publishing business for years, honing my skills and building up experience, hoping that someday I would knock on the door and someone would say, "We're so glad to see you. Come right in."

But in this case, I hadn't even knocked. I just did what I love to do, and the opportunity came to me.

Since she was just starting a new venture, I didn't expect much money. I didn't care. The privilege of working with her, gaining her insights and a first "real" publishing deal were sufficient.

I woke the next morning, eager to put together the brief proposal she requested. "Just write enough to share with my partner," she had said. "I'll do the rest."

I had big ideas popping around in my brain all the time. Now, instead of sharing them with tiny audiences, and writing about them in essays, I could assemble them into a book. Such a project would give me the room to develop my ideas in a complete and methodical way.

I imagined my book answering two questions: "Why have readers suddenly become interested in memoirs by ordinary people?" and, "Why is this a great time to write one?"

Over the next couple of weeks, using the skills I developed at the Writers Room, I wrote an outline, suggestions for chapters, a proposed marketing blurb, and my bio. When I was ready, I met my new editor for lunch at a family-run restaurant with delicious authentic Mediterranean food. The vegetarian selections were fabulous, with tabbouleh, falafel and my favorite, a delicate spinach pie with filo dough that melted in my mouth. It was a perfect place to celebrate my modest success.

The tone of our conversation was collegial, as befits the beginning of a long, creative collaboration. When it was time to pay, she insisted on picking up the tab. "I'm your editor, now," she said.

The following week she emailed her feedback about the proposal. But her original suggestion had morphed from "write your big ideas" to some combination of motivational writing and simple beginner's instructions. This new direction seemed vague at best. I couldn't get a clear image of where she was leading me.

I had heard many stories about the intricate dance between writers and editors, so I set aside my ego and decided I would go wherever she led. I asked her a few questions to guide my revisions.

I sent her my modified proposal, expecting another appointment or phone call in which we could discuss the next step. If I was lucky, I might even get another free lunch.

After waiting a few weeks, I called to ask what she thought. She said she hadn't heard back from her partner. After a couple more weeks of silence, she stopped returning my emails. If something had gone wrong with their new endeavor, I had to figure it out on my own. Another grand attempt at finding my way into the publishing world simply faded away.

And yet… her initial suggestion, "maybe you should write your big ideas" was like a spark landing in tinder. Inspired by her interest in those ideas, I was already on my way to writing another book.

Human University

Ever since starting my blog in 2007, I had become a voracious memoir reader. Scanning titles and cover blurbs at the bookstore, I selected any that caught my attention. These authors, who had come from every conceivable walk of life, shared one thing in common: They had all exerted extraordinary effort to turn a portion of their lives into a book-length story.

By this point I'd read hundreds of memoirs, interviewed many of their authors, and then posted my observations on my blog. I was becoming an expert not only in a literary genre, but also in a way of seeing the human condition.

Now I had to consolidate my ideas into a book. Chapter by chapter, I aimed to show how our culture had ripped off the veil of secrecy and ushered in a new level of mutual understanding.

One of the earliest examples of this new genre was the mid-nineties smash hit, *Angela's Ashes* by Frank McCourt. By the time I started paying attention in the early aughts, bookstores had already expanded their memoir shelves to make room for a slew of new books about ordinary people.

Many of the first wave of memoirs were about the coming-of-age period of life. Soon, memoirs encompassed other important challenges, such as grieving, immigration, and navigating through addiction.

The life challenge that had always interested me was "launching" when kids have to leave the shelter of their parents' home. During my launching period, my little ship faced a mighty storm, taking on water and struggling to remain upright in the turbulence of the Vietnam War protests, the counterculture, and my own psychological foibles.

I'd always thought my chaotic transition was extreme, but in memoirs, I learned that many people had to go through hell to reach adulthood. It was reassuring to know I wasn't the only one. As I had felt so many times during my exploration of memoirs, reading about other people made me feel less alone.

One of the most gripping transitions from child to adult I had ever read was *Infidel* by Ayaan Hirsi Ali, a Black African Muslim woman. She was promised as a child bride to an older relative. Instead of submitting to the plan, she fled to Europe, where generous immigration policies helped her establish a new life. As she adapted to her new home, she fell in love with Western ways of thinking. One of the most revolutionary features of the book for me was that the main character was female.

Up until I began to read memoirs, almost all the books I'd read in my life had been written from a male-centric point of view. As a result, I'd maintained a stunning level of ignorance about what it felt like to be a woman.

My first hint that I might be able to tune into the feminine half of the world came from a scene in Jancee Dunn's memoir, *But Enough about Me*. The author and her younger sister were primping their hair and trading insults about who looked better. I found myself in a private, gender-specific moment I'd never expected to visualize.

Next was a book by Brooke Shields, a star who had intrigued me ever since I spotted her eating in a small restaurant in Princeton, New Jersey. The illusion of knowing her was part of the strange magic of celebrity, but of course in reality the encounter offered no more insight than a photo in a magazine.

By contrast, her memoir, *Down Came the Rain*, was surprisingly open about the vulnerable experience of postpartum depression. By the end of the book, I had witnessed the deep conflicts and longings of a new mother.

In fact, a whole range of emotional situations affected women with far greater intensity than I had ever imagined in my math-drenched male mind. Through memoirs, I felt the vulnerability of a woman who had lost a husband and another who had to care for a disabled one. I felt the shame of being raped and the terror of being stalked. I felt the gut-wrenching, mind-numbing agony of losing a child.

Memoir after memoir acclimated me to the inner worlds of people whose experiences and resulting perspectives differed from mine. And all of this intimate, authentic connection had been made possible by the rise of what at first looked like a literary fad. This was big. I was living through another cultural shift.

I imagined what Joseph Campbell must have felt, gathering myths from all over the world, and then fitting the pieces together into a universal framework. In my own small way, I was doing something similar, gathering memoirs, absorbing each one, and trying to identify the universal characteristics that tied them all together.

The twenty-first century had given birth to a new way of looking at ourselves and one another. Rather than telling stories about gods on mountains, we writers were sharing the stories of our own lives.

The memoir genre had taken me on a grand tour of the courage of being human. I was eager to show how these accounts of climbing to higher versions of ourselves could inspire us all to feel more connected and respectful of one another.

Do-it-yourself sociology

As my book about the trend to write memoirs neared completion, I found myself struggling with some of the same dilemmas I faced when I published my first book. I needed to convey to potential readers what sort of information I was attempting to communicate.

One of the basic rules of book marketing that Jonathan had taught us was that in order to sell a nonfiction book, you need to go to the bookstore and see where it would fit. The answer to this seemingly simple question wasn't obvious.

Since it wasn't a how-to book, it didn't belong in the writing section. And it wasn't a memoir, so it didn't belong on that shelf either. As I methodically ticked off the possibilities, I came across a section called "sociology."

Even in high school, I had been fascinated by cultural trends that swept through entire populations. So in my very first semester in college, in the summer of 1965, I took a course called Sociology 102 about social problems.

The professor taught us about the concept of "anomie"–a fancy word that means that the social order has broken down. To illustrate this condition, he played us a chilling song called *Pirate Jenny*, in which Nina Simone cries out about the horrors of rich versus poor, white versus Black.

Shaken by the song's murderous fury, I stepped outside. On a lovely summer day, on the sleepy college campus, a dozen young people walked in a circle, carrying picket signs. It was the first war protest I'd ever seen. That prophetic encounter would soon blossom into a breakdown in social values that would dominate my life for the next six years.

Back then, I was hardly in a position to make sense of all the historical forces that had been tearing my life apart. Trying to grow up while our culture was undergoing a sea change had been a bewildering experience, and for many years afterward, I tried to forget all about it. Living through that cultural shift had been like bobbing aimlessly on a raft in stormy seas.

Now, decades later, the memoir genre offered another cultural shift, but I was older now and the rise of the memoir genre was anything but chaotic. On the contrary, while my generation in the sixties had been determined to tear things apart, memoir writers fifty years later were trying to build orderly stories out of the rubble of disorganized memories.

To learn what sort of book succeeds on the sociology shelf, I read the bestseller *Bowling Alone* by Robert Putnam. In it, the author observed that communities were more fragmented than ever because people didn't join as many groups as they used to.

If I was going to seek a traditional publisher, I would tell them my book announces an antidote to Putnam's gloomy picture. Whereas *Bowling Alone* warned about the collapse of social groups, my book, the *Memoir Revolution* offered a way to bring people back together.

Even though I felt confident that my book belonged in the sociology section, I was afraid such a placement didn't offer much visibility. The section itself was tiny. Until I looked for it, I didn't even know it existed. Another problem was even more concerning. In the few years since Jonathan had given his advice, bookstores had suffered the same fate as bowling leagues. I doubted my book would ever find a place in the shrinking shelf space of brick-and-mortar stores.

The fading potential for selling in a bookstore made me more confident than ever that self-publishing was the right choice for me. With online publishing, I could immediately make my book available anywhere. And learning the new publishing technologies would give me an opportunity to participate in the "social tsunami" that I and my writing friends had anticipated just a few years earlier.

With the new methods, anyone could turn their memories into a memoir. All they had to do was write a good book and publish it. They didn't need to send endless query letters, land an agent, and then hope for some big publisher who was willing to rescue their particular story from among the growing river of memoirs by ordinary people.

However, self-publishing had its own challenges. Every single detail fell on my own shoulders. Yet thanks to my relentless willingness to network and experiment with various resources, solutions came together.

I found an editor who offered me the kind of support and direction I needed. I designed the interior of the book myself, thanks to many years of experience working with technical writing. A freelance artist in Poland created my book cover. At last, I was ready. I pushed the button and there it was in 2013. *Memoir Revolution* was available to the public.

It all required courage

I'd hoped that visitors to my blog would snap up copies of my book. But frequent visits to the sales dashboard showed little activity. I complained to a fellow writer about my lack of sales and she asked, "How did you launch it?"

"I didn't really launch it. I just added some links on my blog," I said, self-consciously.

She furrowed her brow. "People don't buy books after seeing a link. You need to find a way to make a splash. Let them know that this is a big deal."

She was calling my attention to the same challenge I had been confronting since I decided to escape my computer cubicle. To sell my services, I needed to shout from the rooftops. But I didn't like rooftops, and I wasn't much of a shouter.

Over the years, I'd kept my social anxiety at bay by avoiding public exposure. And yet, that avoidance was blocking me from the very things I was trying to achieve. I felt trapped.

I knew a lot about being afraid of people's responses. I'd faced and overcome many such problems when I'd figured out how to become a therapist, a speaker, and a writer. I hoped I could apply some of the same strategies to help me sell books. And I knew where to go for a refresher course: my first book.

As I flipped through the book, I felt pretty good about what I was reading. These were good, effective strategies and I was proud of the work I'd done to collect them and make them available. Unfortunately, the more I enjoyed the book, the worse I felt about its limited availability. Back when I first published it, Internet distribution systems had not yet become practical. So the book was only available to people who came to my workshops.

Now that the Internet had blown up the publishing world, I dreamt of revisiting that first self-help book to make it more widely available. Of course by focusing on the self-help book, I was avoiding the challenges of selling *Memoir Revolution*. But writing and revising were so much more interesting than selling. I couldn't resist the temptation.

When reissuing the book, I wanted to include a lesson I'd learned from my study of memoirs. The main character or "hero" reached a satisfying conclusion to the story by exerting effort, overcoming obstacles, and reaching a higher version of themselves. I wanted to turn that observation into a self-help technique, encouraging writers to follow the noble upward arc of a hero.

As I continued to modify and update the self-help book, I worried that the original title, *Four Elements for Writers,* was too numerical. I wanted to grow past my hang-up on logic and analysis. Ultimately, I renamed it *How to Become a Heroic Writer.* Embedded in the title was my growing belief that by seeing yourself as a hero, you become one.

To graphically highlight the new emphasis on the indomitable spirit and perseverance of the writer, I reached out to the same Polish artist who designed the cover for *Memoir Revolution*. He modified the image of the protestors that we used on the previous cover, replacing it instead with marathon runners.

When I clicked send, my self-help book instantly became available all over the world. Despite my satisfaction with this achievement, and my pride in having two books, I recognized an irony. I still had not created a splash. No launch meant no sales.

The two publications encouraged writers to be brave. But I had not yet worked up the nerve to follow my own advice. I still preferred to stay hidden. I hadn't even published my own life story yet.

My scary next chapter, 2015

Despite my eroding interest in my computer job, going to work every day had been woven so tightly into the fabric of my daily responsibilities, it never occurred to me that it could end. So when a shuffle of job descriptions meant my time had come, I suddenly found myself in the freefall called retirement.

The notion of retirement had always scared me. Even though I was almost seventy, the word "retire" sounded all wrong. I didn't want to withdraw. I needed to stay active. Do productive things. Make some sort of difference.

I walked out of the building carrying a cardboard box into which I'd thrown a few books and a photo of my wife, the only things worth salvaging from my sparsely furnished cubicle. After depositing the box in my car, I looked around the parking lot in a daze. What would I do to stay busy?

That weekend, I had a long conversation with my wife. She still had several years of work ahead of her, and I worried about the fact that she'd be going off to work each morning while I would still be sitting at my writing desk. She was happy for me, congratulating me for the end of my career. According to her it was a well-earned completion of a lifetime of work.

I bristled.

"You don't understand. Even with all my hobbies, pursuits, and plans, losing that predictable anchor each day is going to be a hardship."

"No," she said. "Going to work was the hardship. You have achieved that wonderful perpetual break that comes at the end of a career."

"I don't see it as a break. Too much spare time scares me. You know how I thrive when I'm immersed in a project."

"Suit yourself," she said. "When I can escape the working world, I will consider it a happy day."

"I doubt it."

One thing we did agree on was that I would expand my range of chores to keep the household running and lift a variety of burdens off her shoulders. And as much as possible, any additional activities I engaged in would be during the weekday hours when she was at work.

And so, together we began a new chapter of our lives: one of us heading off to work each morning, and the other worried about how to fill the stretch of hours ahead.

Surviving without a plan

I woke up at five a.m. each day and wrote for several hours. I went to the gym at lunch, as I'd been doing for years. In the evening. my wife and I enjoyed each other's company.

But when not engaged in these familiar routines, I felt lost at sea, no rudders, no oars, no compass. I could feel my lack of purpose in my bones.

No longer did I know where I would be every day and who I'd be with. Every minute was up to me. The responsibility to fill my days weighed heavily.

I had always been the food shopper and errand runner of the family. Now I could shop during my boring afternoons. But when I searched through the fruit bins for the freshest items, I felt embarrassment that bordered on shame. *Look at that man,* I imagined them thinking. *He should be at work. What is he doing out here just walking around free?*

I recalled the way Toastmasters had stirred me to excel. I thought I'd give it another try. Arriving early, I recognized a few faces amid many new ones. When the meeting started, with its ritual gavel bang and the command to "Come to order," I snapped to attention.

A few sessions later, I delivered my first speech, riding on a wave of anxiety — good anxiety, associated not with fear of disapproval, but with the desire to do my best.

Just as I anticipated, the person offering feedback praised me for delivering the talk without notes. To my delight, he was also impressed by my ability to share anecdotes about myself. Telling stories about my life had become simple, after all these years of tending my memoir manuscript. It felt good to reap a reward from all that work.

As before, though, I also heard the familiar complaint that I seemed a little stiff, a problem I'd never been able to shake. Even though I felt discouraged by someone pointing out what appeared to be my unfixable problem, I wasn't devastated by it. I had come to accept such criticisms as well-intended pointers. I held out a tiny hope, far in the future, when perhaps I might sound more interesting.

The meetings were invigorating, and giving talks fulfilled my craving to do something creative. But they only occupied a few hours a month. I still didn't know where I was going. My only clear goal was to finish my memoir. At the rate I was going, I was afraid that might take forever.

I needed more structure, more emphasis on achieving things. And I wasn't even clear what those "things" might be.

To help me focus, I posted a request on a local forum, asking if anyone wanted to form an accountability group. Such a group would provide an opportunity for us to declare goals and then hold one another accountable for achieving them. Two women responded.

Mary had been in my memoir group a few years earlier and wanted to complete her project.

Gina was a gift from the universe. In addition to being kind, and listening attentively, she possessed a keen intuition about how to connect with people on the Internet. I hoped some of her enthusiasm and faith in the bounty of social media would rub off on me.

The three of us met weekly at a nearby restaurant, using our time together to report our progress and urge one another onward. The meetings were enjoyable, and helped raise awareness about setting and achieving goals. But they only filled two interesting hours each week. On any afternoon when I had no meeting, I felt disengaged and deflated, my motivation just a distant memory.

I tried defeating the doldrums by taking my laptop to a café. The languid comings and goings of the afternoon patrons barely changed my mood. We shared a room, but not a purpose.

While looking for new places to hang out, I learned about a coworking site. For a fee, I could sit at a desk and be around other people in a working environment. It was like having a job, but instead of receiving a paycheck, I would be paying them.

I gave it a try, hoping to sit together with others who, like me, needed to get out of the house. I wasn't sure what I was looking for—perhaps a chat at the water cooler, or a knowing nod from a peer in a situation similar to my own. None of these things materialized. The few people who straggled into the office seemed to be floundering to find their own agendas. Clearly, I had not yet figured out how to survive in this new chapter in my life.

Filling empty days

On my drive into town one afternoon, I noticed a sign in front of a geriatric center: "Volunteers Wanted." Now that I had so many free hours, volunteering sounded like a great way to spend my time.

I called and made an appointment with the volunteer coordinator. After I explained my passion to help people find their stories, she seemed receptive and warm. But instead of responding immediately, she said, "Let's take a walk around the facility."

The building felt modern and clean, with wide, airy hallways and brightly decorated meeting rooms. On our walk, she greeted several of the residents by name, and they smiled at her, as if they were old friends.

My guide thanked one of the residents for playing the piano the previous night. The woman smiled and said, "I did that?" She sheepishly added, "I can't remember anything these days."

After punching a code to enter the more restrictive memory care unit, we entered a large room where residents wandered individually, or sat in chairs. Most of them looked bewildered.

When we returned to her office, she said, "I really appreciate your interest. But I don't believe our residents would be able to take advantage of the kind of program you are suggesting."

After a pause she brightened.

"There was a volunteer once who sat next to one resident at a time. She interviewed them and typed up notes about their lives."

"My passion is to teach people how to pull together their reminiscences into a story."

"I'm so sorry," she said. "As you saw, that won't work here."

Around this time, I received an email from a librarian who remembered me from a talk I gave a few years earlier. She wanted to know if I would lead a memoir group at her library. The relief and joy I felt when reading this invitation provided an insight into my father's later years.

My mother once told me that after my dad retired, one of his greatest pleasures was to work part time at a drugstore. Because of the law that a licensed pharmacist must be on the premises at all times, some of the local family-owned businesses relied on free agents like my dad to fill in for them when they wanted to go on vacation. I pictured Dad sitting around, wondering what he should do, and then feeling a surge of purpose and duty when the call came in. Now it was my turn to feel energized by a call.

The librarian displayed posters for the group, and several people showed up at the inaugural meeting. These were people who, like me, needed daytime activities. When they began to share their stories, I felt like I was exactly where I wanted to be. After the feast of shared stories, we all smiled and chatted, lifted by a glow of connection and warmth.

I committed to doing this group once a month. At least I'd found one ray of light illuminating the otherwise bleak prospect of empty days. And every semester I still taught my brief course at the community college. I wanted more.

Since the very beginning of my experience as a blogger, I'd met memoir writers online. One of them, Linda Joy Myers, had started an organization to support this work, the *National Association of Memoir Writers*. She occasionally invited me to speak to her members, giving me another opportunity to share my passion for life writing.

One day, my sister sent me an article she'd clipped from the *New York Times* about a writing system called "guided autobiography." Since it had some relationship to memoir writing, I looked into it further.

Guided Autobiography (GAB) had been developed by Jim Birren, the founder of the Gerontology Department at the University of Southern California (USC). From what I could gather, the GAB program used life writing as an antidote to isolation. It sounded like a perfect line of inquiry for me.

Out of curiosity, I looked into the gerontology program at USC and discovered that the university offered a distance learning option, but the total cost took my breath away. Fortunately, Cheryl Svensson, one of Jim Birren's first students, offered a certification program in the GAB method at a much more affordable cost. I signed up.

During the training, all of us wrote and shared personal theme-based essays. Our goal was not to produce publishable pieces, but rather to discover the empathy and insight that could be inspired through shared writing.

Learning GAB put me in touch with an international tribe of teachers intent on using lifestory writing to bring people together into a higher awareness of self and others. Even though the system had been developed in the gerontology department, people of any age could benefit.

I thought back to a book I'd read, *Bowling Alone* by Robert Putnam, which warned of the growing isolation of modern culture. I'd certainly feared loneliness when I first stepped out of the office during daylight. Now, thanks to the pervasive influence of life writing, it was beginning to look like memoirs would turn my retirement years into a source of creative joy, self-expression and fellowship.

Therapy for retirement?

Adjusting to retirement proved to be a massive shift in every aspect of my self-image. I didn't want to negotiate this transition alone. It was time to find a new therapist. Each one I'd met over the years had offered a slightly different approach, and I couldn't wait to meet my next one, whoever they might be.

One likely candidate was a woman I'd met in one of my memoir classes several years earlier. When she introduced herself to the class, she told us about her doctorate in psychology and her special interest in life cycle stages. Since she was about my age, she certainly would have a few thoughts about life after retirement. I called her and set up an appointment.

At our first meeting, I told her how desperate I was to stay engaged with my life. Amy said, "You're at an age when many people are thinking about taking it easy."

"Never," I said. "Taking it easy is the enemy. I want new challenges. I need a sense of purpose and community; I want to keep writing about memoirs. I want to increase my teaching and public speaking opportunities."

"Okay, okay," she laughed. "My goal is not to slow you down. I just want you to be sure you feel good about what you do. How will you ever be content?"

"That's a good question. I have to admit I do make myself miserable at times, because I never actually reach a place of contentment. I mainly just want to stay busy doing something meaningful."

"There's something I'd like to show you that might help with your dilemma. In fact, you've already seen it. Remember that deck of cards I showed everyone at that memoir class you were teaching?"

"You are the only student in any of my classes who ever brought in something for 'show and tell'" I said, laughing. "So yes, I do remember. But I was preoccupied with getting through the introductions, so I confess I didn't completely grasp what you were demonstrating."

"It is called SoulCollage©, and is a method of finding inner wisdom," she said. "I think it could help you decipher these pushes and pulls. Here are a few of the cards I've made for myself." She handed me a stack of cards on which a pastiche of images had been cut and pasted.

I told her the cards reminded me of the Tarot, which had entered my life forty years earlier. "We viewed the Tarot cards as a visual vocabulary to help us talk about the spiritual journey."

"I like the way you put it," she said. "A visual vocabulary. And while it's true that some people use SoulCollage for spiritual insight, my main interest is in its application to therapy. Let me show you how it works."

We moved to Amy's craft table, where she placed a stack of blank cards and a pile of magazines.

"The premise is that you can foster deeper insights into your inner world by identifying the various parts of yourself. For example, you can make a card for the part of you that's ambitious and the part that's fulfilled. A part that's a teacher and another that's a writer. For each part, try to find suitable images and paste them on cards."

"That's fascinating," I said. "Where should I start?"

"Because we all start as someone's child, I think it would be instructive to represent that part of you that was a son to your father and mother."

I thought about it for a minute. "Hmm. That's really hard. I'd never thought about myself as a son."

"Exactly," she said. "Look through the magazines for an image in an article or even an ad that evokes that feeling of being a son. It's a kind of visual brainstorming that helps you peer into the unconscious."

"I've seen methods of visual brainstorming in creativity workshops, but this is the first time I've used it to find parts of myself." I was eager to get started.

After perusing a half a dozen magazines, I felt attracted to a photo of an exuberant little boy. Even though I didn't remember feeling as playful as the little guy in the picture, it comforted me to see a child so full of life. Was that really part of me? That little boy's joy made me feel happy. It was an auspicious start. I wanted to know more about this method.

"Perhaps before you come in next time, you could find a few more images for some of the parts we've talked about."

"I don't have any magazines at home," I said.

"You can borrow some of mine. I have a million."

"No thanks," I said, imagining my wife's face if she saw me walking into the house with a stack of magazines. "I already have too many books and papers strewn everywhere."

"Ha ha," Amy laughed. "If you'd like to learn more about those messy habits, we could talk to the part of you in charge of cleaning up."

I sighed. "Another lifelong issue I'd like to resolve. Let's put it on the list."

"But, seriously," she said, "if you'd rather not use magazines, you can also find images on the Internet. Just print them and cut them out."

The next morning, at home, I created a computer file and thought about the various parts I'd discussed with Amy. I was warming to the idea of identifying my inner cast of characters. One that kept nagging at me, begging for better understanding was the part that needed to reach out to the public.

One reason my therapy practice had fallen apart years earlier was my reluctance to let people know I wanted to offer them a service. Similarly, these days, when I thought about selling books or getting students to come to classes, I found myself actively hating the need for publicity.

I'd been asking myself for years to please lighten up and do the perfectly normal process of letting people know about my events and services, but with little success. Now that I was no longer going to an office every day, my old tendency to shrink back into myself would be deadly. If I gave in to my preference for sitting at home waiting for people to come to me, I'd become bored, and boredom was a gateway to depression.

One of the best things I could do for myself at this period in my life would be to overcome my reluctance to reach out to others. But after years of trying, I'd never been able to break through. Perhaps attempting this method of having discussions among parts of myself would give me better results.

After typing keywords into the Internet search engine, I scanned various images of slick salesmen. That wasn't quite right. Then I stumbled on the picture of a man standing on a soap box screaming at a crowd through a hand-held bullhorn. He looked so aggressive, as though he was a circus carny trying to get people to come inside. I hated the image. But it perfectly represented the impression I'd had of my inner marketer.

Now I just had to create a card. But Amy's suggestion of printing the image, cutting it out, and pasting it onto card stock sounded like too much work and clutter. Instead, I just copied it electronically and pasted it into my word processing file.

I knew that keeping my images in a computer file would provide less tactile sensation than holding cards. But since I was already struggling to declutter my office, I thought that my electronic method would be a useful compromise. I hoped Amy would agree with my plan.

Conversing with my inner self

The next time I went to see Amy, I showed her how I had modified her approach. Instead of magazine photos on a physical card, I'd started a computer file with electronic images. "Sure." she said. "If that works better for you."

"Okay. Cool. What do you think about the guy shouting through a bullhorn?"

"This doesn't look like a part of yourself you're in love with."

"Ugh," I said. "I hate this part."

"Hating part of yourself is a good recipe for discomfort," Amy said. "So let's think further about your relationship to this part of yourself."

"How would I do that?"

"Now that you have a visual representation for this guy, you can have a conversation with him."

"Help me understand something," I said, beginning to worry about the direction this was all heading. "I've been working for years to feel more integrated. Now you're telling me to get in touch with parts. Doesn't that run the risk of creating deeper splits?"

"On the contrary," she said. "The parts already exert influence. By inviting them to express what they want, and then listening with respect and curiosity, you can enhance your self-understanding."

I tried to think of any similar system.

"Ahh," I said finally. "I recall learning something like this in a psychodrama workshop, when we imagined speaking with parts of ourselves. And I've heard of something similar in that empty chair technique in Gestalt therapy. Is it anything like that?"

"Yes, externalizing parts of yourself in order to understand your inner world has been around for a while. This method I'm proposing uses writing rather than acting. I've adapted it from Ira Progoff's work. He was one of the real innovators in the field of journal writing."

"Progoff?" I said trailing off into the familiar dreamy state that sometimes washed over me when I thought of all I wanted to learn.

"I can boil it down," Amy said. "For each part, ask these three questions: Who are you? What do you want from me? And what do you offer me? After you pose each question, listen with an inner ear, and imagine how that part might answer."

I closed my eyes and eagerly asked the guy with the bullhorn what he wanted.

"Are you stupid?" I heard him say. "I have to grab people's attention and pull them in. Any moron could see that."

I quickly opened my eyes and told Amy what I'd heard. "What a snarky attitude. And he's so pushy. This is not a very nice part of myself. He's a jerk."

"This is where the method becomes therapeutic," Amy said. "By interacting with these parts, you can discover what they want and find ways to reduce the inner tension."

"This is great, Amy."

"Since you're having such a good time, add some extra credit. See if you can detect a part of yourself that dislikes this marketing part."

I winced. "To see what I don't like about my marketer self, I should conjure up yet another part? Really? I hope I'm not going to get lost in these inner characters."

"Becoming more aware of these inner battles will help you figure out how to bring the sides together into a healthy alliance," she reassured me.

During my morning writing session, I tried to picture the part of me who hated the marketing guy. The image that emerged was a cartoon-like drawing of a bully with clenched fists and a face distorted with rage. I'd stumbled on yet another unattractive part of myself.

When I asked him what he wanted, he responded, "You're no good. You're stupid. No one could possibly love you. You're going to get hurt." He couldn't say enough about all my faults. I couldn't tell if he was talking about me or about my attempt to conduct marketing activities. In any case, I had to forcefully pry myself away from the imagined tirade.

"No wonder I hate selling things," I told Amy at my next session. "Every time I try, I'm terrified, not just of other people, but of this internal bully. Now what?"

"Try to continue the conversation. For example, you could ask additional questions, or offer suggestions and listen to the response."

At home, I tried to get these two parts to reconcile their antagonistic positions, but each one seemed too deeply invested in his own combative stance. So, I set the puzzle aside to work on my other writing projects. Then I went to the gym, ran a few errands, ate dinner, watched television with Janet, and fell asleep.

The next morning, I woke with an entirely different image of being a sales person. I saw myself as a teenager working at my dad's drugstore. Customers walked into the store, picked out items they needed, and handed me money. When they couldn't find what they were looking for, I came out from behind the counter to show them where to look. I knew where everything was, because I was the one who stocked shelves, checked inventory, and even dusted and straightened out the rows. In those rare cases when I didn't know an answer, I could just ask Dad.

When a customer asked for help, I never felt overwhelmed, conflicted, or confused. I was the helper, and I was proud of my service.

At my next session with Amy, I said, "This is a radical departure from everything I thought I knew about my teenage years. Until this moment, I always remembered myself in a classroom or alone in my room, always desperate to prove I was smart. But in this memory in the drugstore... it's all different. I see myself as a decent, hardworking, competent, generous, balanced young man, as if I'm exactly who and where I'm supposed to be."

Amid the anxieties and pressures of my years in high school, I'd completely forgotten that sensation of self-confidence. Now that I'd uncovered this hidden treasure, I wondered how to apply it to the present. Perhaps, instead of worrying about marketing myself, I could concentrate on stocking shelves and serving customers. This was the peaceful path my dad taught me as a young man.

As a therapist, a memoir coach, a teacher, or an author, I pictured myself standing at the counter, waiting for someone to ask for help. Since they knew what they wanted, and I'd spent years stocking the shelves with an ample supply of insights and resources, I could confidently direct them to the place within themselves where they could find that precious sense of purpose, calm, or clarity they had been missing.

What comes after midlife?

By this time in my retirement, my morning routine had expanded into a richly-rewarding work session.

Revise chapters in my own evolving memoir.

Check.

Revise a few essays about memoirs for my blog.

Check.

Review dialogs among my inner parts to discuss in my next therapy session.

Check.

After lunch, I went to the gym. Propping my three-ring binder on the reading stand of the treadmill, I pulled out my pen and started the machine. The rhythm of a brisk walk helped me kickstart my brain, so I could coax another hour of reading, reviewing, and revising out of the day.

By midafternoon, I stopped writing and turned my attention to reading a memoir. As I settled into the familiar sensation of immersing myself in the author's situation, a passage caught my attention. She had joined a group, but she was afraid there were cliques of women who didn't like her. Her upset thoughts about not being included in their conversation felt eerily familiar. I'd thought this way many times.

I'd always enjoyed this sensation of eavesdropping on a character's thought process. Now, in light of my recent therapy, I tried interpreting this inner dialog as an argument among her parts. One part wanted to be included in the group while another part felt rejected.

This dynamic tension between acceptance and rejection perfectly portrayed the workings of her social anxiety. And by allowing me to witness her inner process, she'd made me more aware of my own.

I was thrilled that my study of the memoir genre kept overlapping with what I was learning from therapy. Taken together, the two approaches continued to teach me about how people think.

Throughout history, every new instrument of detection had given birth to new insights. The telescope opened our eyes to celestial objects. The microscope opened our eyes to tiny ones. Medical imaging showed us the inner workings of the body. And now the popularization of memoirs had opened up a vast literary conversation about the inner workings of the mind.

When I told Amy how much I'd been learning about the relationship between memoirs and therapy she grew excited. "That's a great insight, Jerry."

As we talked more about the implications of this observation, she added, "You know, there's another way that parts-of-self relate to the memoir genre. Since our parts change over time, in a sense, each part could write a memoir about itself."

I was intrigued. I'd been picturing each SoulCollage image as though it was frozen in time. Amy's suggestion that each part spread across the lifespan added a rich dimension.

"Okay, I can see how I might write about the evolution of each part. That would be a cool writing exercise. But I don't see how you would use the cards to represent change over time."

Amy grabbed her deck off the shelf, riffled through the cards, and selected two.

"Both of these cards represent my therapist part, one before my fifties, and the other after."

I viewed the two cards, side by side. "Tell me more about the transition. What happened?"

"After I had been working as a therapist for many years, I no longer felt fulfilled," she said, pointing to the card on the left. "Discovering the SoulCollage system of cards and images gave my therapist part a fresh approach." She pointed to the card on the right.

After leaving Amy's office I reflected on her need for renewal. Was she exhibiting the symptoms of the condition called midlife crisis? All I knew about that transition could be captured in the caricature of a guy who drove a red convertible sports car in order to assert his youthful vigor.

But Amy's course-correction didn't fit that stereotype. Rather than craving the veneer of youthful, sexual potency, she'd intensified her commitment to a creative, service-oriented vigor. I too had lurched when I reached fifty and decided to go to grad school. And like Amy, instead of trying to go backward, I planned on an overhaul that would move me forward into a new chapter of my life.

I wondered if this impulse to reinvent one's self at fifty was widespread, but when I scanned my reading list, I could find only one that directly tackled this topic. In his memoir *Accidental Lessons*, David Berner described a period in his life when, similar to me and Amy, he needed to make a fresh start.

But when I shifted my focus from the content of the memoir to the age of the author, I found a motherlode of midlife questioning. Many of the coming-of-age books were by authors later in life trying to make sense of their earlier lives. That was certainly true for me.

Such memoir writers had found a way to flex their own expressive writing muscles. Even if their work never made it to the bookshelf, they'd clearly been attracted by the same sense of creative renewal as I had.

One question lingered. How long would this creative urge last? I hoped the answer was "forever." I was having so much fun in my exploration of the human drama that I hoped it never ended.

Ready to become a drop in the river

For years, I'd converted the heartaches and false-starts of my youth into written pieces. Each segment had benefitted from the suggestions and thought-provoking questions offered by my critique partners. But to link these fragments into a story, I needed more sophisticated feedback.

I remembered the first time I'd hired an editor. A woman in one of my groups had more professional experience than the others, so I asked if she would review an early draft of my manuscript.

When she gave me back the marked-up manuscript, I realized why she charged me so much money. On every page, she'd suggested changes in word choice and phrasing. I brushed past all of those details. I just needed to know if it was a good story.

She thought about it for a minute, and then said the story arc was too long and covered too much ground. Her comment forced me to take another look at the overall scope of the book.

As I originally conceived my memoir, it started during the war protests when, instead of growing up, I was falling apart. In that first model of my story, the rest of the book would explain my lifelong effort to repair the problems that had resulted from that bad start.

But describing the entire journey violated one of the basic rules of the genre. "Don't write about your whole life in one book. That's an autobiography. Write about one period or one specific character arc."

This suggestion sounded right to me. One of my favorite things about reading a good book was the sense of blasting through obstacles toward some intense conclusion. Now, as a writer, I had to offer that same compelling forward momentum to my own readers.

I sketched out stories across various periods of my life and tried to imagine how each one would feel. Finally I decided the best character arc for this first memoir would start from childhood and end when I reached the foothills of young adulthood. Within this more focused timeline, I was able to delve more deeply into the great puzzle of my early life. How had I grown up so ambitiously, fallen apart so pathetically, and regained my footing all in the space of ten years? From the emerging story, it became obvious that coming of age in the late sixties was like trying to thread a needle while rafting down whitewater rapids.

After crafting this segment of my life into a book-length story, I reached out to find yet another reader. A guy from a local fiction writing group generously offered to review this new version for free. Since he didn't know much about memoirs, I wasn't sure if his input would help. In the end, I figured if a fiction writer liked the story, it would be a good litmus test. When he got back to me, I found his feedback to be sensitive and sophisticated.

I asked him if he thought it was ready for publication, he said, "Yes, if you answer one question. What did you learn from your trip to India?"

"How could he not see why I needed to make that trip?" I thought. But instead of quibbling with him, I attempted to understand what he meant. His comment reinforced one of the fundamental tenets of memoir writing. "Be sure readers understand why the events were important to you."

I rewrote the description of my taxi ride from the ashram to the Delhi airport, attempting to evoke what had changed within me during my three months in India. Answering this question added some wonderful depth to the chapter and, in turn, increased the impact of the whole story.

Despite this green light, I still felt vulnerable and incomplete. I longed for one more sign from the cosmos that publishing it was the right thing to do.

Around this time, I attended the Philadelphia Writers Conference, which I had been attending every June for years. One of the speakers at that year's conference published a small literary journal. There was something so "South Philly" about him, I felt his feedback would add valuable regional insight.

We met at 30th Street Station, a Philadelphia landmark only a few blocks away from the University of Pennsylvania. As I stepped off the train, I was assailed by haunting images of my youth, when I used to walk around this part of town, alone, on weekends, imagining the city when it was still just a rustic outpost of the British empire.

Ben Franklin, one of my childhood heroes, had helped transform the city into one of the birthplaces of North American culture. In addition to creating the first public library in the colonies, he was also the father of the University of Pennsylvania. Hundreds of years later, I'd benefitted from his hard work and brilliant mind.

When I spotted my editor wheeling his bike through the busy terminal, I snapped out of my reverie with a laugh. How easily these old buildings carried me back, as if reminding me of things I'd never seen. After a few pleasantries, we sat down, he placed his helmet on the table, and we got right to business.

"Was it a good story?" I asked.

"If you want commercial success, you need to bring readers into the action as close to page one as possible."

I'd heard that advice before, and it always made me wonder how to also insert enough backstory so readers could feel engaged in the early scenes. Hoping he could guide me through these seemingly conflicting requirements, I asked him, "When do you think my story should start?" Instead of answering, he reflected the question back. I was the one who had to decide.

I thought back to my bar mitzvah, the Jewish rite at age thirteen when I announced my entry into adulthood. Instead of pride, I felt smothered by my fears of being seen. Losing my nerve at the threshold of my adult life seemed like a good beginning for a story about a character in search of his true identity.

That raised another problem. Those fears had never completely disappeared. When I imagined announcing myself as a Jewish man, some ancient warning, hidden deep in my bones, counseled me to be silent.

To grow as a person, I needed to push past these fears and just be myself. And I was born at a good time for being outspoken about my identity. All kinds of people had been breaking out of their silence.

Blacks, abused women, gays, indigenous peoples, and immigrants from every part of the world were proclaiming that the time for shame was over. Their strident voices turned public discourse into a sometimes-noisy affair, but they all had one thing in common: They were determined to break down walls and assert their right to speak up, to proudly be themselves.

The laws that protected their right to be different had been crafted just a few miles from where I sat. In this city, the founders of the new nation had established each person's right to worship God in their own way. And one of the things I felt was so important about those idealistic folks was their love for books.

Instead of each generation needing to learn everything from scratch, books enabled us to build our senses of self on the shoulders of those who came before. Publishing my book would honor that tradition, allowing me to contribute my own life experience to the river of humanity as it flowed from the past, through the present, into the future.

"You can hide yours," my Black classmate had said. But I was tired of hiding. How could I honestly love other people if I couldn't also imagine them loving me back? Finally, I was prepared to come out of hiding. A full-circle moment.

I had no more excuses. It was time. The next day I finalized the forms, uploaded the files, and with one click of a button, sent my first memoir out into the world.

Was teaching enough?

Publishing my memoir satisfied my desire to contribute to the new and improved version of civilization which honored every single member. As for sales, my new book hardly made a ripple.

I took a philosophical view of this lack of impact. Even though it was only one drop in the river of knowledge, it was an important one. A healthy society requires a continuous flow of such offerings. Just as my intellectual life had been nourished by contributions from previous writers, I wanted to do my part to ensure the sustenance of future readers.

Anyway, I wasn't sure I wanted anyone to read my first memoir yet, since it ended when I'd staggered onto the shore of young adulthood. In order for it to make sense, I needed to write the second part, about how I'd forged a new life out of the wreckage.

Even though I hadn't promoted my coming-of-age memoir, I'd never stopped looking for places to speak or teach. In front of a room, I could see my audience instead of imagining them. Speaking to real people stretched my social muscles and provided a happy break from sitting alone at my keyboard.

As if in answer to my receptivity, such an offer did fall into my open arms. During a memoir class I was teaching at the community college, one of my students invited me to audition to speak at an annual event celebrating motherhood.

I'd been in front of plenty of classrooms and writing groups, and I'd read hundreds of short pieces aloud to my fellow writers in tiny critique groups. All these listeners had been intent on learning how to write their own stories. This would be the first time I'd be telling a story to listeners who expected to be entertained. Performance storytelling seemed infinitely more intimidating than teaching.

I had to admit, though, that one of my original motivations for writing a memoir had been to overcome my tendency to hide. This opportunity to deliver a story to a live audience would advance my quest for more visibility. "Another mountain," I sighed. But I had climbed many mountains. Perhaps I could add this one to my list.

I submitted a short piece about my relationship with my mother. A few weeks, later, I was invited to read it to a panel of judges. When it was my turn, three women sat facing me across a long table, like a tribunal. But the reality wasn't nearly as scary as it first appeared. The woman who had invited me was one of the panel members and they were all smiling. When I read my essay, one of the judges cried, then apologized for crying. I thought it was a good sign. In a few days, I learned that I'd been accepted.

Since I would be reading from paper, rather than performing from memory, many of the terrors of public speaking vanished. At the appointed time, delivering my essay to a theater full of families on Mother's Day, I felt great. I'd climbed a little higher up the mountain.

Scaling Mount Everest

My successful reading of my speech at the Mother's Day event, felt only partially satisfying, as though I'd only climbed half-way up the mountain. The real test of my ability would be to master the much more difficult type of storytelling in front of a live audience. Delivering such a talk, complete with drama and the need for a relaxed and engaging sense of stage-presence, seemed entirely beyond my capability.

But that was the whole point of a good challenge. Why bother to do it if it was easy? To see if I could take a step closer to that impossible goal, I enrolled in a weekend workshop at Philadelphia's *First Person Arts* organization. The class was taught by Elna Baker, a memoir author and one of the producers of the radio show *This American Life*. I was excited to be following her lead.

I crafted a story about my journey through the sixties and practiced it at home, over and over, trying to create the drama that would hold an audience's attention. To get feedback, I delivered the talk at Toastmasters. Their suggestions and support gave me the courage to try it out in public.

A bar in Bethlehem offered an open mic for storytellers once a month. The small-town environment seemed safe enough. I steeled my nerves, and went one Wednesday night to see if I could muster the gumption.

The room was packed with people who wanted to hear live storytelling. Apparently, such events had already emerged as a sort of oral extension of the Memoir Revolution. I sat alone, awaiting my turn.

When they called my name, I walked up to the mic, hoping I didn't seem too nervous. After I gave the talk, I returned to my seat, a bit shaken. But I felt I had offered a decent performance. At least I hadn't died.

As my storytelling ambition continued to germinate, an editor of an online group, *The Good Men Project*, announced a night of live storytelling in New York City. The group's mission was to promote dialog about becoming a responsible, emotionally mature man. Considering all the work I had done to find my own authentic emotions, I thought I might have something to contribute.

I submitted an application and was accepted. Game on!

Just as I'd been enchanted by my fantasies of early Philadelphia, I had an equally active imagination about early New York City. The vast majority of Jews who immigrated from Eastern Europe passed through this city. While some ethnic minorities moved out to small towns or farmland, Jews had a long history of thriving in the crush of crowded cities. As a result, many of them made New York their home, while others traveled to the nearby city of Philadelphia, where I was born.

In a gesture to the ethnic relationship between the two cities, my Hebrew graduating class took a bus to New York, where we saw the movie, *Bye Bye Birdie*. Thanks to my ability to completely shrink away from social situations, the only memory that remained from the whole trip was a line from the movie in which a character sang the line "I'm going to be on Ed Sullivan," a popular variety show of the time.

That memory fit perfectly with my current situation. As I arrived in New York on a bus to meet the producers for the first time, I imagined belting out my own version. *I was going to perform in New York.*

Coincidentally, the rehearsal took place in a building a few doors away from where my niece, Caroline, and her husband lived on the Upper West Side. Afterwards I met her for lunch, hoping that she would be impressed by her ambitious uncle. Our encounter unleashed a flurry of feelings about fame, since her aunt was one of the most famous women in the world.

The summer after I graduated high school, I attended my brother's wedding. He was marrying Barbara, a woman he'd met while he was in medical school. During the reception at the bride's house, I sat off by myself, shy, awkward, and, as usual, alone. The bride's sister came over and sat next to me. Her welcoming words and warm smile set me at ease. This was long before Joan Rivers was famous. I didn't even know she was a comedian. But her kindness was all I needed to make me a fan.

During the following years, I ran off into the wilderness, first to shatter my own identity and then to repair it. During this detour, I had hardly any contact with my brother's family. After his early death, the opportunities for social interaction diminished even further. But Joan Rivers was an intriguing member of my family tree, and when I began to study memoirs, I read hers.

Enter Talking described how she'd appeared in countless seedy nightclubs in this very town. Her intimate sharing was similar to the strippers for whom she often was the opening act – she was earning a living by exposing her private parts through jokes.

My goal in following in her footsteps was much more modest. I only wanted to expose myself a little. Perhaps I would enjoy it. Perhaps I would be good at it. Perhaps I would even get a chuckle. But I sensed another motivation lurking under the surface.

Perhaps challenging myself to give this talk had emerged from a desire for a second chance, after the fiasco of my very first public performance: my Bar Mitzvah. During that ritual, I was so nervous I could barely see the squiggles on the scroll, much less read them. The Rabbi had to nudge me along as I parroted him, line by line, in a barely audible whisper. Instead of announcing myself as a man, I had shown the world I was a loser.

Now, more than fifty years later, I hoped my performance at the nightclub might send a different message. If I did a good job, perhaps it would mean I'd finally become an adult.

Chasing butterflies

By the day of the performance, I had rehearsed my piece dozens of times. On the noisy bus into the city, I tried to relax, alternating between silently repeating my lines and meditating in order to keep myself centered. Emerging onto the street felt like I'd gone back in time, to the world my grandparents passed through on their voyage to safety.

Arriving at the nightclub, I found myself on a row of brownstone houses. To enter, I had to go down a few steps below street level. My only experience with such places was in movies from the Prohibition era. The doors were not opened yet, and when I knocked, I expected someone to open a peep hole and ask me for my secret code. The low ceilings and dim lights completed the illusion that I had entered a movie set. The exotic environment suited my surreal sense of courage.

Rather than falling prey to my usual pre-performance jitters, I felt a sense of peace, as though the wheels of fate were in motion, and all I had to do was go along for the ride. How was I even doing this?

The producer checked the sound system while we performers sat at a corner table. There was no backstage, no cozy green room, not even a curtain to hide behind. I kept looking at the door, hoping my fans would arrive on time.

My nephew and his wife were driving up from Pennsylvania where they would meet up with my niece and her husband. When the doors opened, I spotted them dash to the front of the room. My fan club. I felt a wave of relief. By the time we were ready to start the performance, the place was packed. I guessed fifty or sixty people.

As the speaker before me drew to a close, I took a few deep breaths and tried to review my opening line. But my brain had turned into mush. I just hoped that when I stood at the mic, my story would come flooding back.

When it was my turn, the bright spotlight in my eyes made the room practically invisible, except for the one table directly in front of me where my brother's kids sat. Perfect. I could focus on them.

I began. "When I was in high school in Philadelphia I fell madly in love"—dramatic pause—"with calculus."

Among the sprinkled laughs I recognized my niece's voice. Knowing that my opening line had tickled her gave me confidence.

The talk traced my journey from an emotionally shut down math nerd to an adult with a growing vocabulary for human kindness and connection. The way I told the story, listening played a significant role, and so did dancing.

As I drew to a close, I said, with as much comical gravitas as I could muster, "So the lesson I wished I'd known in high school, and want to pass on to you, is that when you feel overwhelmed by problems, slow down," I slowed my voice. "Open your ears," I cupped one hand behind my ear. "And dance," I said with a flourish, pointing to the sky and extending my hip as if I was hamming it up at a disco.

I peered into the blinding light and heard some enthusiastic clapping from other parts of the room. At the front, my nephew and niece and their spouses hollered and loudly applauded.

The rest of the performances passed in a blur. I had done it—risen above a mountain of fear in order to reveal my deepest emotions to a room full of strangers. After the show, I bid goodbye to my fellow performers and joined my family for pie at a diner across the street. We stayed up late telling family stories and laughing.

My nephew and his wife offered me a ride back to Pennsylvania. On the walk to their car, we passed through Times Square, which had been cordoned off from car traffic. The festival atmosphere, the connection with my brother's kids, and the bliss of achieving something that my younger, anxiety-riddled mind would never have imagined, all added up to a dreamy moment I would never forget.

I'd done it. I'd performed in New York. And I announced myself as a man, without dying. Despite the apparent success of the event, though, it lacked some of the most rewarding aspects of sharing life stories. After my death-defying performance, I didn't know anything about the people listening to me, and they hadn't learned anything about one another. Rather than search for another similar opportunity, I decided that chasing this butterfly looked suspiciously similar to the climb to nowhere I'd attempted back in my math days.

In the end, it boiled down to this: What was the point of climbing a mountain of excellence unless I anticipated more love or the opportunity to serve others when I reached the top?

Exit interview

Every month or two, my wife Janet and I drove up to the retreat center in the Poconos. In that peaceful environment, surrounded by trees in a place remote enough to forget our everyday lives, we gathered to hear Kathy speak. Due to her deteriorating health, she had been confined to her bed, but fortunately her room was large enough to accommodate the ten or fifteen of us who regularly showed up. Of course, after forty years together, we were not looking for any new insights. Simply the opportunity to enjoy each other's company made the regular trip one of the highlights of my life.

After the meeting, we went downstairs to celebrate those whose birthday happened to be near. We had long ago abandoned any pretense of matching the number of candles to the number of years.

During the festivities, I glanced at the door. Even though Kathy granted fewer individual interviews these days, I was in line for one today. When David gave me the signal, I returned to her room.

When I entered, she turned toward me and smiled. We hugged and sat in silence for a moment, and I asked her how she was. She said she wished she could spend more time with all of us, and was sad that her health was not giving her that freedom. When she asked me what you have been up to, I told her about the memoir classes I'd been teaching, and how rewarding it all felt.

"That's great, Jer. I always said you would help."

When she first made such a comment to me, many years ago, I couldn't imagine helping anyone. But since then, my relentless effort had given me the tools and insights that might help people connect the dots in their own lives.

And yet, as usual, my focus instantly shifted from small personal efforts to the grand scale of suffering I felt in the world.

"My God, Kathy," I said, shaking my head. "The news is so bleak these days. Where is all the harmony?"

"The positive energy is there too. It's just not as easy to see. There's always a balance."

Then, ever my teacher, she brought my attention back from my unanswerable speculation about fixing the world to one of my most magical moments with her.

"Remember when we danced at the Mena House?"

She always had a twinkle in her eye when she mentioned it. Back in the seventies, I had joined her on one of her many trips to Egypt, where she immersed herself in the ancient mystery of that place. On that first day, after settling into the hotel, our small entourage went straight to the Great Pyramid. We were so young, running up the magnificent stone face of that great structure. Officially it was already closing time and no tourists were being admitted.

To my surprise, the guards welcomed her like an old friend and let us clamber down a narrow tunnel into a cave-like room called the Subterranean chamber. The walls and floor seemed rough and unfinished, as if the entire pyramid had been built on the ruins of a small ancient temple even older than the rest. The fact that she wanted us to visit this ragged old relic of a room first, before visiting the far more majestic rooms above, added yet another layer to the already impenetrable mysteries of that place.

I'd always been amazed at the massive enterprise the Egyptians had shown in their determination to connect with a higher plane. The sheer intricacy of their effort made me wonder if they'd left behind any clues that could help the rest of us unlock our relationship to the divine.

If such secrets existed, Kathy seemed determined to find them. On one of her trips, she'd even bribed the guards to let her meditate all night in the Great Pyramid, And yet if she'd reached any esoteric conclusions, she never shared them with me. Instead, on the way back to our hotel, she said "let's go dancing."

Later that night, just a few hundred yards from the Great Pyramid, we entered the nightclub in the famous Mena House, where people from all over the world were rocking to disco music. Setting aside her role as an amateur Egyptologist, Kathy looked as eager to dance as anyone in the room.

I'd heard that in her younger days, before she'd found the spiritual path, she'd been a competitive ballroom dancer. Even though I'd never mastered any of those stylized steps, I had always been able to let loose on a dance floor.

Dancing. What could be more personal? Bodies moving in harmony to each other and also, in rhythm to something higher. Years before I knew how to have any sort of emotionally warm conversation with another person, dancing had provided a preview of how that closeness might feel.

Visiting Kathy by her bedside, forty years later, with even her voice growing thin and weak, the contrast between then and now seemed vast. And yet, her reminder made it easy for me to feel I was back there again, reliving that night in my memory.

After our dance, I watched a group of Israelis in a circle. At first I was amused. Then amazed. Their synchronized movement was indistinguishable from the exercises we'd been doing at the house the year before. During that first year of the group, when Kathy was helping us figure out how to live together in harmony, she led dance workshops that sometimes lasted all night. When our energy flagged, Kathy would shout, "Love one another" into the microphone and we would all cheer.

On the dance floor at the foot of the Great Pyramid, watching the Israelis do the identical moves to what we had been doing at home, time and space dissolved. We could have been in the living room at the house, or on an Israeli kibbutz. In that moment the whole world linked together in the great dance of life.

Through the following decades, whenever I remembered that trip to Egypt, I'd always thought of the mysteries that might still be hidden in those great monuments. But whenever Kathy mentioned the trip, instead of drawing my attention to the piles of carved boulders, she recalled the lively moments on the dance floor.

Perhaps this was the lesson she had been trying to teach me all along; that loving God was important, and serving society was important, but the most important job of all was to learn how to love individuals. I thought I'd made so much progress toward that higher goal, and yet, here at her bedside I was doing it again—slipping away from the person in front of me and into the cosmos.

I reeled myself back in and sat beside her, feeling present in my love for her, and all the different ways she had helped me understand that love. *Remember the dance.* The decades flashed through my mind so quickly I felt it all made sense.

"What a wonderful life we've led together," I said.

I remembered sitting next to my mother in her hospital room, in the last few days of her life. As Mom drifted in and out of delirium, she turned to me, her eyes bright, and she said, "I've lived a good life." My mom's satisfaction arced between us, a fleeting glimpse of wisdom that validated all that had come before.

Now, in Kathy's presence, I felt a similar feeling of completion. *If I had to leave tomorrow, I would be satisfied.*

I turned to her and said, "I've lived a good life." Our eyes met and Kathy started to laugh. "You're not getting off that easy, Jerry. You have a lot more to do, so you'd better get busy."

Science, art, and healing

After my interview, I returned to the party with Kathy's open-ended challenge echoing in my mind. "A lot more to do." But what? All this work with memoirs and memoir writing felt healing, but surely there was more I could contribute to the world before I died.

It reminded me of the sense of responsibility I'd accepted when I first found the path. Right after I became convinced that I needed to focus on my relationship with God, I had to reckon with a second instruction from the teachings, that is, that I had to "do my duty." At the time, I assumed that meant I needed to get a job and earn a living. But I no longer had a job. What was my duty now?

Kathy's suggestion sounded like a continuation of that original instruction. Growing old did not relieve me of responsibility. As long as I was alive, I had a duty to offer as much of myself as I could. As I had done so often in the past, I was back to wondering what I should do to make the most of my time.

Teaching classes and leading memoir groups had certainly given me a wonderful opportunity to help people find their own stories. But I felt that with my training in counseling, perhaps there was some unfinished business, some way to dig deeper and work harder, to help people sort out not only problems in their past but also in the present.

When I spotted Nancy, it occurred to me she would be the perfect person with whom to discuss my quandary. I had known her since the very beginning of our group. Each of us had arrived like wanderers escaping the deserts of our lives. But because Nancy was the artistic type and I was a computer guy, we never seemed to have much to talk about.

Toward the end of the nineties, our interests briefly converged. We both went back to school to become therapists. But rather than bringing us closer together, our paths went off in different directions again. My therapy career ran out of steam and I fell in love with writing, while Nancy kept going strong, earning her doctorate in counseling psychology. By practicing therapy full time, she had found the perfect opportunity to help people. That's what I wanted, too.

In the afterglow of my talk with Kathy, above the din of friends, I told Nancy how I'd been teaching memoir writing and loved the opportunity to show people how to move forward with greater confidence.

"When they begin to see how their lives can be developed into a story, it is as if they have awakened to the power hidden in their own lives," I told her.

"I heard you were writing," she said, "but I didn't know you were using it as a way to help people grow. That's terrific. I use self-expression in my therapy practice, too."

"How so?" I asked.

"I use art and music to help clients ease the effects of trauma. In fact, the neurobiology of trauma was the topic of my dissertation."

Nancy sipped her tea as I let this sink in.

"'Neurobiology' was the last word I expected to hear from you," I said. "You were always such an artist."

"Remember back in the eighties when Kathy taught us lessons about the anatomy and function of the brain?" she asked.

"Sure," I said. I remembered the scene like it was yesterday. We were in the living room, Kathy standing at an easel pointing to a diagram. It was probably the only time I'd ever seen her giving a technical or scientific presentation.

"That was a real turning point for me," Nancy continued. "Kathy's study of the brain led me deeper into the damage that I'd experienced in my own traumatic childhood. And once I figured out it could help me, I wanted to use it to help others."

"I suppose I should have taken those lectures more seriously," I said. "But I was too busy soaking in the comfort I always felt when together with the group. Mostly what I remember was us all laughing."

As we reminisced, I tuned into the laughter and chattering voices around us. Our little group still buzzed with joy all these years later.

"Funny thing," I continued. "To find your adult calling, you picked up on Kathy's challenge and moved toward science. And I went in the other direction, letting go of my obsession with science and following her suggestion to write."

Nancy laughed. "I guess if you live long enough you figure out how to fill in the missing parts of yourself."

"But why 'trauma'? I always thought that word referred to things like being a soldier in combat or the horrors of terror attacks or mass shootings. Do you specialize in people with that kind of extreme damage?"

"Recovering from combat is just the tip of the iceberg. Consider all the emergency workers, firefighters, ER doctors, and nurses who are exposed to violent accidents and crime every day. There are refugees who survive terrible persecution in their native country, and inner-city kids who witness shootings in their own neighborhood. But the majority of my work," she continued, "is to help adults who suffer from the lifelong results of childhood abuse and neglect."

"I've read a lot of memoirs about chaotic childhoods," I said. "But I never associated the word 'trauma' with their experience before."

"It is an intense word," she agreed. "But the research shows how damaging and pervasive it is in the general population."

After years of knowing her as a photographer, an artist, and a piano teacher, I was surprised to hear her speak so authoritatively about this field. "I am impressed by your work, Nancy. Exposing yourself to the raw, painful wounds of your clients must be overwhelming at times. While I sit back and help people write about overcoming problems in the past, you roll up your sleeves and offer them support in the midst of their pain."

"Honestly, I can't imagine not doing it. Helping people feels so good, I don't even think of it as work," she said. "What about you? You earned your master's degree. Now that you have more time, have you considered getting back into doing therapy?"

I cringed, recalling the sense of failure with which I had abandoned my attempt to become a professional therapist. Since then, I had assumed that my calling was in the field of memoir writing. Now, in speaking to Nancy, my original desire to help people cope with their emotional challenges lumbered back into the spotlight.

Perhaps she was right. Surrounded by my friends in this lovely setting in the woods, I felt so safe and comfortable. For a brief moment, I wondered if I could really pull it off this time.

Trying to grapple with this idea, I replied, "When I was first in an office listening to clients, I felt so helpless. They were in the thick of their crises and needed immediate support. I didn't think I knew enough to help them."

As I stood there sorting out my thoughts, Nancy patiently waited. In our early years, we would have interrupted each other mid-sentence, never listening long enough to actually hear. I was as bad as she was back then, or probably worse. Now, as a therapist, she remained quiet while I took the time to think. This new version of Nancy felt safe and helpful. I supposed we'd both grown.

Finally, I continued. "By the time people show up in a memoir class they are back on stable ground. My job is just to help them find the words to explain how they survived," I said. "But therapy?" I turned the word over in my mind. "My memoir groups have taught me so much about encouraging people to talk about where they've come from, and then listening carefully to their answers. But sitting in an office with people, trying to figure out their acute pain and confusion? I wonder if I can muster the courage to pick up where I left off."

"I see it as all one thing," she said. "Healing from past trauma has to take place in the present. You are already doing a lot of the same work I am."

"I'm not sure I see that."

"Come on over to the office next week," Nancy said. "Let's talk about it."

If at first you don't succeed

Nancy's office was in the same building where I'd attempted to start a practice fifteen years earlier, so as I pulled into the parking lot, waves of déjà vu washed over me. My early optimism, my ultimate sense of defeat. When I opened the door and walked in, all thoughts of my past receded. Nancy's office looked like no therapist's office I'd ever seen.

Taped to the walls were large sheets of paper displaying a wild profusion of scrawls and blotches in watercolor, marker, pastels, and colored pencils. A few of the drawings were identifiable as flowers, or beaches, but most were abstract. Some looked outright angry. With so much color and emotional expression on display, I felt I'd entered another world.

"What is all of this?" I asked.

"I ask my clients to paint or draw or scribble what they feel. Putting their work on the wall sets a tone for everyone who walks in. I want every single client to know they can express themselves freely here."

"I envy your ability to get your clients to think visually. I feel more comfortable in the world of memoirs, where images are translated into words.

"Don't sell your writing methods short, Jerry. Stories are more visual than you think," Nancy said. "When you read a story, or write one, visual images play a key role."

"That's true. I always encourage people to describe scenes so a reader can picture them. But, wow. These scribbles are like windows into their souls."

"That's a good way to put it. But the real value comes next, when we work together to make sense of what we see through that window.

And to do that, we must find words. Look," she said lifting up the corner of one of the pages to show handwritten words on the back.

"Ha," I said. "There it is again. Writing…"

"One of my neurobiological heroes, Dan Siegel, says: 'name it to tame it.' According to him, verbally identifying emotions engages the higher brain. In that regard, your memoir writers are doing the same thing as my therapy clients."

"Your therapy system seems so much more immediate than the slower pace of memoir writing. It takes months for memoir writers to peel back the layers of their past. Sometimes years."

"It's true that drawing opens them up and helps us establish a trusting relationship. But growing past their deep pain takes time. I've had plenty of clients who stick with me for months or even years. People grow at their own pace. It's our job to be there for them and use whatever methods are at our disposal."

"Well, I see plenty of overlaps in what you and I are doing. But if I become a therapist, I'd need to learn more strategies for helping people in immediate crisis. Personally, that was the biggest challenge for me."

"It's not an easy profession," she agreed. "But one thing you should be aware of. Since you left counseling, there have been amazing advances in the field. We have so many new tools for relieving psychological turmoil."

"The methods I learned in school were developed in the sixties and seventies. I'd love to learn the latest developments."

"Once you start to read about trauma-informed therapy, I think you'll see how it integrates into everything you already know. It's like an evolution of perspectives. Here's a good introduction to the whole field of trauma therapy," she said, handing me a book. "Read this."

Recognizing the long reach of childhood

From the book Nancy gave me, *The Body Keeps the Score* by Bessel van der Kolk, I learned about a massive study in the nineties that rocked the field of psychotherapy, providing hard data to support the long-term effect of childhood trauma.

He wasn't just referring to the shocking problem of violent or sexual abuse. To an infant, the lack of warmth was perceived as life threatening. And so, even if parents never beat or sexually abused their children, their extreme arguments, excessive drinking, or extended absences created a sense of danger in the developing infant's emotional core.

Later in life, these children grow up with unexplainable insecurities. To cope with their disturbed feelings, they drink or drug too much, or in other ways distract themselves from deep, hidden pain.

Worst of all, without the comfort of early nurturing, they are unable to trust their partner's love. As I'd seen in my earlier work with couples, lack of trust can escalate even small disagreements–instead of talking the problem through, they flail, withdraw, self-medicate, or lash out. Until they figure out how to grow past such ineffective reactions, these adults remain stuck in echo chambers, arguing endlessly without hearing each other.

I recalled the clients who had come to my office soon after I graduated, seeking relief from their terrors, depressions, or addictions. Back then, I felt frustrated by their inability to break out of these painful patterns.

Van der Kolk's book helped me see that even when adults made heroic effort to fix their current situations, the source of the pain emerged from the past. His theories and observations linked what therapists knew about the posttraumatic stress of combat with the much subtler, and far more pervasive aftermath of childhood trauma.

The next time I spoke with Nancy, I asked her to help me understand how these ideas influenced her work with clients.

"They have to retrain their brains," she said matter-of-factly, as if this was a natural and accessible process.

"Okay," I said laughing. I'd spent my whole life wondering about my brain. I hoped I was about to learn a lot more. "How do you do that?"

"It's why I call my practice Brain Smart Therapy," she continued. "I help my clients recognize how their brain was affected by abuse and what they must do to set things right."

"It's amazing how much scientists understand about the brain," I said. "When I first tried to understand myself, psychologists had only a rudimentary understanding of that organ. Now just fifty years later, they know so much."

We both sat quietly for a moment. Finally, I said, "Sorry if I distracted you from your point. I'm so fascinated by all the things that have changed during my lifetime."

"No problem," Nancy said laughing. "I love your insights."

Returning to our conversation she continued, "Once the brain perceives danger, it shifts into fight-flight-freeze or cry-for-help mode. In that state, the thinking part of the brain shuts down."

"No wonder people feel helplessly swept up into emotion when they are triggered. But how do you help?"

"People are comforted when they learn their internal pressures and impulses result from childhood trauma. This knowledge leads to greater self-compassion."

"But if anger and fear are triggered automatically, how do people ever change?"

"Not easily. Fortunately, this field continues to evolve. One recent innovation is the observation that trauma is remembered by the body. So it's not enough just to convince your mind that you are safe," she said. "You have to convince your body, too."

"Ah, right. That's why van der Kolk's book is called *The Body Keeps the Score*. How exactly do you heal trauma stored in the body?"

"There are lots of techniques. Breathing is important. Movement is important. Van der Kolk often suggests yoga to reduce the traumatic feelings in the body. And in therapy sessions, I always ask my clients to identify the part of the body associated with their emotional challenges."

"Could you give me an example?"

"Let's try it right now. Close your eyes and think of a time when you felt upset."

I nodded.

"Now where in your body do you feel that upsetness?"

After scanning my body, I pointed toward my abdomen.

"Great. Now relax and try to remember the first time you ever felt that."

I opened my eyes, remembering all the times as a child I tried to quell the discomfort in my belly by binging on candy. I was impressed by how quickly her simple exercise raised a powerful memory.

"How do you steer through all of these methods," I asked, feeling daunted. "They can't all apply… Can they?"

"There are so many effective systems, Jerry. As a therapist I must become adept at applying the ones that fit each client."

I sat quietly for a few moments, and finally asked the question that had been nagging at me for weeks. "Do you think I'm ready to jump back into this work?"

"You know a lot more than you give yourself credit for. And don't minimize the value of your years of meditating," she added. "Meditation has really taken off as a tool for helping people get in touch with their inner strength. So if you offer it to clients, you'll be able to speak from your own experience."

I grew silent, wondering how I would pull together a lifetime of experience to show one person at a time how to leverage their own strengths.

"Anyway," she said, "the continuing education classes you'll be required to take will provide a constant exposure to innovative ideas."

The fact that the field itself was changing and growing, and I would be required to change and grow along with it, sent a thrill of excitement up my spine. I'd always felt more comfortable climbing than walking on the level.

Finally, I'd found a mountain worth ascending. Unlike math, which led me to a loveless wasteland, and performance storytelling, which glittered but lacked a sense of higher purpose, therapy offered to take me closer to a goal that had been calling me for years–to love people.

The next step seemed obvious. Even though I had my master's degree, I needed to take a few more courses in order to qualify for licensure. It was time to go back to school.

New medicine to heal old wounds

I was the first to arrive in the college classroom just a few miles from my home. As the other students entered, I nodded a casual greeting. I liked being the old guy. Having spent so many years learning, I felt that age was working to my advantage. Then it hit me. Why was I looking for an advantage? These were my fellow therapists, not competitors in a race. But I couldn't shake the impulse. Part of me kept thinking, *I would come in number one. I would win.* Another said, *This is stupid. I don't want these ridiculous thoughts.* As I waited for the class to begin, I decided that in addition to learning about trauma, I would set a second goal for myself— to embrace my fellow students.

The first lessons repeated the information I'd learned from *The Body Keeps the Score,* about the way emotional wounds in childhood resurfaced years later. My hope was that this class would clarify the steps I'd need to take when such wounded people showed up for therapy.

Week after week, the course focused on various aspects of the suffering caused by trauma. I already knew about the damaging and widespread effect of adverse childhood experiences, such as seeing a parent being hit or threatened. But plenty of psychological damage results from events in adulthood, too, such as rape, accidents, and combat. And many emergency workers such as police, firefighters, and EMTs witness violence every day.

One type of trauma pushed me to the limits of my understanding: sex trafficking. The depravity of holding girls and boys in captivity in order to turn them into sex workers sounded like something from a nightmare. And yet, this was a real problem all over the world and a growing one in the United States.

In my pre-memoir days, I would have sat in silence, with little hope that I would ever understand how to assist a person in such dire straits. Now, instead of freezing up, I jumped into the fire, by reading the memoir my teacher recommended.

In *Girls Like Us* by Rachel Lloyd, the author tells of being trapped in this cycle of misery. Thanks to a helping hand, she awakens to her own power and transforms from victim to keynote speaker and activist. The story wraps unthinkable suffering in a container of courage, providing me with the impression that for every evil in society, there are opportunities to reach toward the light.

Lloyd's account of her journey offered a poignant example of the value I'd found in countless memoirs. Each author's willingness to share their humiliation at the beginning, and then to lead me, step by step, to a higher place, had given me a more nuanced appreciation for how people grow.

But I had to go beyond simply appreciating how they'd grown in the past. Taking the class offered an additional layer, showing me how to help people heal in the present.

I was also making progress toward my other goal, to confront my own competitive impulses. During breaks, I listened to my classmates talk about their jobs, where they cared for addicts, abused children, prisoners, victims of crime, and hospice patients.

I felt embarrassed by my earlier assessment. While I'd been congratulating myself for reading books, they had already been working with clients who had been crushed by traumatic experiences. These insights softened, but did not eliminate, my urge to be number one.

To learn more about the origins of these intrusive feelings, I turned my attention inward, quietly listening to my own mental chatter. As I paid attention to my pesky thoughts, I had a flashback of being fourteen years old, in the first few weeks in high school.

During algebra class, my teacher called me to the front of the room to write my homework answers on the board. When he praised my work, such deep pleasure surged through my body, I spent the next four years chasing that sensation. I was unable to see back then that my craving for approval created a barrier between myself and my classmates.

By applying the methods of trauma therapy, I hoped to help that younger version of myself open up to the people around him. In my imagination, I pictured my present-day self, knocking on the door of my ninth-grade algebra class. "Excuse me, Mr. Abrams," I'd say to the teacher. "I need to speak to Jerry." In response to his skeptical look, I would add, "It's important." When young Jerry came out into the hallway, he wouldn't know me, but I hoped some spark of familiarity would make him receptive.

"Look, Jerry. I'll tell you a secret. You think that impressing your classmates will relieve your loneliness. Believe me, it won't work. Instead of trying to convince them you're smart, let them know you admire them. Feel their needs just as you feel your own. Getting to know them will be so much more fun."

I waited for young Jerry to show some sign of recognition, some softening of his isolation. But he looked uncomprehending. I sighed. This method of sending love and wisdom back to my younger self would require more practice. But I felt hopeful. Healing the wounds of childhood seemed like a magnificent project for this chapter in my life. And the more I could help myself, the more I'd be able to help others.

Love the world, one person at a time

It took a year and a half to finish the additional courses I needed to qualify for my license. Then, I rented an office in the same building as before, hopeful that this time, I'd be able to complete what I'd started.

During the years since I'd first tried to pursue a counseling practice, the Internet had expanded the tools for matching clients and therapists. In addition, I had a few referrals coming in from Nancy and from my first supervisor Curt.

When I began seeing clients, I was surprised at how much I'd changed over the last twenty years. Proof of my increased competence was the fact that my clients kept coming back.

One of the reasons I felt so much more confident this time was my dedication to memoirs. Each one had enabled me to accompany an author through the intricately woven account of heart-aches and years of trial and error on their journey to higher ground.

That preparation gave me an incredible boost in understanding how severe psychological problems emerge from earlier trauma, and how those difficulties can be overcome with persistent effort. Witnessing author after author who had achieved that increased level of self-understanding showed me that it could be done.

I was fascinated to realize that the long-term journeys described in every memoir fit perfectly with the principles of trauma-informed therapy–both systems rely on the observation that our feelings each day are framed within the context of everything that occurred before.

But while a published memoir recounts the story of an already-completed leg of the journey, therapy clients were encountering rough terrain in the present. It was my job to help them learn new pathways, find new allies, and uncover new strengths.

During that work in the present, we often uncovered the origins of their current problems by reviewing their stories of growing up. Understanding how their lives worked through the lifespan helped them shift from a stuck sense of helplessness to an empowered sense of hope.

Occasionally, someone came to me carrying an armload of complex memories, wanting to turn them into a readable story. I switched roles. Instead of helping them develop insights into current problems, I worked with them to chart a course through past ones.

I recalled the parting words of my Villanova professor, Steve, who told me I needed to help people cope with their darkest experiences. I had backed away from this challenge once by withdrawing from counseling altogether. In the parlance of the hero's journey, I had refused the call.

Over the intervening years, I inched back toward that challenge. Now, finally I'd crossed the threshold to the next stage in Campbell's Hero's Journey. I'd entered the land of the adventure.

Still and smiling faces

As I continued to see clients in my office, many of their concerns, such as their never-ending loneliness and their obsessive pressures felt eerily familiar. I'd been struggling with similar issues my whole life.

I wasn't sure why my own uneventful childhood should have given rise to some of the same disturbed emotions experienced by victims of violence or sexual traumas. But in order to be as helpful as I possibly could, I needed to find out.

The Lehigh Valley was home to a vibrant group of therapists with whom I stayed in touch through social media. I met Anne at one of those gatherings and was impressed by her deep engagement in the challenges of childhood trauma. Hoping to make further progress with my own inner struggle, I made an appointment to see her.

At my first session with Anne, I told her about my dilemma. Despite decades of regular exercise, meditation, journal writing, and therapy, when I wasn't busy, I could feel myself sliding into despair.

"It happens in the afternoon, after my writing session is finished. If I don't have some errand or responsibility, I just stare at my computer and my brain shuts down. I barely know where I am."

"That sense of disconnection sounds very specific. Does this remind you of any times in your childhood when you felt a similar pattern?"

"Thing is, I remember almost nothing before the age of twelve."

"Forgetting big swaths of your life is called dissociative amnesia. That's a sign of trauma. What was your family life like?"

"I don't recall ever being hit," I said. "Nor was there much yelling. My parents were good people." I was aware that a defensive edge had crept into my voice. "They were busy. I don't think they understood us kids."

"Sometimes trauma is not due to big, violent incidents," she said. "If caregivers didn't instill a feeling of emotional safety, you would not have been able to develop a rich understanding of how to connect with others. Even if you don't remember the specifics, you can gain a lot of understanding about your patterns by reviewing the things you know. Take playfulness, for example. Was there a lot of playfulness in your family?"

"Are you kidding?" I said, grimacing. "Playing was not in our program. We were all so distant from each other."

"The absence of playful connections as a child left you unprepared to have fun with people later."

"That makes sense. Not having fun as a child led me to become withdrawn and serious later. Strange how, after all the work I've done in therapy and memoir writing, I'd never connected those dots."

"What about your ability to connect with other people? As you grew up, did you make friends easily?"

My eyes teared up. "I was terrible at connecting with people," I said. "I've spent most of my life trying to figure out why."

"When babies don't feel securely attached to their caregivers," Anne said, "they have a harder time making friends later."

"I've heard about attachment trauma. Like those babies raised in Russian orphanages who were never held by caregivers. They had horrific issues in adulthood. But that's so extreme."

"Attachment problems are really common, Jerry. If babies don't feel a deep bond with their caregiver, they will grow up unable to form bonds with anyone else." She stood and walked to her bookshelf.

"I have a workbook I use for abused boys."

"No, no, no," I said. "I was not abused. I'll go through the book just to see what it was like for other people, but it's important that you understand, I was never abused."

"I know you don't think so." She calmly handed me the book. "But from my point of view, the absence of warmth is a type of abuse. Let's go through this workbook together and look for insights."

In the following sessions, she had me read pages from the book. Then we talked about the influence these earlier experiences had in my current life. After discussing each topic, she told me to write something about that issue.

"Funny that you want me to write it. We're sitting together. Why not just tell you?"

"You're asking me that question?" she asked, raising her eyebrows. I realized what I'd just said and laughed. I'd been praising the power of writing for years, whether composing letters, or pouring your heart out in a journal, or constructing short stories or chapters in a book. This was my first experience of following a workbook in therapy. I quickly noted the familiar benefits: writing helped me integrate my thoughts and feelings.

In one session, I was describing a recent experience of sitting in a restaurant alone, staring into space. "What does it remind you of," Anne asked.

I remembered exactly what it felt like. I told her about all those afternoons as a teenager when I'd come home from school to an empty house. My brother and sister were away at college and my mom was probably helping Dad at the drugstore.

I'd go up to my room, where I had everything I needed—a small desk where I'd do my homework and for exercise, a set of barbells. Sometimes I lost focus and just stared at my books in a daze.

"That's the thing about trauma. It comes in many forms," she said. "Your childhood sounds remote, distant, cold. Children need hugs as much as they need food and water."

"Here," she said placing her laptop on the desk in front of me. "Watch this."

"What is it?" I asked.

"It's called the Still-Face Experiment," she said.

"If it's what I'm thinking, there's no point in seeing it again," I said feeling a sudden urge to run out of the room.

Her eyes widened, and she gave me a moment to calm down. "So, let's look at it together. I want you to see it," she said gently.

Giving in, I nodded.

In the video, a one-year-old child is in a high chair, facing her mother. The two of them are smiling and interacting. Then a researcher instructs the mother to stop reacting. The mother abruptly stops smiling or responding. The baby quickly becomes agitated, and then frantic as she urgently tries to regain her mother's attention. When that doesn't work, the baby arches her back and screams as if in pain.

Her suffering made my whole-body tense up. I wanted to cry.

After a signal from the researcher, the mother resumes her loving interaction. The baby quickly returns to normal, smiling and gesturing contentedly toward Mom.

When it was over, I felt drained.

Anne said, "Look at how sensitive babies are to parental cues. They really need lots of feedback from parents in order to know they are loved."

"Yes, I saw that video years ago, and it upset me then, too," I said. We sat in silence for a few moments as I tried to collect myself.

"I can't remember my mom's interaction with me when I was little," I finally said. "But when I try to remember looking at her, or smiling with her, I draw a blank. She wasn't exactly unhappy though. I recall she laughed a lot with Dad."

"Body language is the only thing babies know." Anne grew silent.

I continued to mull over the video. "I can't remember my own early years, but I have reason to believe my mom was not warm and cuddly. When my sister had her first child, she handed her infant son to Mom. Mom held the baby out at the end of her knee, avoiding contact. This made my sister ask how much Mom held us as children."

"Mom told my sister, 'I didn't hold you at all when you were a baby because you didn't like to be held.' My sister was horrified by this response."

Anne took a moment to let this observation hang in the air. She looked sad.

"Without that cuddling, babies must try to fend for themselves. Then later in life, when they feel agitated or disconnected, they don't turn to other people for support."

"That explains a lot," I said.

"Just to be clear, we're not blaming anyone. Your mother had her own reasons for behaving the way she did. If she had been traumatized in her own childhood, that would explain why it was hard for her to bond with her baby. That's the way we pass our traumas from one generation to the next."

"Pretty much all my ancestors fled from anti-Semitic riots in Russia. I never heard details of the beatings, rapes, and murders that sent them running for their lives, but if trauma can be passed down through generations, surely those experiences affected my mom."

"Trauma across generations is a reality," Anne said softly.

"When I try to remember my mom, I think of her as always being vaguely scared of something," I said.

"Perhaps she was."

"I guess I was ignoring my early childhood because I couldn't remember it. But ignoring it hasn't really helped me, has it?"

Each session with Anne awakened an ache in my chest. Whenever we reviewed the things I could remember, it became brutally apparent that my childhood provided close to zero preparation for relating emotionally to other people. But now, instead of hating myself for those missing social skills, I could feel compassion for that young man who entered the world so profoundly clueless.

In addition to the work I was doing with Anne, I also had a role model to help me with one very important aspect of healing my inner child. As I'd recently learned in therapy, children need smiles, and I happened to be living with a genius in that regard.

Neither my wife Janet nor I had ever had children, but when our nephews and nieces started having babies, I discovered her masterful ability to engage with them.

As soon as a baby entered the room, without hesitation, Janet sat on the floor to play with them at their own level. Her expressive face instantly made them smile. She used loving language and touch. Each child seemed hypnotized by the attention she showered on them.

I told Anne about Janet's ability to relate to these little people. "It's like watching a secret ritual I didn't even know existed. How could I have gone my whole life without noticing this simple connection?"

"You're never too old to learn about love," Anne said.

"Now that I've seen Janet with babies, it helps me understand why the two of us laugh so much. I think she knows how to speak to my inner child."

My painful inheritance

The distressed look on the little baby's face in that video awakened an ocean of understanding about the long, painful journey I'd been forced to travel as a young man. Far from blaming my parents for my fate, though, I felt more compassion than ever for the turmoil they must have experienced in their own childhoods. And yet, despite my renewed awareness of the way their childhoods must have influenced them, I knew almost nothing about what they'd been through. Until the end, they'd maintained a wall of silence about the past, allowing only tiny fragments to leak through.

I knew my mother's mother had to drop out of school as a teenager to support the family. Her father's death must have been a devastating blow. But as difficult as her life had been, her fate seemed easy compared with my father's mother. From the vaguest of hints, I heard about my aunt as a little girl, hiding in the basement while Russian soldiers swept through town looking for Jewish women to rape and Jewish men to conscript.

My parents never talked about hatred, or anti-Semitism, or the challenges my grandparents endured. But their silence protected me far less than they realized. From history books I learned that for a thousand years, Jews had been chased out of their homeland, by armed rioters as well as state-orchestrated persecutions, only to settle into a new country where they were again seen as intruders.

When my ancestors arrived into the relative safety of the U.S., they had to start from nothing, but under the watchful eyes of the haters. Restaurants all over the South displayed signs No Jews Allowed. And, since so many of Jews saw education as a way out of their predicament, colleges imposed strict limits, so as not to be overrun by these strange, non-Christian people. This whole history of not fitting in reached a crescendo when Hitler tried to exterminate them like vermin.

Even though my parents pretended such problems didn't exist, the ancestral pain had apparently been bequeathed to me like a birthright. And it all emerged at a war protest on a fall day in 1967. It's true we were blocking a campus building, so in that sense it was unlawful, but we were kids, and we meant well. We thought if we screamed loudly enough the U.S. would stop bombing innocent civilians, and we could go back to normal life.

But everything changed when the police stormed in, swinging billy clubs. Most of us fled and regrouped outside. The unlucky ones were carried to the hospital in a stream of ambulances.

Enraged by the violent response, the growing crowd worked itself up into a frenzy. Random screams coalesced, and in unison with hundreds of others I heard myself screaming *Sieg Heil* and snapping my arm to attention in the Nazi salute. The chanting, screaming, and saluting sent the horror of the Holocaust coursing through my body.

Those images of Hitler's armed minions, goosestepping through the streets, had apparently fused in my mind with the police who had stopped our protest. We screamed and wailed, hoping to alert them to a higher moral duty, as though we were possessed by a desperate desire to stop history from repeating itself.

Despite all those frantic appeals for peace, the next morning the world carried on as before. Instead of relieving the subterranean pressures that had driven me to the edge of sanity, my grand gestures brought the pain closer to the surface.

Certainly, some of my terror was aroused by witnessing armed men clubbing students. But the throbbing felt even bigger than that, like an echo from an unseen past, as though my ancestors' anguish still burned in my heart, hissing like a volcano ready to erupt.

In the twenty-first century, my peers were discovering a new way to express those hidden pains. Instead of competing to be the loudest, or to scream out with the most venom, memoirs let us join together in fellowship, blending our voices in an effort toward mutual understanding.

While I continued to mourn the punishing cruelty of war, poverty, disease, and greed, I came to see, through the magic of stories, that moving toward kindness, goodness, and dignity created the real substance of our lives, and that evil was merely an obstacle that slowed, but didn't stop our climb.

This new response to the past was far healthier than my morbid fascination with despair that almost destroyed me in my younger years. Whether through written stories or talk therapy, I hoped I could help others find their own healing versions of the past. Perhaps by working with them, and pointing them toward the positive potential of the human condition, I could help them move forward into their own strengths.

Growing old. Coming home.

Sometimes my conversations with my sister jogged long-forgotten memories. Other times we commiserated on how little we remembered. Like the Hardy Boys, that sibling detective team I'd envied in my youth, my sister and I peered into the darkness hoping to solve our own childhood puzzles.

"I wish Mom had written more about those early times," she sighed one day. "Toward the end of her life, she wrote every morning. What was she writing that was so important? I've only ever found fragments of her papers."

"I think she was mostly preparing the talks she gave at her ladies' clubs," I said. "It's a shame she passed just before I discovered memoirs. There is so much I could have asked her."

Shaking off that regret, I added, "Even though she didn't leave behind much for us to read, we have somehow inherited her joy. She often said her morning writing session was the best part of her day. I feel the same way."

These conversations about Mom's writing always led back to our own. Like me, Marilyn found that joining writing groups helped motivate her. One day, she mentioned that the group she attended was too far away. "The ideal location would be the continuing education program at my synagogue, but they don't have a memoir group."

"Then let's start one," I said.

"How would that work?"

"You've had experience leading other types of groups. This is just a different kind. I'll come down and teach some introductory sessions, and then once it gets going, you can run it."

Marilyn asked the woman in charge of the adult enrichment program if she could list a memoir class in her brochure. Twelve people signed up. Our memoir group was born.

I had set foot in a synagogue only a few times since I was a teenager, so just walking into the building stirred up waves of nostalgia. The lovely architecture, the six-pointed stars, and hallways lined with photos of rabbis and Hebrew school students made me feel like I'd come home.

When we introduced ourselves, without any filters on our heritage, my new writing club also awakened feelings of my youth, when I'd been surrounded by people just like me. I attended public school with mostly Jewish teachers and classmates, got vaccinations from my Jewish doctor, and bought ethnic foods at the local Jewish deli. Nearly every family on my block had Yiddish-speaking grandparents who had fled Eastern Europe. Like their ancestors for thousands of years, they were searching for a place to feel safe.

Every one of us experienced the synagogues, the rituals, the dietary laws, a flair for irony, our love for culture, our horror of the Holocaust, and hopes for peace in Israel. Was it legal to feel this connected to strangers? Even though I wasn't a member of the synagogue, I was a member of the tribe.

The group, which began as a favor to my sister, offered me the first opportunity in my life to explore my relationship to my cultural roots with others who had been through similar experiences. I decided to stay.

Month after month, my short pieces described the culture shock I'd experienced when I left my ethnic neighborhood in Pennsylvania, and landed in college, surrounded by the northern Europeans of Wisconsin. In that environment, my bubble of sameness burst. I felt exposed. Different. Other. I could no longer ignore that Easter and Christmas felt like national holidays. I was an outsider.

In response, I pretended religion was irrelevant. But pushing my Jewishness out of sight didn't make me feel more accepted. On the contrary, the denial of my heritage made me feel empty and invisible.

When spirituality offered a way out of that darkness, I came to see myself as a universal human being, with empathy for others. And after many years of work, I finally embraced the belief that others felt empathy for me. But even in those happier times, when I'd worked so hard to see the importance of mutual respect among all people, I continued to assume that hiding my religion was the safest path. Now, participating in this group offered an opportunity to review my contradictory views.

At first, I was self-conscious about revealing my conflicted feelings about my Jewish identity. But as our meetings progressed, I discovered that sharing my experience as a Jew with other Jews was a natural and healthy way to open up about that part of my self.

At one meeting, after I read a chapter about Central High, one of the guys said with nostalgic reverie that he too attended that school. Suddenly, I was straddling two worlds, my isolation back then and the congeniality of our story sharing in the present.

When I told him about the isolation I felt in the honors class, his tone changed to wonder. "Wow, you were in the honors class? I always thought you guys were geniuses." *He knew about the honors class!* Time collapsed and I was back in high school. This time I was seventeen, and getting close to graduation.

Throughout my four years at Central, I'd taken classes with the same thirty boys, almost every one of them Jewish. But instead of seeing them as a band of brothers, I barricaded myself against them.

Even worse than the way I distanced myself from my classmates was the way I remained aloof from everyone else in the school. Of the hundreds of other boys at my grade level, I couldn't recall being curious about a single one. By my senior year, the only other guy I'd met was the one who always sat next to me in homeroom.

Inside my self-constructed prison I congratulated myself for being smart, but it took me years to realize that no matter how much I justified my isolation, it still hurt. Once I acknowledged the misery I'd been causing myself, it took more years to figure out how to tear down or climb over my own walls.

Now, in this quirky little writing group, among people who were trying to grasp the stories of their own past, this gentle man ignored my overwrought system of self-aggrandizement. For him, intelligence was a point of admiration rather than separation. His attitude highlighted the absurdity of my competitive stance. With a slight shift in perspective, I could have had friends all along.

My preoccupation with intelligence had been only one of the many walls I'd built and then hid behind. Exaggerating the importance of being Jewish was another one. It was true that my religion was different from a lot of other people. But like being good at math, it was only one of thousands of parts of myself.

Memoirs had taught me how to love people by appreciating the way they wove many qualities and experiences into good stories. I needed to apply that principle to myself. Instead of focusing on one or two parts, I could learn to love myself as a whole person by weaving all the parts together.

If I labeled myself as just one thing, it would be easy to imagine that some people hated that thing. By extending my definition of myself to the whole mix of experience, I could dodge the hater's fallacy. I wasn't just smart, or just Jewish or for that matter just a computer guy, a therapist, a writer, a husband, or an uncle. There were also long-neglected playful parts, and many ancient buried fears. By embracing all these parts, the walls began to shimmer in the light. They were only real as long as my fears of others kept them alive. As I outgrew my fears of being the Other, I could walk right through them.

This was the answer to Joseph Campbell's abstract suggestion that modern heroes should follow their bliss. I'd discovered that my bliss was to learn the story of life, my own and everyone else's. Each story contained many unique features, but instead of creating separation and fear, our curiosity about those stories brought us together. After all these years, my quest to learn how to love people boiled down to the simple act of sharing stories.

Epilogue: Surrounded by heroes

After my last interview with Kathy, a growing contentment about my age convinced me to stop dying my hair. Letting it turn white helped break the illusion that I was going to live forever. But the following year, Kathy fell ill and after suffering a breathtaking sequence of complications, she was the one who departed.

Those of us who looked to her for support and inspiration were in shock. Our hero had left us behind. We gathered at the retreat center to celebrate our lives together. Most of those who had come together at the beginning of the group were still here all these years later, along with about the same number of others who had trickled in over the intervening decades.

One after another, we recalled the ways her creative energy had given us a head start toward hope and purpose, and how much more socially aware and engaged we'd become since we first met her.

When it was my turn, I told about my first encounter with her, not in person but in the pages of her book. It was in 1971, when I wondered if my fall into chaos could go much lower. In one last desperate act, I reached out to an old friend. The book he gave me turned my attention upward. My first act, on my journey back to sanity was to move closer to my parents. That's where I met Kathy and David, who lived only a few miles away.

"No coincidences," someone in the room said, and everyone laughed. I paused to look around at all the familiar, smiling, faces.

"In addition to showing me how to relate to you all," I continued, "Kathy's guidance continued to help me grow. From her suggestion to write in a journal in the seventies, to her suggestion to see a therapist in the eighties, to the inspiration she offered by getting her graduate degree in the nineties, her ideas and leadership kept guiding me to my own best self. It all started by reading her book."

After sharing my recollection, I sat down to listen to the ways others had been touched by knowing her. As if wrapping up a good story, we shared our tales of fulfilling lives, in both spiritual and worldly dimensions.

The thought flitted through my mind how this type of speaking, in front of a group, even of my close friends, would have been impossible when I first showed up at the house. Now, it was not only easy, it made me happy to be able to share all I'd been through.

It was only then, while looking around at this group of grateful individuals, that I realized that even though Kathy's book had been published in the sixties, it fit the modern memoir genre perfectly.

Like the main character in Joseph Campbell's *The Hero's Journey*, her quest for deeper wisdom pushed her beyond the boundaries of the world in which she'd grown up. She traveled to India, where she found what she'd been looking for. Then, to fulfill the final requirement for a heroic journey, she returned to offer her wisdom to others.

I already had so many reasons to be grateful for having known her. And here was one more. Her willingness to turn her experience into a story created a model that had motivated me to keep growing and learning in this chapter in my life.

After the speaking portion of the meeting, we went out to the meadow, where we assembled in a human chain around a garden built in the shape of an *ankh*. Kathy had long ago identified that symbol, in the shape of a T with a tear drop on top, as an indication of her reverence for all spiritual traditions, not just in our time, but across the millennia.

In a final farewell, we joined hands as the magical sounds of *Amazing Grace* floated through the air. After a signal from our choir director, we all began to sing. It was the same song that marked the high point of our big Christmas gathering each year. This was the first time we would be singing it without Kathy.

The truth of the lyric, "I once was lost but now I'm found," moved me every time I heard it. Our voices, rich with shared emotion, swelled at those words, as if we were sending our combined gratitude to heaven.

I recalled just how lost I'd been when I was twenty-four. Bereft of all meaning, blind and starving by my own choosing, hating everything, and prepared to leave civilization behind. I had lost my way. The swelling of the singing voices around me, and the hands I held in this healing circle, reassured me that I was no longer alone.

Books cited

Alterations of Temperature, Sleepiness, Mood, and Performance in Residents Are Not Associated With Changes in Sulfatoxymelatonin Excretion by K. H. Sharp, G. M. Vaughn, P. W. Cosby, C. E. Sewell, D. J. Kennaway, Nov. 1988, Journal of Pineal Research Volume 5, Issue 6, 1988.

Accidental Lessons: A Memoir of a Rookie Teacher and a Life Renewed by David W. Berner

Angela's Ashes by Frank McCourt

The Body Keeps the Score: Brain, Mind, and Body in the Healing of Trauma by Bessel van der Kolk, MD

Bowling Alone: The Collapse and Revival of American Community by Robert D. Putnam

But Enough About Me: A Jersey Girl's Unlikely Adventures Among the Absurdly Famous by Jancee Dunn

Down Came the Rain: My Journey Through Postpartum Depression by Brooke Shields

Enter Talking by Joan Rivers with Richard Meryman

The Feeling Good Handbook by David D. Burns, MD

Girls Like Us: Fighting for a World Where Girls Are Not For Sale: A Memoir by Rachel Lloyd

The Greatest Salesman in the World by Og Mandino

The Theory and Practice of Group Psychotherapy by Irvin D. Yalom

The Hero's Journey by Joseph Campbell

If You Want to Write: A Book About Art, Independence and Spirit by Brenda Ueland

Infidel by Ayaan Hirsi Ali

Introducing NLP: Psychological Skills for Understanding and Influencing People by Joseph O'Connor

1984 by George Orwell

The Publish-It-Yourself Handbook: Literary Tradition and How-To from Pushcart Press (Bill Henderson, ed.)

Robinson Crusoe by Daniel Defoe

The 7 Habits of Highly Effective People: Powerful Lessons in Personal Change by Stephen R. Covey

Short-term Couples Therapy by Wade Luquet

The Soul of a New Machine by Tracy Kidder

Story by Robert McKee

Trading Secrets: Seduction and Scandal at the Wall Street Journal by R. Foster Winans

The Trial by Franz Kafka

Wherever You Go, There You Are: Mindfulness Meditation in Everyday Life by Jon Kabat-Zinn

Jerry Waxler

The Writer's Journey: Mythic Structure for Writers by Christopher Vogler

Acknowledgements

Writing this memoir has been a journey of ever deeper gratitude to the many hundreds of people who have contributed to my social, intellectual, literary and spiritual wellbeing. As in the expression "it takes a village to raise a child"–I've seen within the pages of my own and hundreds of other memoirs that it takes a village to raise an adult as well. The point of the book was to honor them all in narrative form. In this brief page, I will try to list a few of the most important.

Thanks to every one of the hundreds of published memoir authors and hundreds of aspiring ones who have preceded, accompanied, or will follow me on the journey of turning life into story.

Gratitude for spiritual guidance goes to Charan Singh whose philosophy pulled me from the depths of despair, by showing me in Eastern language how this life is simply one short leg of a much longer journey, and Kathy and David Sharp who helped me integrate those mystical teachings into a creative, fulfilling, loving life in the West.

Nick Rosa, the Villanova professor kept throwing pearls of insight at me, and when I trampled them into the ground, they turned out to be the seeds of future understanding. Another professor, Stephen Weinrach, admonished me not to skim past the deep underlying pain of mental suffering. It took me two decades before modern advances in therapy, and my own desire to fight the good fight finally enabled me to rise to his challenge.

Author and NLP trainer, Joseph O'Connor who, in addition to introducing principles of NLP, returned at exactly the right moment to get me started on understanding the mental game of becoming a writer. To continue that journey, I joined a swarm of aspiring writers at the Writers Room in Bucks County, created by Foster Winans, followed by Jonathan Maberry who dropped an astonishing number of redwood seeds into my mental compost heap and changed my life.

My many therapists, including Craig Soskin, who ushered me into the world of my own mental order, and Lyndra Bills, MD, who, in addition to being an awesome talk therapist, was, along with Sandra Bloom, MD, one of the pioneers of modern trauma informed therapy.

Linda Joy Myers, founder of National Association of Memoir Writers, whose dedication has helped many hundreds of authors transform ordinary life into the shape of a story, and the legions of my own group members and workshop attendees who, by sharing their lives, enriched mine. Amy Miller Cohen, my SoulCollage guru who introduced me to the parts of self and Nancy Lubow who opened my eyes to the goals and methods of trauma-informed therapy. Note: SoulCollage© is a trademarked, copyrighted name.

This book has benefitted from dozens of beta readers and critique partners, spread across almost two decades of my evolution as a writer. Professional editors lifted it to the next level; especially Kathryn Craft who kept pushing me to improve the story. With additional advice and editing from Brooke Warner, Lorraine Ash, and Dianna Sinovic.

My wife who has offered an endless supply of support and inspiration. My older sister Marilyn, a valued fellow-detective in the mystery of growing up, and my older brother Ed, who went blazing ahead of me on his journey, and at a very young age left on his gravestone the wisdom that gives me goose bumps every time I write it. "Ad astra per aspera"–to the stars through effort and hardship–which sums up the journey of every hero throughout the ages.